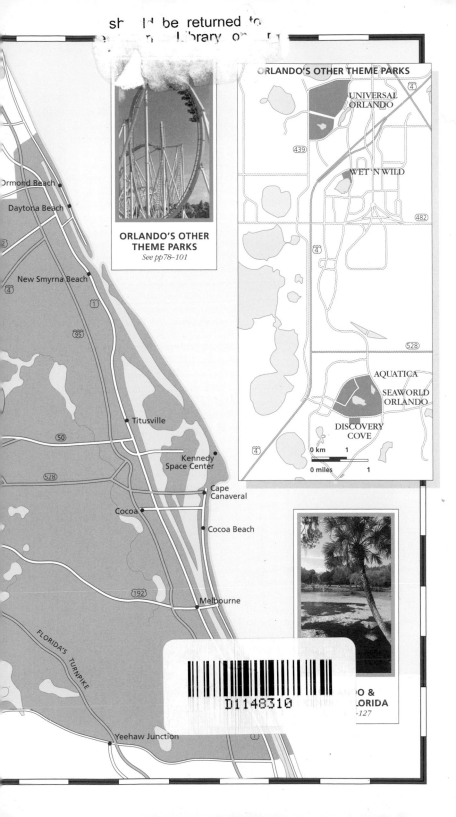

Ormond Beach

Daytona Beach

New Smyrna Beach

Titusville

Kennedy
Space Center

Cape
Canaveral

Cocoa

Cocoa Beach

Melbourne

FLORIDA'S TURNPIKE

Yeehaw Junction

ORLANDO'S OTHER THEME PARKS
See pp78–101

ORLANDO'S OTHER THEME PARKS

UNIVERSAL
ORLANDO

WET 'N WILD

AQUATICA

SEAWORLD
ORLANDO

DISCOVERY
COVE

0 km   1

0 miles   1

DO &
LORIDA
-127

EYEWITNESS TRAVEL

WALT DISNEY WORLD® RESORT & ORLANDO

EYEWITNESS TRAVEL
WALT DISNEY WORLD®
RESORT & ORLANDO

DK

LONDON, NEW YORK,
MELBOURNE, MUNICH AND DELHI
www.dk.com

MANAGING EDITOR Aruna Ghose
ART EDITOR Benu Joshi
SENIOR EDITOR Rimli Borooah
EDITOR Shahnaaz Bakshi
DESIGNER Kavita Saha
PICTURE RESEARCHER Taiyaba Khatoon
CARTOGRAPHER Suresh Kumar
DTP COORDINATOR Shailesh Sharma
DTP DESIGNER Vinod Harish

MAIN CONTRIBUTORS
Phyllis and Arvin Steinberg, Joseph Hayes, Charles Martin

CONSULTANT
Richard Grula

Reproduced by Colourscan (Singapore)
Printed and bound in China by L. Rex Printing Co. Ltd

12 13 14 15 10 9 8 7 6 5 4 3 2 1

First published in Great Britain in 2005
by Dorling Kindersley Limited
80 Strand, London WC2R 0RL

Reprinted with revisions 2006, 2007, 2008, 2009, 2010, 2012

Copyright 2005, 2012 © Dorling Kindersley Limited, London
A Penguin Company

Front cover main image:
Fireworks over the castle at Magic Kingdom®,
Walt Disney World® Resort, Orlando

MIX
Paper from
responsible sources
FSC
www.fsc.org   FSC™ C018179

A ride at Universal Orlando's
Islands of Adventure *(see pp96–7)*

CONTENTS

INTRODUCING
WALT DISNEY
WORLD® RESORT
& ORLANDO

Cinderella's Castle, a fairy-tale
fantasy at Magic Kingdom® *(see p34)*

◁ **Spectacular fireworks above Cinderella's Castle at Magic Kingdom®, Walt Disney World® Resort**

Primeval Whirl®, at Disney's Animal Kingdom® *(see pp64–7)*

WALT DISNEY WORLD® RESORT & CENTRAL FLORIDA AREA BY AREA

Highway patrol insignia

TRAVELERS' NEEDS

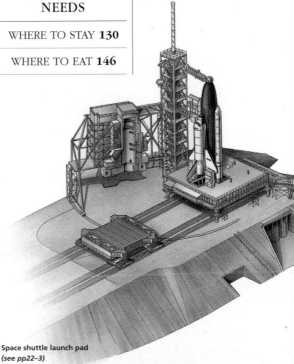

A boardwalk trail at Blue Spring State Park *(see p114)*

Space shuttle launch pad *(see pp22–3)*

INTRODUCING WALT DISNEY WORLD® RESORT & ORLANDO

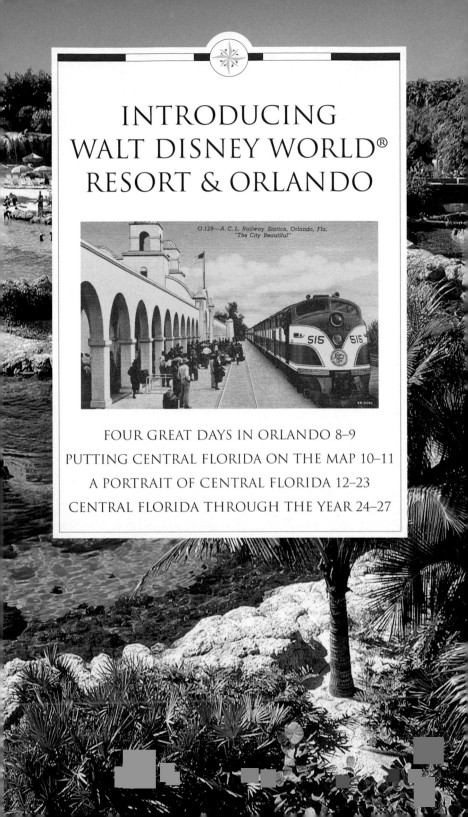

O.129—A. C. L. Railway Station, Orlando, Fla.
"The City Beautiful"

FOUR GREAT DAYS IN ORLANDO

Orlando's family-oriented selection of attractions includes a world-famous concentration of theme parks with enough larger-than-life personalities and adrenaline-pumping thrills to dazzle even the most jaded imagination. Assuming Mickey Mouse and Co. represent just one part of your Orlando visit, with some forethought you can easily accommodate the region's other

Ponce de Leon Inlet Lighthouse

highlights. The following four itineraries guide you to the area's best, whether you are traveling with young children or in a group of adults, with an eye towards the Space Coast or looking to go no further than Disney's Main Street, USA®. Key sights have page references so you can check for more details. Price guides include the estimated cost of travel, food, and admission charges.

The façade of the impressive Mission: SPACE at Epcot®

BEST OF DISNEY

- **Go international at Epcot®**
- **Ride the rails on Big Thunder Mountain**
- **Enjoy Main Street's lights and delights**

FAMILY OF 4 allow at least $425

Morning
Try to arrive at **Epcot®** *(see pp42–53)* an hour before the official opening time. Pick up a Fastpass for Test Track *(see p46)* if you are with young children, or Mission: SPACE *(see pp44–5)* for older children. While waiting for your allocated Fastpass time, explore Innoventions East *(see p43)* for some high-tech video gaming. After the rides, stroll around World Showcase *(see pp50–3)*. Either find a pavilion that is of particular interest to your group, or join the line for Spaceship Earth *(see p43)*.

Afternoon
Take the monorail to the **Magic Kingdom®** *(see pp34–41)* and hop aboard the steam train at Main Street, USA® *(see p36)* which takes 20 minutes to skirt the perimeter of the park. Disembark at Fantasyland® *(see pp38–9)* for classic child-friendly attractions such as Dumbo the Flying Elephant and "it's a small world" or, for older children, at Frontierland® *(see p37)* for Big Thunder Mountain Railroad and the exhilarating Splash Mountain®. For the latter two, secure Fastpasses before sitting down to affordably priced sandwiches and salads at Pecos Bill's. After the rides, head to Adventureland® *(see pp36–7)* and get a Fastpass for Pirates of the Caribbean, one of the park's best original

rides. Alternatively, take a leisurely Jungle Cruise with a highly entertaining boatman. Once the thrills are over, stroll back to Main Street, USA® to witness the dazzling late-afternoon parade.

ORLANDO FOR ADULTS

- **World-famous golf courses**
- **Priceless pre-Columbian art**
- **Picnic in idyllic Lake Eola Park**

TWO ADULTS allow at least $200; $600 for golf/basketball itinerary

Morning
Weather permitting, golf enthusiasts can shoot a round of nine at one of Central Orlando's award-winning courses. **Falcon's Fire Golf Club** *(see p176–7)* offers top-quality rental equipment as well as online tee-time booking. Alternatively, aesthetically

Falcon's Fire, one of Orlando's premier golf courses

Dragon Challenge®, popular with coaster addicts at the Islands of Adventure®

inclined visitors will enjoy the pre-Columbian, Mesoamerican, and Impressionist collections at the **Orlando Museum of Art** (see p107).

Afternoon
Golfers might wish to return to their hotels to freshen up. They and museum visitors should then head to **Thornton Park** (see p108) to carry out lunch from one of the more casual establishments located in this charming neighborhood, such as **Dexters** (see p151). Browse the shops here before heading to nearby **Lake Eola Park** (see p108). After picnicking amid the quaint footbridges and gorgeous palmetto trees, take a relaxing trip around the lake in a fairytale-perfect, swan-shaped paddleboat built for two.

Evening
Even for sold-out games, the box office of the **Amway Center** (see p179) often releases Orlando Magic basketball tickets on game-day; call ahead to confirm. Alternatively, gastronomes and non-sports fans can head to **Downtown Disney®** (see pp74–5) for a casual feast of regional seafood delights at popular **Fulton's Crab House** (see p148), followed by a stroll among the Marketplace shops or a drink at one of the bars in the area.

SLIDES & RIDES

- **Splash at Wet 'n Wild®**
- **Hollywood thrills at Universal Studios Florida®**
- **Shopping and people-watching on CityWalk®**

FAMILY OF 4 allow at least $400

Morning
Head to **Wet 'n Wild®** (see pp100–101), where there are numerous attractions for young children as well as for older thrill-seekers. Grab lunch at one of the many concessions in the area.

Afternoon
Given the wildly different experiences offered by **Universal Studios Florida®** (see pp88–93) and **Islands of Adventure®** (see pp96–7), choose the one that best suits your needs. At Universal, families should head to Shrek 4-D™ (see p89), one of the top attractions, and then to Woody Woodpecker's Kid Zone (see p92) to experience ET Adventure®. Bigger kids will be more interested in the revolutionary roller coasters at the Islands of Adventure® – particularly those of Marvel Super Hero Island® (see p96). Explore The Lost Continent® and The Wizarding World of Harry Potter™ (see p97) before an evening of winding down on **Universal City-Walk®** (see pp98–9).

COASTAL FLORIDA

- Stroll and swim the Space Coast
- Blast off at Kennedy Space Center
- Get acquainted with killer whales at SeaWorld®

TWO ADULTS allow at least $200

Morning
Equipped with swimsuits, sunblock, snacks, and water bottles, head to Florida's beautiful Space Coast, approximately a 45-minute trip from the resorts. Tour the emblematic **Ponce de Leon Inlet Lighthouse** (see p117) and its surrounding trail network. The waves here are reliably gentle if you want to swim, but riptides occur so do not venture far from shore.

Afternoon
Spend the early part of the afternoon at **Kennedy Space Center** (see pp126–7) and visit the Astronaut Hall of Fame. Take lunch in the cafeteria before setting out for **SeaWorld® Orlando** (see pp82–5). Enjoy the surprising acrobatics of killer whales at the One Ocean show, the faithful replications of Caribbean habitats at Key West at SeaWorld®, and the popular Manatee Rescue exhibit. Journey to Atlantis® and the ridiculously fast Kraken® ride will satisfy even the most discriminating adrenaline addict.

A killer whale diving during SeaWorld's® One Ocean show

Putting Central Florida on the Map

At the approximate geographic center of Florida, the Greater Orlando area covers around 2,850 sq miles (7,380 sq km). Flanked by beaches, peppered with lakes, and blessed with exceptional weather, the area's 2.1 million residents play host to over 51 million visitors a year. Walt Disney World® Resort and the region's other theme parks are the top attractions for the majority of vacationers. A sizeable number also visit the surrounding Central Florida area – including the beaches on the east, Ocala National Forest to the north, and the Kennedy Space Center on the Space Coast, named for its heavy concentration of space and defense industries.

Fireworks in Walt Disney World® Resort's Magic Kingdom®

The state seal of Florida

0 km   50

0 miles   50

0 km   5000

0 miles   5000

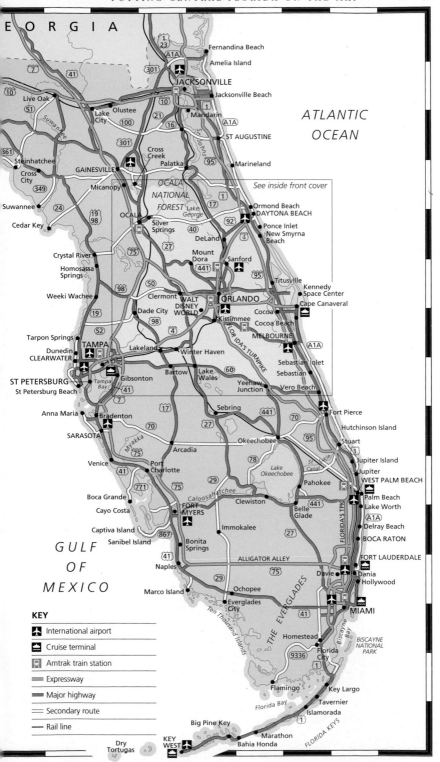

GEORGIA

Fernandina Beach
Amelia Island
JACKSONVILLE
Jacksonville Beach
Live Oak
Lake City   Olustee
Mandarin
ST AUGUSTINE
Steinhatchee
Cross City
GAINESVILLE
Cross Creek
Palatka
Marineland
Suwannee
Cedar Key
Micanopy
OCALA NATIONAL FOREST
Lake George
Ormond Beach
DAYTONA BEACH
Ponce Inlet
OCALA
Silver Springs
DeLand
New Smyrna Beach
Crystal River
Mount Dora
Sanford
Homosassa Springs
Weeki Wachee
Clermont
Titusville
Kennedy Space Center
Cape Canaveral
Dade City
WALT DISNEY WORLD
ORLANDO
Cocoa
Tarpon Springs
Kissimmee
Cocoa Beach
MELBOURNE
Dunedin
CLEARWATER
TAMPA
Lakeland
Winter Haven
Sebastian Inlet
ST PETERSBURG
Gibsonton
Bartow
Lake Wales
Sebastian
St Petersburg Beach
Yeehaw Junction
Vero Beach
Anna Maria
Bradenton
Sebring
Fort Pierce
SARASOTA
Hutchinson Island
Okeechobee
Stuart
Venice
Arcadia
Jupiter Island
Port Charlotte
Lake Okeechobee
Jupiter
Pahokee
WEST PALM BEACH
Boca Grande
Clewiston
Palm Beach
Cayo Costa
Belle Glade
Lake Worth
Captiva Island
FORT MYERS
Immokalee
Delray Beach
Sanibel Island
Bonita Springs
BOCA RATON
ALLIGATOR ALLEY
FORT LAUDERDALE
Naples
Davie
Dania
Ochopee
THE EVERGLADES
Hollywood
Marco Island
Everglades City
MIAMI
Ten Thousand Islands
Homestead
BISCAYNE NATIONAL PARK
Florida City
Biscayne Bay
Flamingo
Key Largo
Florida Bay
Tavernier
Islamorada
Big Pine Key
FLORIDA KEYS
KEY WEST
Marathon
Bahia Honda
Dry Tortugas

ATLANTIC OCEAN

See inside front cover

GULF OF MEXICO

Tampa Bay

Suwannee R.
St Johns R.
Myakka R.
Caloosahatchee R.
St Lucie Canal

FLORIDA'S TPKE

KEY

- ✈ International airport
- ⚓ Cruise terminal
- 🚆 Amtrak train station
- ▬▬ Expressway
- ▬▬ Major highway
- ▭▭ Secondary route
- ──── Rail line

A PORTRAIT OF CENTRAL FLORIDA

Sun-drenched beaches with aquamarine waters and the never-ending amusement offered by its theme parks make Central Florida the ultimate family vacation destination. Adding to the mix are scenic nature preserves, unique cultural and historic attractions, fantastic shopping, and evening entertainment options.

In the last 50 years, Orlando and Central Florida have witnessed a spurt of development unmatched by any other region of the state. The initial fillip to this primarily agricultural community was provided by the increased employment opportunities associated with the space program at Cape Canaveral.

Juan Ponce de Leon

Then Walt Disney World arrived on the scene, opening its first theme park – Magic Kingdom – in 1971. The rest, as they say, is history.

HISTORY

The first Europeans to set foot on the Florida peninsula were Spanish explorers who sighted land between Cape Canaveral and the Matanzas Inlet in 1513. On April 2, 1513, Ponce de Leon claimed the territory for King Phillip of Spain and named it La Florida – the Place of Flowers. Spain, France, and England ruled the region in turns. The 20-year British rule, from 1763 to 1783, is notable for the growth of a flourishing plantation economy: the Daytona Beach area, for instance, successfully produced cotton, sugarcane, rice, and indigo. In 1819, Florida was finally ceded to the United States by Spain. The plantation system soon entered the Industrial Revolution, with the application of steam power to sugar and rum processing: the first steam-operated mill was at the Dummett Plantation in Ormond Beach.

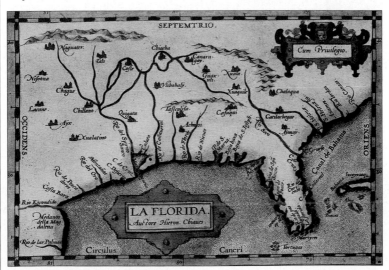

A 16th-century map of Florida and the Gulf of Mexico

◁ A lifeguard sits on duty at Daytona Beach, one of the country's most popular beaches

Attempts by the Americans to remove the Seminole Indians, who had settled in the area in the 17th century, continued for decades. Central Florida's plantation economy suffered major losses when the Seminole Indians destroyed many plantations and sugar mills during the seven-year Second Seminole War, which ended in 1842. Orlando was born during this period, developing around an Army post, Fort Gatlin.

With ample land available for grazing, Central Florida fostered a thriving cattle industry. By the early 1860s, cattle and cotton were the mainstays of the region's economy. The Civil War, however, sounded the death knell of the cotton industry by taking away much of its workforce. Then came a hurricane in 1871, which wiped out the whole crop. Farmers turned to citrus, which was easier to grow than cotton. The region's citrus industry grew by leaps and bounds, helped along by developments such as the extension of the South Florida Railroad into Central Florida in 1880. Freezing weather in 1894–95 hit Central Florida's citrus

Oranges, Central Florida's juiciest crop

industry very hard, but it recovered and continued on course to make the region one of the world's leading producers of citrus fruit.

During the hard freezes, an innovative citrus grower, John B. Steinmetz, converted his citrus packing house into a skating rink, built a bath-house and picnic area, and created a toboggan slide that led into a spring. Thus was set up the region's first entertainment complex, a precursor of things to come.

With the advent of electricity in 1900, telephones in 1901, and the first cars in 1903, Central Florida entered the 20th century. The Orlando Municipal Airport opened in 1928. A major turning point was in 1955, when the NASA space program was launched at Cape Canaveral near Orlando. The Glenn L. Martin Company set up a missile factory south of the city in 1956, and became the area's largest employer before Walt Disney arrived.

The success of Disney's Magic Kingdom® led to a proliferation of theme parks. SeaWorld® Orlando opened in 1973, while Walt Disney World® continued to expand with the setting up of Epcot®, Disney-MGM Studios®, and Animal Kingdom®. In 1977, Wet 'n Wild®, the world's first water park, opened with a splash. In 1990, Universal Orlando® entered the arena with Universal Studios Florida®, followed a few years later by Universal CityWalk® and Islands of Adventure®. The Wizarding World of Harry Potter™ opened at Universal Orlando® in 2010. This wealth of entertainment options has earned Orlando the title of "Theme Park Capital of the World," and has firmly entrenched it as one of the world's topmost vacation spots.

BEYOND THE THEME PARKS
Central Florida's tourist appeal is not limited to its theme parks. The great outdoors beckons along the East Coast and the forests and waterways of the interior. Pristine beaches, lush state and county parks, and natural sanctuaries are all within easy reach of the

A dizzying thrill ride at SeaWorld® Orlando

A Disney Cruise Line® ship at a gleaming terminal in Port Canaveral

highways and at times run parallel to them, making driving in the area an enjoyable experience. Another way to enjoy the region's natural beauty is to board a seaplane from Orlando: rides and tours take passengers from the water to the air for amazing sightings of alligators, eagles, deer, and other wildlife in their natural habitat.

Outdoor activities are available in plenty, from biking, hiking, and golfing to swimming, angling, boating, and most other watersports. Additionally, outstanding professional sports bring tourists to the region in droves. The cruise industry is also flourishing, with Port Canaveral, the world's second largest multi-day cruise port, just 45 minutes east of Orlando. Thousands of visitors take the Disney Cruise Line ships and other luxury cruises from this port to destinations around the world.

Along the Space Coast is the Kennedy Space Center, home to NASA. Opened to the public in 1996, it attracts more than 1.5 million visitors each year to explore the workings of space technology.

Farther north up the Space Coast is Daytona Beach, synonymous with car racing. From 1903 to 1935, all of the world's land speed records were set here. Stock cars began racing at Ormond Beach in 1936, and the first Daytona 200 motorcyle race took place there the following year. In 1959 Daytona International Speedway opened, and racing on the beach was

A Florida Film Festival poster

abandoned. The speedway hosts numerous sports car, motorcycle, and go-karting races, attracting racing aficionados from all over the world.

Apart from the big theme parks, Central Florida offers countless smaller entertainment venues, ranging from the old-fashioned to the ultra-glitzy. Trendy nightspots, dinner shows, rodeos, fine dining, and a surfeit of shopping options add to the Orlando area's charm. There is plenty of cultural activity as well, with art and history museums dotting the area, and a highly active theater, opera, ballet, film, and live concert scene.

Central Florida's weather plays no small role in the region's appeal. Many people think of the area as a place where the sun always shines and the temperatures are warm, but this is not always so and there are days and

Shuttle launch at Kennedy Space Center

Glittering high-rises reflected in the placid waters of Lake Eola in Downtown Orlando

evenings in December, January, and February when it can get extremely cold. However, this in no way detracts from Central Florida's status as a year-round destination.

ECONOMY & TOURISM

For most of its history, the main source of revenue of the region – and the entire state – has been agriculture. Improved communications and transportation have kept the citrus and cattle industries buoyant. The area along the Kissimmee River is Florida's principal cattle ranching country, and the town of Kissimmee is known as the state's "Cow Capital." The region has contributed hugely to making Florida second only to Kentucky in the raising of beef cattle in the Southeastern states. Central Florida also continues to be the state's major supplier of citrus fruits; here, fruit trees stretch as far as the eye can see. The high-tech

Tourists riding a trail at a resort in Orlando

industry has also become a significant factor in the region's economy.

However, it is tourism that is now the mainstay of the economy of Central Florida. Theme parks dominate the region's tourism industry, but Orlando has also emerged as one of the country's leaders in the meetings and conventions industry. The city's Orange County Convention Center is one of the country's largest. The broader Orlando area has more than 115,000 hotel rooms, testifying to the huge numbers of visitors drawn by its many entertainment and business opportunities. Today, tourism is the largest employer in Metropolitan Orlando, accounting for around 27 percent of the jobs.

PEOPLE & CULTURE

The state "where everyone is from somewhere else," Florida has always been a mix of cultures and nationalities. The Seminole Indians, who arrived in the 17th century, now live mostly on reservations. The best candidates for the title of "true Floridian" are probably the Cracker farmers, whose ancestors settled in Central Florida and its environs in the 1800s; their name comes perhaps from the cracking of their cattle whips or the cracking of corn to make grits. However, visitors rarely encounter a Cracker in Orlando or the nearby heavily populated areas.

North Americans have poured into Florida since World War II; the 20th most populous state in the US in 1950, Florida is now ranked fourth. The largest single group to move south has been the retirees, for whom Florida's climate and leisurely lifestyle hold great appeal after a life of hard work. They take full advantage of Central Florida's abundance of recreational and cultural opportunities. Many seniors can be seen playing a round of golf, fishing, or browsing around the state-of-the-art shopping malls. An increasing number of new arrivals are young people who see Central Florida as a land of opportunity because of its booming tourism industry. They find it easy to get jobs as tour guides, hotel staff, theme park workers, and numerous other posts related to the thriving tourist-oriented economy.

From 1959 on, there has also been massive immigration from Latin America. There are many Mexican farm-workers as well as a large Cuban population in Florida. Many businesses in Central Florida hire employees who speak Spanish in addition to English because of the numerous residents and vacationers from Latin American countries. This ethnic diversity is celebrated in the local food, which features genuine re-creations of Caribbean and other ethnic dishes. Several exciting and innovative dishes have also originated in the region as a result of the craze for cross-cultural cuisine.

Zora Neale Hurston, leading writer of her time

The diversity of Central Florida's people is also celebrated in many festivals held throughout the year, such as the Native American Festival in September in Silver Springs, the Epcot® International Food and Wine Festival in October and November, and Viva la Musica at Sea-World® in March and April. Another significant cultural event is held in Eatonville, the oldest incorporated African-American community in the US. This festival is named for its famous resident Zora Neale Hurston (1891–1960), a well-known novelist, folklorist, and anthropologist.

Relaxed and laidback are the words that best describe the people of Central Florida. It is also the area's dress code: rarely will visitors come across a place that requires them to wear a jacket and a tie. People are often seen in the fanciest of restaurants in blue jeans and tennis shoes. Central Florida is a place where tourists can ask a native for directions, and get a friendly smile and an answer, no matter how complicated the question. Folk here are rarely in a rush to get anywhere. They came to Central Florida to escape the harsh winters in the north and elsewhere. They are here to relax and have fun, and they are quite proficient at it.

A cabin owner fishes from his front porch at the Wekiva River Corridor near Orlando

Theme Parks

The attractions at Walt Disney World®, Universal Orlando®, SeaWorld®, Discovery Cove®, and Wet 'n Wild® give a whole new meaning to the word "fun." There is something for everyone, young and old, at these amazing theme parks. On offer are the high-voltage excitement of rides – including roller coasters as well as simulator and flume rides – the thrill of animal encounters and Space Age attractions, the magic of fairy-tales and the movies, the visual extravaganza of parades and fireworks, and much more, with one theme park usually specializing, or scoring over the others, in a particular area.

Parades
Magic Kingdom® has the biggest and best parades, along Main Street, in the afternoons and evenings. Spectacular affairs, they feature grandiose floats, with colorfully clad Disney characters and special effects.

Fireworks
Dazzling displays against the superb setting of Cinderella's Castle make the fireworks at Magic Kingdom® difficult to beat.

Kid's rides at their best are to be found at Magic Kingdom®'s Fantasyland®. Most of them are based on classic Disney films.

Science attractions at Epcot®'s Future World win hands-down. One of the most popular is the simulated adventure Mission: SPACE, designed with the help of professional astronauts.

Lake Tibet

Lake Mabel

Lake Sheen

WINTER GARDEN-VINELAND ROAD

Bay Lake

Magic Kingdom® Park
(See pp34–41)

WALT DISNEY WORLD® RESORT

WORLD DRIVE

EPCOT CENTER DRIVE

Epcot®
(See pp42–53)

Downtown Disney®
(See pp74–5)

Disney's Hollywood Studios
(See pp54–63)

Typhoon Lagoon
(See p71)

Disney's Animal Kingdom®
(See pp64–7)

Blizzard Beach
(See p70)

424

ESPN Wide World of Sports®
(See p178)

4

Wildlife
More than 1,700 animals crowd the best theme park in which to view wildlife, Animal Kingdom. Glimpse hippos, giraffes, and zebras on a jeep ride through a re-created African landscape on Kilimanjaro Safaris.

Sports
With facilities for more than 30 sports – including baseball, basketball, tennis, and much more – ESPN Wide World of Sports® overshadows all other sports venues at theme parks.

Thrill Rides
Universal Orlando® reigns supreme in thrill rides, using amazing special effects. One of the best is Revenge of the Mummy® – The Ride, a high-speed indoor roller coaster that takes guests into an ancient Egypt of curses and horrifying creatures; the set is a masterpiece of design and the effects are mind-blowing.

UNIVERSAL
ORLANDO
Universal Studios Florida® (4)
(See pp89–93)

Islands of Adventure
(See pp96–7) (439)

Universal CityWalk®
(See pp98–9)

Wet 'n Wild
(See pp100–101) (482)

TURKEY LAKE ROAD

APOPKA VINELAND ROAD

Big Sand Lake

BEE LINE EXPRESSWAY (528)

SeaWorld Orlando®
(See pp82–5)

Discovery Cove
(See pp86–7)

INTERNATIONAL DRIVE

Lake Bryan

(4)

(417)

0 km   1
0 miles   1

Water Rides
Wet 'n Wild® takes the honors as the water park with the best rides – though suitable only for older children and adults. Its big-thrill water rides include the Flyer, a six-story toboggan ride with plenty of exciting watery curves.

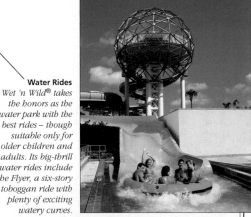

Sealife
SeaWorld® is the park for those who want close encounters with sea creatures. See incredible live shows with highly trained dolphins, whales, sea otters, penguins, and more.

Wildlife & Natural Habitats

Central Florida's great variety of habitats and wildlife is due to the meeting of temperate and subtropical climates in many areas, complemented by its humidity, sandy soils, low elevation, and proximity to the water. An amazing diversity of habitats is found within several wildlife preserves, such as Merritt Island National Wildlife Refuge, and numerous state and county parks. Native flora in Central Florida ranges from longleaf and slash pines to various palms and cypress trees, while the region is home to more than 4,000 species of wildlife – from alligators and loggerhead sea turtles to brown pelicans and red-bellied woodpeckers.

Oranges
This introduced plant has thrived in Central Florida. The state's citrus industry supplies the bulk of the nation's crop.

SCRUBS & SANDHILLS

Called "Florida's Ancient Islands," the ridges of Central Florida were formed along the backbone of peninsular Florida millions of years ago when ocean levels were much higher than they are today. The sandy, porous soils of the ridges are home to two types of high and dry plant communities – scrubs and sandhills. Several species of plants and animals unique to Central Florida are found in this habitat.

Scrub oaks *are generally less than 10 ft (3 m) in height. These hardy plants produce plentiful acorns for the region's fauna.*

The gopher tortoise, *the only type found in Florida, has a large, thick shell and heavily scaled legs.*

PINE FLATWOODS

Pine flatwoods are the most common plant community in Central Florida. Dominated by an overstory of pines, the subcanopy of flatwoods is comprised mainly of saw palmetto shrubs, but there may be 50 to 75 different plant species per acre. Pine flatwoods are often interspersed with swamps and other habitats, and thrive when periodically swept by fire. The plants and animals here have adapted to survive the difficult conditions.

The bobcat *has a distinctive short tail with a dark tip, facial ruff, and spotted coat, and hunts by both day and night.*

Palmetto *is one of the most widespread plants in Florida. The saw palmetto variety is harvested and used for medicinal purposes.*

PROTECTING THE SEA TURTLE

From May through October, the East Coast beaches of Central Florida are host to three species of sea turtles – green, loggerhead, and leatherback turtles. These magnificent animals emerge from the surf at night to lay their eggs in nests, dug into the dry sand, then return to the sea. Two months later, about 100 baby turtles emerge from each of these nests and crawl to the ocean. To protect these gentle creatures, beach driving, parking, and lighting on beachfront properties are regulated.

At Marine Science Center, Ponce Inlet

Avoid walking or cycling in places posted as nesting areas, and never disturb the protective screening over turtle nests.

Loggerhead turtle hatchlings heading to sea

FRESHWATER MARSHES & SWAMPS

Freshwater marshes and swamps are usually inundated with water throughout or during a portion of the year. Such wetlands once comprised about 50 percent of the land area in Central Florida. Freshwater swamps are dominated by cypress or bay trees, while marshes tend to be open, vegetated mostly by rushes and sedges. They are rich in bird life, such as varieties of herons, storks, and warblers.

RIVERS

The floodplain – the low land along either bank that is periodically flooded – of a Central Florida river contains forests of water-tolerant trees or low marshes. Some rivers "bubble up" from natural free-flowing springs while others start slowly as small streams. As rivers make their way toward the sea, they form brackish estuaries that support saltwater fish and wildlife.

Pitcher plants *grow in acidic, saturated soil. The species found in Central Florida is called Sarracenia minor, and has gracefully curved yellow flowers.*

Bald cypress, *one of the largest trees in North America, is a long-lived wetland species, known for its "knees" – projections from its submerged roots – and buttressed trunk.*

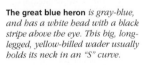

The great blue heron *is gray-blue, and has a white head with a black stripe above the eye. This big, long-legged, yellow-billed wader usually holds its neck in an "S" curve.*

The bald eagle, *an endangered species found by the ocean, lakes, and rivers, has a distinctive white head and tail and a dark brown body. Its wings span 7 ft (2 m).*

The Space Shuttle

Shuttle mission insignia

The Space Coast's Kennedy Space Center was NASA's launch headquarters and the home of the space shuttle program until the last mission in 2011. The program was begun in the late 1970s, by which time the cost of sending astronauts into space had become too much for the American space budget; hundreds of millions of dollars were spent lifting the Apollo missions into space, with little more than a scorched command module ever returning to earth. It was time to develop a reusable spacecraft made for years of service, whose main cost after production would lie in maintenance. The answer was the space shuttle – *Columbia* was launched into space on April 12, 1981.

When in orbit, *the shuttle's cargo doors are opened. The Hubble telescope was one of its payloads.*

The flight deck *of the shuttle is extremely complex – even more so than the shuttle itself, which is built along the lines of an aircraft. You can get some idea of how the shuttle is navigated at the Launch Status Center (see p127).*

Tracks enable the tower to be moved away before liftoff.

The Crawlerway *is a double pathway, 180 ft (55 m) wide, specially designed to withstand the weight of a shuttle as it was taken to the launch pad by gigantic crawlers. The rock surface overlies a layer of asphalt and a 7-ft (2-m) bed of crushed stone.*

The Crawler backs away once the shuttle is in place.

SHUTTLE CYCLE

The Space Shuttle has three principal elements: the main orbiter spacecraft (with its three engines), an external tank of liquid hydrogen and oxygen fuel, and two solid-fuel booster rockets, which provide the extra thrust needed for liftoff. When operational, the shuttle reached its orbit in stages.

1. Prelaunch
The external tank and rocket boosters are fitted to the orbiter in the Vehicle Assembly Building. Then it is moved to the launch pad.

2. Launch
After a final check, the shuttle blasts off, using its own three engines and its two booster rockets.

The service tower gives access for fueling and cargo installation.

The access arm is a corridor through which the astronauts board the shuttle.

Orbiter

Solid Rocket Booster

The flame trench channels the burning gases away from the vehicle.

THE SHUTTLE LAUNCHES

Since the shuttle's maiden voyage in 1981, there have been many missions shared between the *Columbia, Challenger, Discovery, Atlantis,* and *Endeavour* vehicles. The program was severely crippled when *Challenger* exploded shortly after liftoff in 1986, and again when *Columbia* disintegrated on re-entry in 2003. The last shuttle launch, of *Atlantis,* took place in 2011 and the shuttle fleet has been dispersed to new homes in US museums. *Atlantis* will be on permanent display at the Kennedy Center. There are plans for future launches of private industry rockets.

Shuttle clearing the launch tower

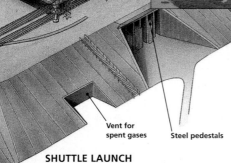

For landing *back on Earth, the shuttle re-enters the atmosphere and begins to glide with its engines off. It heads toward the Space Center and proceeds to land on the runway at an incredible speed of 220 mph (360 km/h).*

Vent for spent gases

Steel pedestals

SHUTTLE LAUNCH

The launch pad is made up of 183 million cu ft (52,000 cu m) of reinforced concrete, supported by six steel pedestals. The flame trench is flooded with cooling water when the engines ignite, producing an immense cloud of steam.

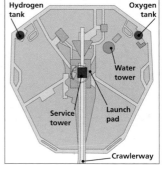

PLAN OF THE LAUNCH PAD

Hydrogen tank

Oxygen tank

Water tower

Service tower

Launch pad

Crawlerway

3. Separation
Two minutes later, the boosters separate and are parachuted back to earth. At eight minutes, the external tank detaches.

4. Orbital Operations
Using its own engines, the shuttle maneuvers itself into orbit and begins its operations. The mission may last between 7 and 18 days, flying at an altitude of 115–450 miles (185–725 km).

5. Re-entry
The shuttle re-enters the atmosphere backward, using its engines to decelerate. It turns nose-first as it descends into the stratosphere. Parachutes slow it down.

CENTRAL FLORIDA THROUGH THE YEAR

One of Central Florida's biggest attractions is its year-round mild weather. The region's climate has long been its top drawing card for tourists and residents. The average annual temperature is a comfortable 72.4°F (22.4°C) and the average rainfall is 50 in (1,270 mm), keeping the area green with flowering plants and trees year-round. The busiest time in the Orlando area is from November to December, when tourists come in huge numbers to enjoy the mild winters. Summer can be somewhat hot, but Orlando's theme parks still attract families with kids on school vacations, with some hotels offering special summer rates for families, including free transportation to the theme parks. Whatever time of year you visit, you will encounter an entertaining festival of some kind. For a complete schedule of festivals, contact the local tourist offices.

Livestock show, Central Florida Fair

Motorcyclists show off their bikes during Bike Week, Daytona Beach

SPRING

Starting in late February, students from all over the US head for Florida's coastal resorts, such as the Daytona Beach area, for spring break. For six weeks these areas are bursting, putting pressure on accommodation. Major League Baseball's "spring training" camps are also a big attraction in Central Florida.

MARCH

Orlando Bike Week *(first weekend)*. Harley enthusiasts throughout the globe eagerly anticipate this annual event, headquartered at the Orlando Historic Factory dealership.
Bike Week *(first weekend)*, Daytona Beach. A huge and popular motorcycle event brimming with shows, concerts, and exhibits.

Central Florida Fair *(early Mar)*, Orlando. Held since 1914, this large fair features more than 90 rides and exhibits, including livestock and horticulture displays, arts and crafts, and numerous food stalls.
SeaWorld®, Bud & BBQ Fest *(early Mar)*, Orlando. Two weekends of fun, food, and racing at this park-wide event.
Florida Strawberry Festival® *(early Mar)*. Music, rides, livestock shows, contests, and cookoffs; a piece of Americana dating back to 1930.
Annual Winter Park Sidewalk Arts Festival *(mid-Mar)*, Orlando. The most prestigious outdoor fine arts festival in Southeastern USA, this features three days of art, food, music, hands-on children's activities, and jazz.

Antique Boat Festival *(late Mar)*, Mount Dora. Display of more than 150 classic and historic boats.
Annual Downtown Antique Fair *(late Mar)*, Mount Dora. Treasures on display in downtown streets.
Florida Film Festival *(late Mar)*, Orlando. Ranked among the best film festivals in the world, this features more than 100 films, documentaries, and shorts from around the globe.
Orlando Shakespeare Theater *(Jan–Mar)*, Orlando. Performances take place at the state-of-the-art John & Rita Lowndes Shakespeare Center *(see p107)*.
Epcot® Flower & Garden Festival *(Mar–May)*. Epcot® blooms with elaborate gardens and topiary displays. You can attend gardening workshops.

FLORIDA FILM FESTIVAL

Florida Film Festival logo

APRIL

Sailboat Regatta *(early Apr)*, Mount Dora. This is the oldest sailing regatta in the State.
Spring Fiesta in the Park *(Apr)*, Orlando. Booths full of regional arts and crafts line the shores of Lake Eola.
Maitland Spring Festival of the Arts *(mid-Apr)*. The juried arts and fine crafts show highlights original artwork by the finest craftsmen in Southeast USA.

Boats on display at the Antique Boat Festival, Mount Dora

Annual Taste of Winter Park *(mid-Apr)*. Sample cuisine from more than 30 local restaurants.

Indian River Festival *(mid-Apr)*, Titusville. Live music, carnival rides, food, arts, crafts, and antiques are some of the highlights here.

Cracker Day *(late Apr)*, DeLand (near Daytona Beach). Celebration of Florida heritage with games for the entire family. Features a cattleman's barbecue.

Morse Museum *(late Apr)*. Explore the country's largest collection of Tiffany artworks, including glass, jewlery and paintings.

MAY

Viva La Musica *(mid-May)*, SeaWorld Orlando. Two spicy weekend fiestas of Latino music, dance, culture, authentic arts and crafts, and great food.

Orlando International Fringe Festival *(mid-May)*. The 10-day festival of theatrical performances showcases original works; premiere performances; and first-class improvizational comedy, musicals, drama, mime, and dance in 500 shows by performers from around the world.

Florida Music Festival *(mid-May)*, Downtown Orlando. A program of shows by emerging and established indie and rock bands takes place in clubs and on outdoor stages along Downtown Orlando's Orange Avenue.

SUMMER

Many families head to Orlando for the summer season and for good reason. The hotel rates are discounted for families and the theme parks stay open for a longer period, giving tourists more time to enjoy the attractions. The big summer holiday is of course Independence Day on July 4, which is celebrated with fireworks, parades, and picnics.

JUNE

Silver Spurs Rodeo *(early Jun)*, Kissimmee. One of the area's largest rodeos attracts some of the world's best riders. Visitors wear their rodeo finery to watch bull and bronco riding, barrel racing, and bareback riding. There's a barbecue cook-off too.

Fiesta San Juan en Wet 'n Wild® *(late Jun)*. Wet 'n Wild® celebrates Latin culture in this family-friendly fiesta

of dancing, music, Latin food, competitions, and local Latin entertainment. Activities culminate at midnight when everyone takes a big splash.

JULY

Lake Eola Picnic in the Park *(early Jul)*, Orlando. Celebrate the Fourth of July at this Downtown Orlando tradition with games and entertainment. Fireworks wrap up the show at 9pm.

Coke Zero 400 *(early Jul)*, Daytona Beach. NASCAR racing on Daytona International Speedway during the Independence weekend. Other activities include concerts and beach parties.

Christmas in July Craft Fair *(mid-Jul)*, Lakeland. Shop from local vendors for beautiful handmade gifts for family and friends.

AUGUST

Ocala Shrine Club Rodeo *(mid-Aug)*. Cow-roping, steer-riding, and more, are on offer at this action-packed annual attraction, held at the Livestock Pavilion.

Ocala Sturgis Rally & Bike Show *(mid-Aug)*. Field events are open to spectators.

Downtown Concert Series *(late Aug)*. Free outdoor concerts featuring international artists are held at City Hall Plaza.

A contest at Fiesta San Juan en Wet 'n Wild®

Display of glass at the Festival of the Masters, Downtown Disney®

FALL

The theme parks are less crowded in the fall and the temperatures are cooler, making this an ideal time to visit Central Florida. Halloween is the big fall holiday in Orlando, with several theme parks offering special celebrations. Thanksgiving is the other major holiday. Fall is the best time for bird-watching and visiting the region's wildlife preserves.

SEPTEMBER

Viva La Musica *(mid-Sep)*, SeaWorld® Orlando. A celebration of Hispanic food and culture during Hispanic Heritage Month. Live performances by hot Latino bands. **Christian Rock Festivals** *(mid-Sep)*. Two concerts held at different theme parks on the same night showcase some of the most powerful voices

in contemporary Christian music: Night of Joy at Disney's Magic Kingdom®, and Rock the Universe at Universal Orlando®. **Lake Mirror Classic Auto Festival** *(mid-Sep)*, Lakeland. All types of classic automobiles on display.

OCTOBER

Epcot® International Food & Wine Festival *(Oct–Nov)*. The temptation to dine your way around World Showcase is intensified by cooking demonstrations, samples of exotic dishes, and international wines and desserts. **Bicycle Festival** *(second weekend)*, Mount Dora. Attracting 1,500 cyclists, this is Florida's oldest and largest bicycling event. **Beertoberfest** *(mid-Oct)*, Orlando. This day-long event featuring beers made by more than 40 brewers from the USA and around the world, as well as great food and live music, turns Downtown Orlando's Church Street into Florida's largest beer garden. **Biketoberfest** *(third weekend)*, Daytona Beach. International motorcycle show, demonstrations, and concerts. **Craft Fair** *(fourth weekend)*, Mount Dora. More than 350 craftspeople and 250,000 visitors come from all over the nation for this fair.

NOVEMBER

ICE! At Gaylord Palms *(early Nov–early Jan)*. This spectacular ice display features holiday figures such as Santa Claus and Rudolph the Red Nosed Reindeer. Dress warmly when visiting this popular attraction. **Winter Park Concours d'Elegance** *(early Nov)*, Park Avenue. Event showcasing and judging more than 200 of the world's most exotic cars and motorcycles. There is also a car parade.

Fall Fiesta in the Park *(first weekend)*, Downtown Orlando. Enjoy 550 booths full of regional arts and crafts along Lake Eola. One of the top five outdoor arts and crafts shows in Florida. **Halifax Art Festival** *(early Nov)*, Daytona Beach. This annual festival features the works of more than 250 artists, plus live entertainment. **Native American Festival** *(early Nov)*, Silver Springs. A celebration of Native American culture, arts, crafts, and entertainment. **Festival of the Masters** *(mid-Nov)*, Downtown Disney®. More than 200 artists participate in this three-day festival of the fine arts. Music and food round out the activities. **Daytona Turkey Run** *(late Nov)*. Car show and swap meet on the Thanksgiving weekend at the Daytona International Speedway. **Birthplace of Speed Celebration** *(late Nov)*, Ormond Beach. Gaslight parade of antique cars, as well as a car show. **Light Up Mount Dora** *(Nov 28)*. Close to two million sparkling lights switch on in celebration of the holiday season. Festivities include singing by the community choir, ballet, and other entertainment, at Donnelly Park.

PUBLIC HOLIDAYS

New Year (Jan 1)
Martin Luther King Day (3rd Mon, Jan)
Presidents' Day (3rd Mon, Feb)
Memorial Day (last Mon, May)
Independence Day (Jul 4)
Labor Day (1st Mon, Sep)
Columbus Day (2nd Mon, Oct)
Election Day (1st Tue, Nov)
Halloween (Oct 31)
Veterans Day (Nov 11)
Thanksgiving (4th Thu, Nov)
Christmas Day (Dec 25)

CLIMATE OF ORLANDO

°F/°C	Apr	Jul	Oct	Jan
high	83/28	91/33	85/29	71/22
low	59/15	73/23	66/19	49/9
☀ (hrs)	10 hrs	10 hrs	10 hrs	9 hrs
☂ (in)	1.8 in	7.2 in	2.4 in	2.3 in

Zora Neale Hurston Festival of Arts & Humanities, Eatonville

WINTER

The crowds multiply in winter as the flood of "snowbirds" from the north intensifies. The celebrities arrive too, some to relax, others to perform during the region's busiest entertainment season. The parks are all aglow with Christmas lights and festivities – there are special Christmas parades. Magic Kingdom® is at its most colorful.

DECEMBER

Mickey's Very Merry Christmas Party *(Nov–Dec)*, Magic Kingdom®. Evening of seasonal fun complete with snow and enchanting Christmas-themed parades.
Festival of Trees *(early Dec)*, Ocala. Decorated trees and wreaths are displayed at the Appleton Museum of Art, along with crafts and decorations created by local artisans, which are for sale.

Festival of Lights *(mid-Dec)*, Silver Springs. Follow millions of sparkling lights through a maze of illuminated gardens, twinkling topiaries, and dozens of holiday scenes.

JANUARY

Birding & Wildlife Festival *(Jan)*, Titusville. This festival features birding trips, wildlife seminars, workshops, an art competition, and paddling adventures.
Central Florida Scottish Highland Games *(mid-Jan)*. Pipe bands, dancing, athletic competitions, and food.
Renninger's Antique Extravaganza *(third weekend, Jan, Feb & Nov)*, Mount Dora. An antique lover's dream, this event held at Renninger's Twin Markets has more than 1,500 dealers.
Zora Neale Hurston Festival of Arts & Humanities *(late Jan)*, Eatonville. This festival highlights the life and works

of one of America's most celebrated collectors and interpreters of Southern rural African-American culture. Features art exhibits, theatrical performances, and educational programs.

FEBRUARY

Mount Dora Arts Festival *(first weekend)*. Celebrated on the streets of Mount Dora since 1977, this festival showcases the works of more than 300 juried artists. Artists compete for awards in painting, printmaking, photography, jewelry, sculpture, and various other categories. There is also live entertainment, children's activities, and food.
Speedweeks *(first three weeks)*, Daytona. Daytona International Speedway becomes the World Center of Racing during three weeks in February. Action kicks off with the Rolex 24 Hours at Daytona, followed by events leading up to the Daytona 500.
ArtsFest *(mid-Feb)*, Orlando. Showcases Central Florida's best in arts and culture, with more than 50 planned events, which range from symphony and ballet performances to art exhibits and lessons in Central Florida's history.
Mardi Gras at Universal Orlando *(mid-Feb–mid-Mar)*. Music and pageantry, colorful costumes, parades, food, and high-energy excitement at this Mardi Gras celebration at Universal.

Daytona 500 race at Daytona International Speedway, during Speedweeks

Moss-covered oaks in Lake Kissimmee State Park ▷

WALT DISNEY WORLD® RESORT & CENTRAL FLORIDA AREA BY AREA

WALT DISNEY WORLD® RESORT

The largest entertainment complex on earth, Walt Disney World® Resort sprawls across 47 sq miles (121 sq km), encompassing four theme parks renowned for their imaginative and state-of-the-art attractions. Two water parks, a sports complex, a cruise ship line, and a range of hotels, restaurants, nightclubs, golf courses, and shops combine to make it the complete vacation experience.

Unless you're a cynic, Walt Disney World® will amaze you. Peerless in its creativity and attention to detail, the resort offers a respite from the real world and takes you on a trip into a realm of fantasy and wonder.

Disney's first theme park, Magic Kingdom®, opened in 1971. Consisting of seven "Lands," it remains one of the most popular theme parks of all time. In 1982, the ever-evolving Disney set up the 300-acre (120-ha) Epcot®, an international and futuristic showplace, which focuses on discoveries and scientific achievements, and also provides an insight into the cultures of 11 nations across the world.

Disney's Hollywood Studios® (previously Disney MGM Studios®) followed in 1989. The smallest of the four parks, it celebrates films and television. Disney's Animal Kingdom® covers 500 acres (200 ha) of jungles and savanna featuring exotic creatures, safaris, and trails. Then there are the water parks, Typhoon Lagoon and Blizzard Beach, with their ingenious landscaping and some thoroughly enjoyable rides. Downtown Disney® amalgamates shows, restaurants, and shops into a vibrant entertainment area that pulsates at night.

Its cruise line offers two luxury ships with various amenities and cruise options. A sports lover's paradise, the resort boasts the massive ESPN Wide World of Sports® complex, 18-hole and mini golf courses, and activities such as hiking, horseback riding, tennis, watersports, and race car driving. Accommodation options are equally varied and include several resorts and a camping ground.

The Primeval Whirl®, a thrilling ride at Disney's Animal Kingdom®, Walt Disney World® Resort

◁ Cinderella's Castle, a fairy-tale fantasy in full bloom at Magic Kingdom®

Exploring Walt Disney World® Resort

Let your imagination take flight at this world-class entertainment center, where there is something for everyone, regardless of their age. Plan to spend at least a day in each of Disney's "big four" – Magic Kingdom®, Epcot®, Disney's Hollywood Studios®, and Disney's Animal Kingdom®. Don't miss a chance to cool off at the two water parks – Blizzard Beach and Typhoon Lagoon. Or you might choose to let off steam at ESPN Wide World of Sports® complex; golf courses; hiking and riding trails; and pools and lakes for swimming, boating, and waterskiing. With more than 30 resorts on the premises, you can go back to your hotel to rest before returning to one of the parks for the fireworks or checking out a show at Downtown Disney®.

SIGHTS AT A GLANCE

Blizzard Beach ❺
Disney's Hollywood Studios® ❸
Disney's Animal Kingdom® ❹
Downtown Disney® ❽
Epcot® ❷
Fort Wilderness Resort & Campground ❼
Magic Kingdom® ❶
Typhoon Lagoon ❻

0 meters   500
0 yards   500

Magic Kingdom®
Seven Lands of fantasy and adventure encircle the stunningly beautiful Cinderella's Castle.

MAGIC KINGDOM® ❶

Ticket and Transportation Center

DISNEY'S ANIMAL KINGDOM® ❹

Blizzard Beach

Winter Summerland ❺

TAMPA

IRLO BRONSON MEMORIAL HIGHWAY

192

Disney's Animal Kingdom®
Experience the thrill of the wild through encounters with animals, as well as the pure fun of African safaris, river rafting, treks, and some enjoyable rides.

KEY

🅿 Parking
⛽ Gas station
⛳ Golf course
— Monorail
═ Interstate highway
▬ Major highway
═ Secondary route

Blizzard Beach
Thrilling rides and exhilarating water slides are on offer at this cleverly designed and delightful 66-acre (27-ha) water theme park.

Epcot®
Travel across continents, blast into space on a rocket to Mars, embark on an underwater adventure, and take a peek into the future with remarkable discoveries and inventions.

Disney's Hollywood Studios®
There's no business like show business at Disney's Hollywood Studios, where guests of all ages are immersed in the glitz, glamor, and magic of Hollywood.

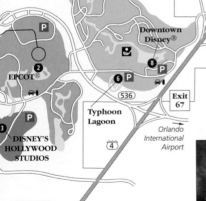

Fort Wilderness
Resort &
Campground

ORLANDO

Downtown
Disney®

Exit
68

EPCOT®

Exit
67

536

Typhoon
Lagoon

Orlando
International
Airport

DISNEY'S
HOLLYWOOD
STUDIOS

ESPN Wide
World of Sports®

Exit
64B

← KISSIMMEE

TAMPA

▦	Magic Kingdom Resort Area
▦	Epcot Resort Area
▦	Disney's Hollywood Studios
▦	Disney's Animal Kingdom Resort Area
▦	Downtown Disney Resort Area

SEE ALSO

• *Where to Stay* pp138–40

• *Where to Eat* pp148–50

GETTING AROUND
An extensive, efficient transportation system handles an average of 200,000 guests each day. The transportation hub of Walt Disney World is the Ticket and Transportation Center (TTC). Monorails, ferryboats, and motorcoach shuttle services operate daily. Additionally, hotels outside the resort area offer free shuttle services to the parks. For further details, see page 76.

Downtown Disney®
Themed celebrity restaurants, shows, and the largest outlet for Disney merchandise – all this and much more are on offer at this exciting entertainment and shopping complex.

Magic Kingdom® ❶

As Disney's quintessential theme park, Magic Kingdom® makes a popular reappearance in similar form in California, Japan, and France. Cartoon characters and nostalgic visions of how the world, and particularly America, once was and how it might be again fill its relentlessly cheerful 107 acres (43 ha). The park is made up of seven Lands evoking a particular theme or era, such as the Wild West, Colonial America, and the future. Symptomatic of the park's effervescence are elaborate parades, entertaining musical street performers, and three-dimensional Disney characters.

TOP TIPS

• If you're an early entry guest, try and reach the rope barrier next to Peter Pan and It's a Small World about 15–20 minutes before the official opening time.
• In order to reduce the number of guests in the attractions prior to closing, much of the internal queuing areas are roped off so the lines of waiting guests appear long from the outside.
• The Fastpass system works as an incredible timesaver. Reduce the waiting time by up to an hour (sometimes more) at most of the popular rides by obtaining complimentary passes at dispensers near the entrance to the ride in question. Return within a scheduled "window" (usually an hour) to get into a much shorter line. Prioritize carefully as you get only one Fastpass at a time.

TACKLING THE PARK

Unless you are a guest at one of the Disney hotels, plan your visit at midweek or toward the end of the week as the park is busiest on weekends and early in the week. If you are staying at a Disney resort, you are in luck. As their guest, you will have access to early entry privileges on certain days at certain parks. Take this excellent opportunity and reach the entrance turnstiles an hour and a half before the official opening time. This will allow an extra 90 minutes of precious time to enjoy Fantasyland and Tomorrowland before the rest of the park opens.

Upon arrival at the park, you will receive a map showing the Lands and rides as well as the timings for the shows and parades. A notice board at the top of Main Street also offers this information and, additionally, gives a list of waiting times at various attractions. Getting around the park is relatively easy as the Lands emanate from the central hub, in front of Cinderella's Castle.

The most popular attractions are situated at opposite ends of the park, a considerable distance apart. As a result, you will probably end up walking more than you might expect. However, there are also other, more novel forms of transport. Main Street has a series of vehicles which, in keeping with the Disney storytelling ideal, serve to tell the story of transport from the horse-drawn tram to the motor car. A steam train makes a 20- minute circuit of the park, stopping at Main Street and Frontierland.

EATING & DRINKING

The park offers a wide selection of fast foods and an equally vast range of quick service places to choose from. For a reasonable meal, try the Liberty Tree Tavern.

Visitors on Main Street, USA® with Cinderella's Castle in the background

If you would like a quieter dining experience, the Crystal Palace is a good option. Cinderella's Royal Table, located within the castle itself, gives you a taste of royalty with its stately and regal ambience. Their specialty is prime ribs and, overall, the food is agreeable. The frequent appearances by Disney characters keep the kids entertained and makes for a magical meal. However, it is a good idea to make advance reservations in order to ensure a table at this popular eatery.

If you're looking for sandwiches, Aunt Polly's on Tom Sawyer Island is one of the best places to head for. However, this is the only fare on offer here.

WALT DISNEY'S VISION

Walt Disney (1901–66), the father of Mickey Mouse, was a pioneer in the field of animation. Watching his children at play in a squalid amusement park, Disney was struck by his ultimate inspiration – to build a place that was clean and filled with various attractions that parents and kids could enjoy together. He envisioned a theme park revolving around five Lands: Main Street, a setting plucked from late-19th/early 20th-century America; Adventureland, imbued with the mystery of exotic locales; Frontierland, a homage to the pioneers; Fantasyland, a place of whimsy inspired by the song "When You Wish Upon A Star;" and Tomorrowland, with a futuristic theme fit for the emerging Space Age. Disney picked a 160-acre (65-ha) site in Anaheim, California, and oversaw every aspect of the planning and construction of Disneyland. When Magic Kingdom opened its gates in 1955 and 28,000 people stormed in, tears reportedly streamed down Walt Disney's cheeks – his great dream had finally become a reality. Today, the Disney empire stretches across the globe, with theme parks in Paris and Tokyo. Orlando's Walt Disney World® Resort opened on October 21, 1971.

1 DAY ITINERARY

If you really want to cover the Magic Kingdom® in one day, be warned, it's a daunting task because of the distances involved. This is specially true in the summer.

1. After leaving the turnstiles, head immediately for the central hub. If the entire park is open, turn right and head for **Space Mountain®**. There might be ropes across areas at the hub. If so, wait at the rope entrance to Tomorrowland and head for Space Mountain® when the rope drops. This is an exciting ride for those looking for thrills. Alternatively, if you'd prefer a tamer start, make a beeline for **Buzz Lightyear's Space Ranger Spin**.
2. After Space Mountain®, choose between the **Tomorrowland® Indy Speedway** and the **Tomorrowland Arcade**. If you have preschoolers, you should head for Fantasyland through Tomorrowland (keep the speedway on your right and turn left at the Mad Tea Party) and ride **The Many Adventures of Winnie the Pooh**.
3. After Winnie, turn left and head across Dumbo the Flying Elephant toward **Peter Pan's Flight** and enjoy the ride.
4. Exit left, head to Liberty Square and visit **The Haunted Mansion®** on the right.
5. On leaving Haunted Mansion®, turn to the right and continue to **Splash Mountain®**. If the waiting period is more than half an hour, it might be a good idea at this point to get a Fastpass for this ride. Turn right from here and cross to the **Big Thunder Mountain Railroad**.
6. Take the exit from Big Thunder and cross the bridge bearing right to **Pirates of the Caribbean®**. Take the ride.
7. Now you can return to ride the Splash Mountain®.
8. After Splash Mountain®, backtrack to the **Jungle Cruise**. If the time slot is right, ride, otherwise see the **Enchanted Tiki Room Under New Management**.
9. Obtain a Fastpass for **Mickey's PhilharMagic** and grab a light lunch.
10. By the time lunch is over, you should be due to see Mickey's PhilharMagic.
11. Afterward, younger children and pre-schoolers will find plenty more to enjoy in Fantasyland®: **it's a small world**, **Snow White's Scary Adventures**, **Dumbo the Flying Elephant**, **Ariel's Grotto**, or the **Mad Tea Party**.
12. Cross the central hub to Tomorrowland and obtain a Fastpass ticket for **Buzz Lightyear**.
13. Visit the **Monsters Inc. Laugh Floor Comedy Club** and choose between **Astro Orbiter®** and **Walt Disney's Carousel of Progress**.
14. Return to ride Buzz Lightyear.
15. Cross the central hub to Frontierland, and find a comfortable, vantage spot to enjoy the full splendor of the **afternoon parade**.
16. Following the parade, you have a chance to take one last relaxing ride before dinner. Choose between the **Jungle Cruise** in Adventureland or climb aboard the **Liberty Square Riverboat**.
17. Following dinner, don't miss the **Main Street Electrical Parade**. If the park is closing early, view the parade from the Town Square. If it's open late, it's a good idea to see the parade from Main Street on the Tomorrowland side so that, when the parade has passed, you can return to the attractions in Tomorrowland and Fantasyland® to catch any rides you missed (or ride particular favorites again).
18. Finally, enjoy dinner at the California Grill (see p150) and watch the fireworks in comfort from the restaurant's wall of windows overlooking Magic Kingdom®.

TOP 10 ATTRACTIONS

MAIN STREET, USA®

On entering Main Street, take a step into Disney's fantasy of a small-town Victorian America that never was. As you walk down Main Street, you pass beneath the Main Street Station. From here, you can catch the train for a ride around the park. The trains run every ten minutes. Beneath the station are lockers where, for a small fee, you can store valuables and bags.

As you enter the Town Square, **City Hall** lies to your left. This is a good place to visit first if you are looking for information regarding the shows being performed and any special events that might be taking place during your stay. The **Town Square Exposition Hall** lies to the right as you enter the square. You can pick up film rolls and other camera supplies here, but the main shops are, as you would expect, along Main Street.

Main Street itself is a magnificent melange of color, shapes and music, all in astonishing detail. At night, the entire street assumes a magical ambience as thousands of glittering lights bring a resplendent glow to the spotlessly clean sidewalk. It's also an excellent place to see the popular **Main Street Electrical Parade** *(see p39)*, a shimmering fantasy of music, live action and illuminated floats.

ADVENTURELAND®

Lush foliage, evocative drumbeats, and Colonial buildings combine to conjure up vivid images of Africa and the Caribbean. Reached via a wooden bridge from the central hub, Adventureland is an exciting and entertaining fusion of the exotic and the tropical.

One of the first attractions you come across in this Land, the **Swiss Family Treehouse** is a great way to start your tour of this area of the park. The large, man-made replica of the elaborate treehouse described in the beloved 19th-century children's tale is magnificent to behold. Replete with little details and small signs, the tree is reminiscent of the ingenuity and Christian values of the fictional castaways. Climbing the tree provides you with a splendid overhead view of this section of the park. The exhibit also offers a refreshingly shady and breezy educational tour that is certain to capture the interest of pre-teen kids.

Guests enjoying The Magic Carpets of Aladdin ride, Adventureland®

The **Jungle Cruise** boat ride takes its guests around a variety of animatronically designed settings of deepest Africa, India, and South America. A much sought-after ride, it owes a huge part of its popularity to the immense entertainment value of the "boatman" whose often wacky and infectious humor never fails to amuse.

The **Enchanted Tiki Room Under New Management** is an amusing and cleverly animated attraction. It is also a pleasant way to spend 20 minutes or so out of the heat. Featuring characters from *Aladdin* and *The Lion King*, it is certainly worth a visit, just to see the walls change shape.

The **Pirates of the Caribbean®** is an extremely entertaining and remarkably detailed voyage. This thrilling

The Jungle Cruise, a journey into deep forests with a zany boatsman

journey takes you on a seemingly realistic cruise through crumbling, underground prisons, past fighting galleons of the 16th century, and through scenes of debauchery and mayhem. The colorful characters and loving detail have ensured that it remains one of the best of the original rides. Following the runaway success of the film version, this ride has recently been given a facelift and now may be too scary for young children. Although it has been said that it is not as good as the version presented in Disneyland Paris, the Audio-Animatronic® effects are well done and the ride is a favorite with park visitors.

In another popular ride, **The Magic Carpets of Aladdin**, four-passenger carpets circle around a giant replica of a genie's bottle; the carpets move at the "command" of the riders, while whimsical camels "spit" at the airborne guests.

At the exit, you will find one of the most interesting stores in the park. An excellent selection of essential Disney accessories and memorabilia is available for purchase here.

The careening Big Thunder Mountain Railroad ride

TOP TIPS

- *The Swiss Family Treehouse's pinnacle offers some spectacular picture opportunities of the rest of Adventureland®.*
- *Most Magic Kingdom® parades begin in Frontierland, near Splash Mountain®, so this is the best place to watch them.*
- *Try to arrive there about 45 minutes before the parade begins to get a good viewing spot and wait for the Disney characters to arrive.*
- *Daytime parades run from the Splash Mountain® area to the Town Square and the nighttime parades usually perform this route in reverse.*
- *To visit Splash Mountain® first, board the train at Main Street before the park opens. The train departs at opening time and reaches Frontierland 7 minutes later. This station is next to Big Thunder and Splash Mountain®.*

FRONTIERLAND®

Set in a Hollywood-inspired Wild West, this Land abounds with raised walkways and trading posts. The **Frontierland Shootin' Arcade** is reminiscent of both the Wild West and of country fairs gone by. The **Country Bear Jamboree**, on the other hand, provides a completely animatronic musical animal show, much liked by youngsters, and a welcome respite on a hot summer's day.

A stunningly conceived and superbly executed journey through America's Wild West on an out-of-control mine train, **Big Thunder Mountain Railroad** remains one of the park's enduring attractions. In roller coaster terms, it's a relatively gentle experience, although the rear cars provide a wilder ride than the front. It acquires long lines of people from early in the day, so this is a ride to be enjoyed sooner, rather than later.

Opposite Big Thunder Mountain is the landing stage from where a raft can be taken to **Tom Sawyer Island**. Complete with a fort, swinging bridges, waterfalls, and tunnels, this is a child's dream adventure playground.

An outstanding attraction which threatens to get you a lot wetter than it actually does is **Splash Mountain®**. This is the epitome of what Disney does best, with a seamless integration of music, special effects, and beautifully crafted creatures. This, combined with a multitude of small drops prior to the big one, makes it one of the finest flume rides in the world. Guaranteed to make you want to repeat the adventure, the ride soon develops long queues that remain until closing. Fastpasses for Big Thunder Mountain Railroad and Splash Mountain® are highly recommended.

Plunging down on the thrilling Splash Mountain® ride

LIBERTY SQUARE

The smallest of all the Lands, Liberty Square is set in post-Colonial America and hosts three attractions: the **Liberty Square Riverboat**, **The Hall of Presidents**, and **The Haunted Mansion®**. The Liberty Square Riverboat is a relaxing trip back in time to the days of the new frontier, the Louisiana Purchase, and the birth of Southern culture. The ride is usually not very crowded and is a great way to beat the summer heat.

Another interesting option is a visit to the never-crowded Hall of Presidents. This is an impressive animatronic show that features the recorded voice of the current president joining in on readings by the great presidents from the past. The animatronic portion is preceded by a multimedia film showcasing the trials and tribulations of the early days of the United States. The film takes an unusually honest and candid look at slavery and ends on a stirringly patriotic note.

The first ride constructed at Walt Disney World®, The Haunted Mansion® still holds its own as one of the best. While the scare factor has ebbed noticeably over the years, the clever introduction, ingenious ghost-projection, 3-D effects, and attention to detail throughout the ride still warrant admiration. The ride's ability to take in large groups of people nearly continuously ensures that even long lines – now rare – move quickly. Very young children may still be frightened by some of the sudden "gotchas," but most others will find this more wonderfully amusing than frightfully scary.

Prince Charming Regal Carousel, against the backdrop of the Castle

FANTASYLAND®

Dominated by the soaring spires of Cinderella's Castle, this Land forms the core of the Magic Kingdom®. The delightfully designed attractions inspire feelings of amazement and enchantment in even the most cynical.

TOP TIPS

• A little known shortcut from Fantasyland® to Tomorrowland® is just to the right of the train station.

• A great place to see the nightly fireworks display and leave ahead of the crowds is right at the park entrance on Main Street, looking towards Cinderella's Castle.

• The Tomorrowland® Arcade (see p40) can be a useful place to "park" easily bored youngsters while you take toddlers to savor the delights of Dumbo the Flying Elephant or take in some of the quieter shows.

A relaxing ride on the Liberty Square Riverboat

SHOWS & PARADES

Don't miss checking out at least one of these amazing events. The shows – Mickey's PhilharMagic, a wonderful 3-D film experience, and The Enchanted Tiki Room – are superb in their own right but the parades are unique. Floats of towering proportions, surrounded by a multitude of actors and dancers, travel on a set route between Frontierland® and Town Square on Main Street. There is always an afternoon parade and, during the peak holiday season, the Main Street Electrical Parade takes place twice in the evenings, usually at 8:30pm and 10:30pm. The evening also features the Wishes™ Nighttime Spectacular, a brilliant choreography of fireworks and music.

This Land is usually the first destination for kids as their favorite storybook characters come to life here. **Dumbo the Flying Elephant** is a compelling draw for young children whilst the **Prince Charming Regal Carousel**, a genuine 1917 restoration, entices both old and young onto its gallopers. **Snow White's Scary Adventures**, which recounts the fairy-tale, is a basic tracked ride and may be slightly frightening for very young children. **Peter Pan's Flight**, however, is deservedly popular, combining the feeling of flying with the delight of perfectly matched music and movement. Opposite this is **it's a small world**, a waterborne journey through a series of animated tableaux.

Situated at the entrance to Cinderella's castle is the main attraction, **Dream Along with Mickey**, a musical stage show where Mickey and the gang invite everyone to join in the music and dancing.

The Many Adventures of Winnie the Pooh incorporates the latest in ride vehicle technology, lighting, and multi-channel sound effects. A popular attraction, it is worthy of its Fastpass status.

Inspired by the Mad Hatter and the March Hare's nonsensical "unbirthday" party in *Alice in Wonderland,* the **Mad Tea Party** ride has guests sitting in teacups that go right and left in circular motions. This musical ride is a must for young children and teens.

The 3-D film, **Mickey's PhilharMagic**, embodies the high standards associated with Disney, though it might be overwhelming for young children. Of all the 3-D films

shown around the Disney parks, it may also be the most perfected. It features a strong plotline – Donald Duck getting into trouble after appropriating Mickey's Sorcerer's Hat during a warm-up for an enchanted symphony. This sends the duck spiraling through several of Disney's most popular animated musicals, trying to undo his mischief. The music is magnificent, the addition of 3-D to beloved scenes from Disney's stable of hits is incredible, and the sensory enhancement at certain times is used very well and often for comic effect.

Ariel's Grotto hosts the "interactive fountain" and greeting area. Here, small children can play in an aquatic environment, meet the Little Mermaid herself, and get totally soaked.

Pooh's Playful Spot is a "splendiferous" playground

from Winnie the Pooh, where children can bounce like Tigger and play like Roo.

Other attractions incude **Fairytale Garden** for a relaxing storytime, and **Bibbidi Bobbidi Boutique** where children can be pampered.

A major expansion of Fantasyland® is currently under way that will almost double its size. The expansion will occupy the former Mickey's Toontown Fair®. Visitors can now greet Disney's most famous characters, Mickey and Minnie at the main entrance, where guests are guaranteed a photograph. Goofy's Barnstormer coaster will remain, rethemed as The Great Goofini, with a Big Top and other circus-themed play elements.

The headliner feature of the expansion is a Little Mermaid dark ride that will carry guests through Ariel's underwater realm. Nearby will be the Beast's Castle, high on a hill, where children can play a role with Belle in a performance in the library. Other celebrated Disney princesses and heroines will be showcased in areas where children can share Aurora's birthday with the Good Fairies, dance with Cinderella, meet Tinkerbell, and take a rollicking ride with Snow White and the Dwarfs on the Mine Train.

Whirling round in teacups on the Mad Tea Party ride

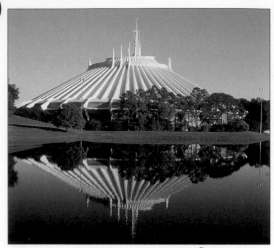

The futuristic building that houses the Space Mountain® ride

TOMORROWLAND®

Based on a futuristic theme, Tomorrowland® has undergone numerous reformations in Disney's attempts to revitalize the Land. Management continues to routinely close, replace, or add rides in its efforts to find the right mix. **Space Mountain®** is a fast ride through tight bends and sharp drops in the dark against projections of asteroids and the like. The impression of traveling through space is excellent, but the ride, though wilder than Big Thunder Mountain (see p37), may seem somewhat tame for seasoned thrillseekers.

Next door to Space Mountain is **Tomorrowland® Arcade**, an enormous showcase of video games and various high-tech demonstrations. **Walt Disney's Carousel of Progress** is a sit-down attraction where the auditorium rotates around a central stage. It examines the transformations in domestic life through the times and, although rather quaint, is a firm favorite, particularly late in the evening.

Guests find the power of laughter in an interactive adventure inspired by Disney-Pixar's **Monsters, Inc. Laugh Floor Comedy Club** as they match wits with the one-eyed hero Mike Wazowski and his friends at the Tomorrow in

the Magic Kingdom® theater. **Stitch's Great Escape!™** is another theater experience featuring multisensory mayhem (including smells) with the madcap alien; surprises throughout the performance may unnerve smaller children.

Weary adults and kids will find unexpected entertainment while enjoying a meal at **Cosmic Ray's Starlight Café**. Sonny Eclipse, a giant animatronic alien, holds court at a piano on a rising bandstand, amusing the whole family while they tuck into Cosmic Chicken and Blast-off Burgers. It's a great place to escape the heat and rain, or to watch the fireworks.

Visitors can soar high on silvery rockets on the **Astro Orbiter** ride, which affords an excellent view of Tomorrowland. The **Tomorrowland®**

Transit Authority is a serene, quiet, and interesting 10-minute ride, which affords great views of the park and an opportunity to relax. Almost never busy, it travels through Space Mountain® and offers glimpses inside several other attractions as well.

Buzz Lightyear's Space Ranger Spin is an extremely fast loader and one of the park's best rides. This highly addictive journey pits you and Buzz against the evil Emperor Zurg. You sit in a two-seater car, fitted with laser cannons and electronic scoreboards and a control allows you to rotate the car rapidly for a better aim. Shooting at all the targets with a red laser beam causes bangs, crashes, and rapid increases in your scores. One turn is not enough on this ride, and it's one of the few rides that kids have to tear their parents away from. Located on the border is the new **Tomorrowland® Indy**

Guests fly high in the sky during a ride on the Astro Orbiter®

The peaceful Tomorrowland®
Transit Authority ride

SHOPPING

There are shops everywhere in the Magic Kingdom® and they sell just about every type of clothing, confectionery – except chewing gum! – and badged merchandise imaginable. All Lands have their own shops selling items based on the theme of the Land and on the nearest ride. Much piratical memorabilia can be purchased near Pirates of the Caribbean, for instance. Do your shopping on your way out so that you don't have to carry your purchases around with you all day.

Speedway, a large, safe course where kids and adults 4.3 ft (1.3 m) and taller can drive their own race cars around a twisting track – smaller children must have an adult drive with them. Nowhere near as difficult, or as thrilling as Epcot®'s Test Track *(see p46)*, the ride is more in line with family-oriented go-kart race courses.

RIDES & SHOWS CHECKLIST

This chart is designed to help you plan what to visit in the Magic Kingdom®. The rides and shows are listed within each Land.

		WAITING TIME	HEIGHT/AGE RESTRICTION	BUSIEST TIME TO RIDE	FASTPASS	LOADING SPEED	MAY CAUSE MOTION SICKNESS	OVERALL RATING
	ADVENTURELAND®							
R	JUNGLE CRUISE	○		11am–5pm	➡	❷		▼
R	THE MAGIC CARPETS OF ALADDIN	○	3 yrs +	9am–7pm		❶	✓	▼
R	PIRATES OF THE CARIBBEAN®	○		10am–5pm		❷		◆
S	THE ENCHANTED TIKI ROOM	◗		noon–4pm		❷		▼
	FRONTIERLAND®							
R	BIG THUNDER MOUNTAIN RAILROAD	●	3 ft 4 in	9am–7pm	➡	❶	✓	★
R	SPLASH MOUNTAIN®	○	3 ft 4 in	9am–7pm	➡	❶		★
S	COUNTRY BEAR JAMBOREE	○		10am–7pm		❶		▼
	LIBERTY SQUARE							
R	THE HAUNTED MANSION®	◗		noon–7pm		❶		◆
R	LIBERTY SQUARE RIVERBOAT	◗				❶		▼
S	THE HALL OF PRESIDENTS	○				❶		▼
	FANTASYLAND®							
R	DUMBO THE FLYING ELEPHANT	○		10am–4pm		❷		▼
R	IT'S A SMALL WORLD	○		9am–7pm		❷		★
R	MAD TEA PARTY	○		10am–6pm		❶	✓	▼
R	THE MANY ADVENTURES OF WINNIE THE POOH	○		10am–5pm	➡	❷		◆
R	PETER PAN'S FLIGHT	○		10am–5pm	➡	❷		★
R	SNOW WHITE'S SCARY ADVENTURES	○		10am–5pm		❷		◆
S	MICKEY'S PHILHARMAGIC	○		10am–6pm	➡	❶		★
S	DREAM ALONG WITH MICKEY	○		10am–7pm				◆
R	THE GREAT GOOFINI	○		10am–6pm		❶		◆
	TOMORROWLAND®							
R	ASTRO ORBITER®	○			➡	❶		▼
R	BUZZ LIGHTYEAR'S SPACE RANGER SPIN	◗	3 ft 8 in	10am–7pm	➡	❶	✓	◆
R	SPACE MOUNTAIN®	○	3 ft 8 in	9am–7pm	➡	❸		▼
R	STITCH'S GREAT ESCAPE!™	◗	3 ft 4 in		➡	❷	✓	▼
S	COSMIC RAY'S STARLIGHT CAFE ALIEN PIANO SHOW	○		10am–7pm				▼
R	TOMORROWLAND® INDY SPEEDWAY	○	4 ft 4 in	10am–7pm		❸		◆
R	TOMORROWLAND® TRANSIT AUTHORITY	○				❷		◆
S	WALT DISNEY'S CAROUSEL OF PROGRESS	○				❷		▼
S	MONSTERS, INC. LAUGH FLOOR COMEDY CLUB	○						◆

Key: Ride – R Show – S; Waiting Time Short – ○ Average – ◗ Long – ●; Loading Speed Fast – ❶
Leisurely – ❷ Slow – ❸; Overall Rating Good – ▼ Excellent – ◆ Outstanding – ★

Epcot® ②

Epcot®, an acronym for the Experimental Prototype Community of Tomorrow, was Walt Disney's dream of a technologically replete, living community. It was intended to represent a utopian vision of the future but, by the time it opened in 1982, several changes had been made to the original dream and Epcot® opened as an educational center and permanent world's fair.

The 250-acre (100-ha) park is divided into two distinct halves: Future World with an emphasis on entertainment and education and World Showcase which represents the art, culture, and culinary expertise of different countries around the globe.

Test Track, one of the most popular rides at Epcot®

TACKLING THE PARK

Epcot® is two and a half times the size of Magic Kingdom®, which means that at least a day and a half are needed to cover most of the attractions here. World Showcase is not normally open until 11am so the early-morning crowds fill Future World and then gradually migrate to the rope between the two parks waiting for World Showcase to open. As with everything Disney, arriving early is the key to a successful visit. If you are entitled to early entry privileges, arrive one hour and 40 minutes before the official opening time.

Although there are really only a small number of rides in Future World, two of these – Test Track and Mission: SPACE – are besieged from the outset, so it's best to get to them early. Pick up a Fastpass for one and ride the other. To reach them, bear left through the huge Innoventions East building. It sometimes helps to think of

Future World as a clock face; if the main entrance is at 6 o'clock, then Mission: SPACE is at 9 o'clock and Test Track at 11 o'clock. This is roughly the equivalent of walking from the entrance of Magic Kingdom® right through to Splash Mountain®/ Big Thunder Mountain Railroad.

After leaving the Mission: SPACE/Test Track area, retrace your steps back through Innoventions East, cross immediately through

Innoventions West, and emerge to the Imagination! Pavilion (clock face position roughly 1 o'clock). After this, you can return to Spaceship Earth (6 o'clock) if the lines have shortened or make your way back across to the excellent Ellen's Energy Adventure (7 o'clock) and Wonders of Life (seasonal, 8 o'clock) pavilions. Though this seems like a lot of backtracking, you should enjoy a little glow of satisfaction when you see the lines later in the day.

Visit Soarin and the Seas with Nemo & Friends later in the day after a visit to World Showcase, more interesting for children now that it hosts the clues to the Kim Possible World Showcase Adventure, an interactive scavenger hunt. There are also Kidcot Fun Spots in several pavilions where kids can draw and

PIN TRADING

This answer to many a parent's prayer was introduced when Disney noticed that the lapel pins it had produced for special events were re-selling at several times the market value. In a flash of inspiration, they created Pin Stations, small booths in every park selling the hundreds of different Disney pins. Epcot's Pin Station Central, near Spaceship Earth, is the largest booth. The pins usually cost $6–$15 each. Following this with a stroke of genius, Disney created Pin Traders – cast members who could be persuaded to swap pins with guests – and surmounted the whole idea with a set of very simple trading rules, which cast members could break in favor of the guest. This has captured the imagination of children who happily spend hours tracking down the pin they don't have and swapping another for it.

Spaceship Earth, the 180-ft (55-m) geosphere at Epcot®'s entrance

have fun, and the diversionary tactic of buying each child a "passport" to have stamped can prove a blessing. There are minor rides – usually boat rides – in some pavilions and several others show films. The dining at some pavilions is excellent and can be booked ahead through your hotel. The transportation system in the park is not very efficient – you'll always get where you want faster by walking, so good, comfortable shoes are essential. There is also not much shade, so be sure to wear a hat.

FUTURE WORLD

As you enter the turnstiles, dominated visually by the giant geodesic dome that is home to the Spaceship Earth ride, you'll notice **Leave a Legacy**. This millennium-related project used images of more than 500,000 real guests engraved onto metal tiles to cover a series of modern stone and steel structures. Future World itself comprises a series of huge, modernistic buildings around the outside, the access to which is through Innoventions East and West. Some buildings house a single ride attraction while others afford the opportunity to browse various exhibits – usually hands-on – and enjoy smaller rides within the main pavilion. Most attractions here are sponsored by major corporations, which will be evident from the signs.

Spaceship Earth

Housed in a massive, 7,500-ton geodesic sphere, this continuously loading ride conveys you gently past superbly crafted tableaux and animatronic scenes portraying mankind's progress in technology. Almost as interesting as the ride is the dome which cunningly re-circulates rainwater into the World Showcase Lagoon.

Innoventions

Both buildings, East and West, form a hands-on exhibition of products of the near future which, through ties to electronics manufacturers, is constantly updated. It is an excellent "quick visit" you can return to throughout the day as you wait for your Fastpass time window or for lines to shorten. Some of the original games have moved to Downtown Disney® *(see pp74–5)* but there's still plenty for kids to do, while parents take in the "live informercials" that show off the latest gadgets. East Innoventions features Epcot Character Spot, where you can meet Mickey.

TOP 10 ATTRACTIONS

1. ILLUMINATIONS
2. MISSION: SPACE
3. TEST TRACK
4. SOARIN'
5. ELLEN'S ENERGY ADVENTURE
6. KIM POSSIBLE WORLD SHOWCASE ADVENTURE
7. SPACESHIP EARTH
8. THE SEAS WITH NEMO & FRIENDS
9. MAELSTROM
10. GRAN FIESTA TOUR

1 DAY ITINERARY

1. *Arrive 1 hour 40 minutes before the official opening time on an early entry day or an hour before on a normal day.*
2. *Head straight toward **Test Track** and pick up a Fastpass for later. Get in line for **Mission: SPACE**.*
3. *Upon leaving Mission: SPACE, use your Fastpass for Test Track, then cross the park to the **Imagination Pavilion** and take the **Journey into Imagination with Figment**. Visit **Innoventions** if you have a bit of time to kill.*
4. *Upon leaving the Imagination Pavilion, head for **Spaceship Earth**.*
5. *Turn right from Spaceship Earth and head toward **Turtle Talk with Crush**, a state-of-the-art 3-D experience. Otherwise, you could visit Innoventions if you have not done so already.*
6. *Next, head to **Ellen's Energy Adventure**.*
7. *Head toward **World Showcase** and wait for the rope drop on the left.*
8. *At rope drop, head to **Mexico**. Ride **Gran Fiesta Tour**.*
9. *Leave to the right and go to **Norway**. Ride **The Maelstrom**.*
10. *Now it's time for a late lunch. Pick a pavilion other than the one you have in mind for dinner, and use the time after lunch to select and make dinner reservations. Time your reservation for two hours prior to the start of IllumiNations if possible. Once the reservations are made, visit **China** (movie), **France** (movie), and **Canada** (movie).*
11. *Return to Future World and visit **The Land** pavilion. Ride **Soarin'** or, if the wait is too long, pick up a Fastpass for Soarin and experience the other attractions here while you wait.*
12. *Leave The Land pavilion to the left and head for **The Seas with Nemo & Friends Pavilion** and experience the two attractions there.*
13. *Exit The Seas with Nemo & Friends Pavilion and head for the **Epcot Character Spot** for a chance of autographs and photos with kids' favorites.*
14. *Ride Soarin when your appointment time arrives and finish exploring Innoventions, or pick up a Fastpass for a repeat ride. Head for dinner, which should allow you a half-hour to find a good spot for **IllumiNations**.*

Epcot: Mission: SPACE

On one of the newest thrill rides at Epcot, guests go on a journey to the heavens that culminates with a crash landing on Mars. This popular attraction is the ultimate in simulator thrill rides, combining high-speed spinning – to simulate g-forces – with a simulator and a 3-D visual interactive storyline. The result is a mesmerizing and convincing rocket launch and high-speed trip to Mars, which also involves a ride around the moon. Particularly impressive are the wholly realistic re-creations of a liftoff into space and a problem-fraught landing. The most technologically advanced of Disney's attractions, the ride is a creation of Disney imagination, but is based on scientific fact and theory provided by astronauts, scientists, and engineers. You can choose between a more intense journey or a milder voyage with everything but the spinning.

INTERNATIONAL SPACE TRAINING CENTER

The story is set at the International Space Training Center (ISTC) in the year 2036. In this future time of space exploration, many countries have joined together to train a new generation of space explorers. Mission: SPACE participants become astronaut candidates on their first training mission.

The ISTC building is a gleaming, metallic affair, complete with curved walls and a state-of-the-art, Space Age look. The curvy steel exterior surrounds the courtyard, called **Planetary Plaza** – from the moment visitors step into this courtyard, they are taken straight into a futuristic world. Huge replicas of Earth, Jupiter, and the moon fill Planetary Plaza, and its walls feature quotations from historical figures about space

travel and exploration. The moon model displays brass plaques indicating the location of every US and Soviet manned and unmanned touchdown during the 1960s and 70s. The interior of the ISTC is compartmentalized into various areas for different levels of training. There are four ride bays, with ten capsules in each bay; each capsule can hold four guests.

TRAINING

Before embarking on their flight, the explorers must follow a series of procedures in order to prepare for their "mission." These training and briefing sessions also go a long way in making the wait times for the show seem shorter, as they keep the crowds entertained prior to the actual ride portion of the show: the ambience is well-executed and slightly

militaristic – a rare feature at Disney parks. At the **ISTC Astronaut Recruiting Center**, explorers learn about training and view a model of the X-2 Trainer, the futuristic spacecraft they will board for their journey into space.

The second station of the mission is the **Space Simulation Lab**, a slowly spinning 35-ft (10-m) high gravity wheel containing work quarters, exercise rooms, sleeping cubicles, and dining areas for space teams. One of the highlights of the lab is an authentic Apollo-era Lunar Rover display unit on loan from the Smithsonian National Air and Space Museum, which describes mankind's first exploration of the moon.

Participants then enter the **Training Operations Room**, which bustles with the activity of various training sessions in progress. Several large monitors show live video feeds of ongoing ISTC training sessions. In **Team Dispatch**, a dispatch officer meets participants. Here, participants are split into teams of four people and sent to the **Ready Room**. This is the point at which each team member accepts an assignment: commander, pilot, navigator, or engineer. Each member is supposed to carry out the tasks associated with his or her assigned role

Replicas of planets standing out dramatically against the metallic façade of the Mission: SPACE building

during the flight. It is here that the explorers meet Capcom – the capsule communicator – who will act as the astronauts' guide through the flight. In the **Pre-flight Corridor**, explorers receive their final instructions for the mission. A uniformed flight crew member then escorts the team to a capsule – the X-2 Space Shuttle.

FLIGHT & LANDING

The team members board the X-2 training capsule and are securely strapped in, with individual "windows" just inches away. The countdown begins and then there is a pulse-racing liftoff: the roar of engines, the clouds of exhaust, and the motion of the capsule all combine to generate in the participants sensations similar to those that astronauts feel during actual liftoff.

The cabin's windows are actually state-of-the-art video flat screens that use a combination of LCD glass and electronic video cards to present an ultra-sharp full-motion video based on actual data taken from Mars-orbiting satellites. The spectacular

views of planets Earth and Mars that participants glimpse through the capsule windows, reinforce their illusion of traveling through space.

The members of the space team must work in unison, performing the roles of pilot, commander, navigator, and engineer in order to successfully face challenges and accomplish their mission to Mars. Throughout the flight, crew members receive instructions from Capcom regarding their duties, which consists of pressing buttons; the capsule obeys the commands very convincingly. Unexpected twists and turns keep participants on the edge of their seats, and call for tricky maneuvers with joysticks. Apart from the exhilarating "slingshot" around the moon, other thrills include a brief experience of "weightlessness" and dodging asteroids on the way to Mars.

The four-minute ride comes to a crashing finale with the Mars landing, complemented by superb sound effects that are achieved by the use of a stereo woofer built right into the back of the space capsules. Pioneering astronauts such as Buzz Aldrin and Rhea Seddon have taken their turn on the ride, comparing it favorably to actual space travel.

The g-forces that come into play during Mission: SPACE are, in fact, of lower intensity than in a typical roller coaster but they are of much greater duration.

ADVANCE TRAINING LAB

After the ride, guests can go around the Advance Training Lab, a colorful interactive play area where they can test their skills in space-related games for people of all ages. You can explore this area even if you choose not to go on the ride itself. There is no minimum height requirement here.

In **Space Race**, two teams are involved in a race to be the first to complete a successful mission from Mars back to Earth. The teams are

VISITORS' CHECKLIST

Future World, between Test Track & Wonders of Life.
Tel (407) 934-7639.
◐ 9am–9pm daily. **www.** disneymissionspace.com

composed of up to 60 guests, who are required to work together to overcome numerous challenges and setbacks in their mission. **Expedition: Mars** is another fun endeavor at the Advance Training Lab. In this sophisticated video game, the player's mission is to locate four astronauts stranded on Mars. **Space Base** is targeted at junior astronauts. It is an excellent interactive play area where kids can climb, slide, crawl, explore, and get rid of excess energy. You can also send **Postcards from Space** at a kiosk in the Advanced Training Lab. Here, guests make a video of themselves in one of several space-related backdrops to create a fine memento of their Mission: SPACE experience, and can email the result to friends and family.

Beyond the Advance Training Lab is the **Mission: SPACE Cargo Bay**, a shopping area spreading over 1,500 sq ft (139 sq m). A 4-ft (1.2-m) high 3-D figure of Mickey Mouse dressed as an astronaut greets visitors, and the area is dominated by a 12-ft (3.6-m) mural depicting various Disney characters in space gear on the surface of Mars. Here, visitors can purchase a large variety of souvenirs, from inexpensive to costly, as a remembrance of their "space experience."

TOP TIPS

• *This is the first ride created with Disney's Fastpass system in mind. Avoid a lengthy wait at this popular attraction by using the Fastpass, which is available at the entrance to Mission: SPACE. Two times will be posted. If the wait is too long, guests can obtain a Fastpass ticket with an assigned return time.*

• *Read all the warning signs at the entrance to Mission: SPACE and take the ride only if you are sure you'll be able to handle it.*

• *The ride has a minimum guest height requirement of 3 ft 8 in (1.1 m).*

• *The entire Mission: SPACE experience, from pre-show to the Advance Training Lab, can last from 45 minutes to more than an hour. The ride to Mars lasts approximately 4 minutes from capsule door closing to it reopening.*

CAUTION

This ride is not for everyone, and certainly not for anyone prone to motion sickness or sensitive to tight spaces, loud noises, or spinning. Younger children may find it too intense, and expectant mothers and people with high blood pressure or heart problems would be well advised to forgo it. Remember: there is no backing out after liftoff.

FUTURE WORLD CONT...

Ellen's Energy Adventure
A passably entertaining film is enlivened by some fascinating technology and hosts Ellen DeGeneres and Billy Nye. The entire theater rotates before breaking into self-powered, moving sections, which take the audience through a prehistoric landscape. The ride is a journey through the creation of the universe: see and hear the explosive Big Bang; travel around, between, and under giant Animatronic dinosaurs; narrowly escape streams of molten lava, and float far above Earth with satellites and atoms before finally exploring a future filled with fusion power.

The Seas with Nemo & Friends Pavilion
The technology behind this attraction is quite stunning in its own right, but the reason most come here is to visit Sea Base Alpha, Epcot®'s most ambitious research project. A pre-show presentation prepares you for your journey to the bottom of the ocean, after which you take the "hydro-lators" to the sea bed. There you board a continuously moving train of small cars, which carry you past astonishing views of sharks, dolphins, giant turtles, and manatees. **The Seas with Nemo & Friends**, inspired by the movie, is a fun-filled story where guests board their own 'clamobiles' to join Marlin, Dory and other memorable characters in their search for Nemo. There is

also a popular and fun interactive show called **Turtle Talk with Crush**, a live, 15-minute show in which, with state-of-the-art 3-D voice-activated computer animation, Crush the turtle takes questions and chats with members of the audience.

Test Track
One of the most popular rides at Epcot®, Test Track uses the most sophisticated ride vehicle technology available, placing you in a simulator that moves on tracks at high speed. Essentially, you are the passenger in a six-seater prototype sports car being tested prior to going into production. Although the ride puts you through brake tests, hill climbs, sharp turns, near crashes, and paint spraying bays, the climax is the outside lap of the ride where the vehicle exceeds 66 mph (102 km/h) on a raised roadway around the outside of the Test Track building. However, the system has frequent stops – usually because the advanced safety systems have cut in and halted the entire run. While this may be reassuring, it results in the lines outside continuing to grow until, by the evening, you can expect a wait of between 90 minutes and 2 hours. The ride itself – just 4 minutes long – is so good you will want to try it again and again, but be aware that the Fastpass machines outside the entrance have normally exhausted their allocation by lunchtime.

The Imagination Pavilion
The Imagination Pavilion houses a show, a ride, and

an interactive demo area. The show is a revival of **Captain Eo**, the 3-D spectacular starring Michael Jackson, the ride is **Journey into Imagination with Figment**, and the interactive showcase is a playground of audio-visual sensory games and demonstrations.

The Journey Into Imagination with Figment ride is an upbeat, light-hearted trip in search of ideas in the arts and sciences. However, it is overcomplicated and overlong. You move past several different animated scenes which present optical illusions and sound effects.

The **ImageWorks Lab** offers visitors a chance to manipulate sound and vision interactively, from making music by waving your arms to experimenting with fast- and slow-motion video to making music by doing aerobics. Highly recommended for the kids, it appeals to adults as well.

Feeding time for the residents of The Seas with Nemo & Friends Pavilion

The Land

Ecology and conservation form the main themes and permeate the attractions housed around the fast food restaurant. As a consequence, these attractions become much busier during lunchtimes. *The Lion King* characters lead **The Circle of Life**, a hymn to conservation expressed through film and animation. Dangers to the environment as well as potential solutions are presented through this entertaining and inspirational show. **Living with the Land** is a 14-minute boat ride that explores the past and present of US farming and showcases agricultural advances in the rain forest, Africa, and beyond. Set sail on a voyage of discovery through living laboratories as you cruise past the American plains, a tropical rain forest, and the African desert to witness the latest developments in aquaculture and desert farming. Float by experimental greenhouses, where produce native to

Guests experience the illusion of flight at Soarin' in the Land Pavilion

many cultures, including rice, sugar cane, and bananas is grown – some of it destined for the Epcot® restaurants – and take a fascinating first-hand look at an aqua environment, the Aquacell, with alligators and fish. A walking tour accompanies the boat ride.

The greatest attraction in the Land pavilion – and the newest thrill ride at Epcot® – is **Soarin'**. Passengers are lift-

ed high off the ground in this simulated hang glider. Wind whips through your hair, your feet dangle above tree-tops, and the scent of pine forests fills the air as you experience the sensation of flying over California's breathtaking natural wonders, including the Golden Gate Bridge and Yosemite National Park. Be warned that Soarin is not for those with a fear of heights.

RIDES & SHOWS CHECKLIST

This chart is designed to help you plan what to visit at Epcot®. The rides and shows in Future World and World Showcase are listed below.

		WAITING TIME	HEIGHT/AGE RESTRICTION	BUSIEST TIME TO RIDE/ATTEND	FASTPASS	MAY CAUSE MOTION SICKNESS	OVERALL RATING
FUTURE WORLD							
R	JOURNEY INTO IMAGINATION WITH FIGMENT	◗		11am–2pm			◆
R	MISSION: SPACE	●	3 ft 8 in	All day	➡	✓	★
R	SPACESHIP EARTH	◗		9am–noon			★
R	TEST TRACK	●	3 ft 4 in	All day	➡	✓	★
S	CIRCLE OF LIFE	○		noon–2pm			▼
S	TURTLE TALK WITH CRUSH	◗					▼
S	ELLEN'S ENERGY ADVENTURE	◗		10am–1pm			◆
S	THE SEAS WITH NEMO & FRIENDS	○		11am–3pm			◆
S	LIVING WITH THE LAND	○		noon–2pm	➡		◆
R	SOARIN'	●	3 ft 4 in	All day	➡	✓	★
WORLD SHOWCASE							
R	MAELSTROM	●		11am–5pm	➡		◆
R	GRAN FIESTA TOUR STARRING THE THREE CABALLEROS	○		noon–3pm			◆
R	KIM POSSIBLE WORLD SHOWCASE ADVENTURE	◗		9am–noon			▼
S	THE AMERICAN ADVENTURE	○					▼
S	IMPRESSIONS DE FRANCE	○					◆
S	O CANADA!	○					◆
S	REFLECTIONS OF CHINA	○					★
S	MATSURIZA TAIKO DRUMMERS AT JAPAN PAVILION	○					★

Key: Ride – R Show – S; Waiting Times Short – ○ Average – ◗ Long – ●;
Overall Rating Good – ▼ Excellent – ◆ Outstanding – ★

The gateway of the China pavilion

WORLD SHOWCASE

The temples, churches, town halls, and castles of these 11 pavilions or "countries" are sometimes replicas of genuine buildings, sometimes merely in vernacular style. But World Showcase is much more than just a series of architectural set pieces. Every pavilion is staffed by people from the country it represents, selling high-quality local products as well as surprisingly good ethnic cuisine.

At set times, which are given on the guide map, native performers stage live shows in the forecourts of each country: the best are the excellent acrobats at China and the bizarre and comic Living Statues at Italy. Only a couple of pavilions include rides, while a number have stunning giant-screen introductions to their country's history, culture, and landscapes. A few even have art galleries, though these often go unnoticed.

The fastest way to get around the 1.3 mile (2 km) perimeter is to walk, but the easiest way to get from the entrance to the back end, where the American pavilion is located, is to take the ferries that crisscross the lagoon, linking

the Canada pavilion to the Morocco pavilion and Mexico to Germany.

Mexico
A Mayan pyramid hides the most remarkable interior at World Showcase. Musicians and stalls selling sombreros, ponchos, and papier-mâché animals *(piñatas)* fill a plaza bathed in a purple twilight. The backdrop to this is a rumbling volcano. Hidden among the splendor of the main area are little art galleries and an arts-and-crafts play space for children.

The **Gran Fiesta Tour Starring the Three Caballeros** is a delightful boat ride in a shady lagoon at the foot of a smoking volcano, while the restaurant outside the pavilion offers a great viewing spot for IllumiNations *(see p52)* later in the day.

Norway
The architecture in this pavilion includes replicas of a stave church – a medieval wooden building – and the 14th-century fortress above Oslo harbor called Akershus Castle, arranged attractively around a cobblestone square.

You can buy trolls and sweaters and other native crafts, but the essential

element here is **Maelstrom**, a short but exhilarating journey down fjords in a longboat into troll country, and across an oil-rig-flecked North Sea – before docking at a fishing port. The ride is followed by a short film about Norway. The film is not mandatory – you can pass through the theater and exit directly if you choose – but it is a well-done look at the past and present of the country.

China
In this pavilion the *pièce de résistance* is the half-size replica of Beijing's well-known landmark, the Temple of Heaven. The peaceful scene here contrasts with the more rowdy atmosphere in some of the nearby pavilions.

For entertainment, there is **Reflections of China**, a Circle-Vision film shown on nine screens all around the audience simultaneously, which makes the most of the country's fabulous, little-seen ancient sites and scenery. Note that you must stand throughout the film. China, the country, also sends a near-continuous stream of acrobatic and other performing troupes that put on mini-shows throughout the day all year long.

The pavilion's extensive shopping emporium sells everything from Chinese lanterns and painted screens to tea bags. Unfortunately, the restaurants are nothing to write home about.

Model buildings from various countries on display at World Showcase

◁ The unmistakable globe of Spaceship Earth, the focal point of Future World

Architectural elements of Venice at the Italy pavilion

Germany

The happiest country in World Showcase is a mixture of gabled and spired buildings gathered around a central square, St. Georgsplatz. They are based on real buildings from all over Germany, including a merchants' hall in Freiburg and a Rhine castle. If you have children, try to time your visit so that it coincides with the hourly chime of the *glockenspiel* in the square.

An accordionist sometimes plays, and the shops are full of quirky or clever gifts such as beautifully crafted wooden dolls. However, you really need to dine here to get the full flavor of Germany.

Italy

The bulk of Italy's relatively small pavilion represents Venice: from gondolas moored alongside candycane poles in the lagoon to the tremendous versions of the towering redbrick campanile and the 14th-century Doge's Palace of St. Mark's Square; even the fake marble looks authentic. The courtyard buildings behind are Veronese and Florentine in style, and the Neptune statue is a copy of a Bernini work.

The architecture is the big attraction, but you should also stop off to eat at one of the restaurants or browse around the shops where you can pick up pasta, amaretti, wine, and so forth.

USA

This is the centerpiece of World Showcase, but it lacks the charm found in most of the other countries. However, Americans usually find **The American Adventure** show, which takes place inside the vast Georgian-style building, very moving. For others, it will provide an interesting insight into the American psyche. The show is an openly patriotic yet thought-provoking romp through the history of the United States up to the present day. It incorporates tableaux on screen and some excellent Audio-Animatronics figures, particularly of the author Mark Twain and the great 18th-century statesman, Benjamin Franklin.

WORLD SHOWCASE: BEHIND THE SCENES

If you'd like more than just a superficial view of Walt Disney World, its behind-the-scenes tours may appeal. In World Showcase, two-hour Segway tours provide a closer look at the architecture and traditions of the countries featured in the park, while during the Flower and Garden Festival, Gardens of the World tours explain the creation of the World Showcase gardens; you are even given tips on how to create a bit of Disney magic back home. These tours cost $60–$99 per person. If you have $219 and seven hours to spare, you might want to sign up for the Backstage Magic tour, which includes all three theme parks. One of the highlights is the visit to the famous tunnel network beneath Magic Kingdom®. Call up for information on all Disney tours *(see p77)*.

The lovely architecture and landscaping at the Japan pavilion

---

MORE PAVILIONS IN THE WORLD SHOWCASE

Japan
This is a restrained, formal place with a traditional Japanese garden, a Samurai castle, and a pagoda modeled on a seventh-century temple in Nara – whose five levels represent earth, water, fire, wind, and sky.

The Mitsukoshi department store, a copy of the ceremonial hall of the Imperial Palace in Kyoto, offers kimonos, wind chimes,

bonsai trees, and the chance to pick a pearl from an oyster. Kabuki theater troupes and other performers appear throughout the day. However, Japan really only comes to life in its restaurants, where visitors can sample delicacies such as sushi and tempura. On the second level of the pavilion, chefs work dexterously with flashing knives, demonstrating the Japanese art of tableside cooking.

Morocco
Morocco's appeal lies in its enameled tiles, its keyhole-shaped doors, its ruddy fortress walls, and the twisting alleys of its *medina* (old city), which is reached via a reproduction of a gate into the city of Fez. The use of native artists gives the show a greater sense of authenticity.

Morocco offers some of the best handmade crafts in World Showcase. The alleys

of the old city lead you to a bustling market of little stores selling carpets, brassware, leatherware, and shawls.

There are several interesting dining experiences on offer. The Tangerine Café serves a variety of Moroccan sandwiches and specialty pastries. Try the couscous, steamed and served with lamb or chicken, at the Restaurant Marrakesh. It is also the place to see belly dancers perform in a stimulating show.

France
A Gallic flair infuses everything in the France pavilion, from its architecture to its upscale stores. Architectural highlights include a one-tenth scale replica of the Eiffel Tower, Parisian Belle Epoque mansions, and a rustic village main street. Among the authentic products from France sold here are

---

ILLUMINATIONS: REFLECTIONS OF EARTH
The one Epcot show that you mustn't miss is the nightly IllumiNations. Presented near closing time around World Showcase Lagoon, it is a rousing *son et lumière* show on an unbelievably extravagant scale with lasers, fire- and waterworks, and a symphonic soundtrack that highlight the 11 featured nations. Best viewing spots are a seat on the veranda at the Cantina de San Angel in Mexico, the outside restaurant balcony in Japan, and the International Gateway bridge near the United Kingdom.

Detailed replica of the famous prayer tower in Marrakesh at the Morocco pavilion, across a promenade

The Canada pavilion, featuring examples of Canadian architecture

perfumes – such as the famous Guerlain range – wine, and berets. Excellent French food can be sampled in a couple of restaurants in the pavilion and a patisserie selling sinfully rich croissants and cakes.

A film entitled **Impressions de France** is the main entertainment. The film, shown on five adjacent screens and set to the sounds of French classical music, offers a whirlwind tour through the country's most beautiful regions.

United Kingdom
The Rose and Crown Pub is the focal point in this pavilion. It serves traditional English fare such as Cornish pasties, fish and chips, and even draft bitter – chilled to suit American tastes. There's also a "chip shop" takeaway booth next door for those in a hurry or wanting a smaller, less expensive meal. The pub also sports a genuine singalong most evenings. Pleasant gardens surround the pub, as well as a medley of buildings of various historic architectural styles. These include a castle based on Hampton Court, an imitation Regency terrace, and a thatched cottage.

There is not much to do here in this pavilion other than browse around the shops, which sell everything from quality tea and china to sweaters, tartan ties, teddy bears, and toy soldiers. The terrace of the Rose and Crown, however, offers good views of IllumiNations.

Canada
A Native Indian village with a log cabin and 30-ft (9-m) high totem poles, a replica of Ottawa's Victorian-style Château Laurier Hotel, a rocky chasm, and ornamental gardens make up the large but rather staid Canadian pavilion.

The country in all its diversity, and particularly its grand scenery, comes to life much better in the Circle-Vision film **O Canada!** – though China's Circle-Vision film is even better. The audience stands in the middle of the theater and turns around to follow the film as it unfolds on no fewer than nine screens. Shops at Canada sell a wide range of Native Indian and Inuit crafts and various edible specialties, as well as wine. Le Cellier Steakhouse restaurant serves tasty Canadian seafood and steaks along with wines and beer from Canada.

EATING & DRINKING

Dining well is fundamental to visiting Epcot® and particularly World Showcase. Some of the latter's pavilions have decent fast-food places, but the best restaurants (including those listed below unless otherwise stated) require reservations. Call Dining reservations *(see p77)* as soon as you know when you'll be at Epcot® or book early in the day. Most restaurants serve lunch and dinner; try unpopular hours such as 11am or 4pm if other times are unavailable. Lunch is usually about two-thirds of the price of dinner, and children's menus are available at even the most upscale restaurants.

Recommended in World Showcase are:
Mexico: the San Angel Inn serves interesting but pricey Mexican food. It is the most romantic place to dine at Epcot. Ask for a riverside table to get the best view.
Norway: Restaurant Akershus offers a good-value *koldtbord* (buffet) of Norwegian dishes in a castle setting based on a real 14th-century castle in Oslo.
Germany: the Biergarten has a beer hall atmosphere, with a cheap and plentiful buffet and hearty oompah-pah music.
Italy: Tutto Italia Ristorante offers pasta and fine Italian specialties, or try Via Napoli for hand-tossed pizzas.
Japan: you can eat communally, either in the Teppan Yaki Dining Rooms around a grilling, stir-frying chef, or at the bar of Tempura Kiku for sushi and tempura (no reservations).
France: there are three top-notch restaurants here: the upscale Bistro de Paris (dinner only); Les Chefs de France, the most elegant restaurant in Epcot®, with haute cuisine by acclaimed chefs *(see p149)*; and the Boulangerie Patisserie for pastries, quiches, and coffee.
United Kingdom: Harry Ramsden's "chippy" booth sells only modest-sized, inexpensive pub fare; it makes for a great "lunch on the go" and the terrace adjoining it is the most relaxing spot in the World Showcase.

Recommended in Future World are:
The Land: the revolving Garden Grill passes a re-created rainforest, prairie, and desert.
The Seas with Nemo & Friends: at the expensive Coral Reef you can eat fish and watch them through a transparent, underwater wall.

Disney's Hollywood Studios ❸

The smallest theme park in Walt Disney World Resort, Disney's Hollywood Studios (formerly known as Disney-MGM Studios) was launched in 1989 as a full-fledged working film and TV production facility. In January 2004, however, the animation department was shut down, and the "working" side of the equation has been almost completely abandoned, although some film and TV production – mostly for the Disney cable channel – is still undertaken here. Regardless of these changes, the park remains a famed tourist destination, with top-notch shows and rides based on Disney and Metro-Goldwyn-Mayer films and TV shows, which offer a tribute to the world of Hollywood and showbiz. Constantly evolving, the park has introduced new and spectacular shows, such as Fantasmic! and Beauty and the Beast – Live on Stage, which have taken its popularity to new heights. Like its competitor Universal Orlando *(see pp88–99)*, Disney's Hollywood Studios' educational yet highly entertaining interactive experiences are geared toward adults and teenagers.

(see pp88–99)

TOP TIPS

• *The best place to watch the afternoon parade is on the bench nearest the popcorn and drinks stand located opposite Sounds Dangerous. You still, however, have to get there first.*
• *During the parades, most of the other attractions are quiet, but almost impossible to reach if you're not on the correct side.*
• *Avoid parking in the Disney-Hollywood or Animal Kingdom lots if you are visiting multiple parks throughout the day. Trams to these parking lots stop running long before the last show at the Magic Kingdom and it can take a long time for you to get back.*

TACKLING THE PARK

The layout of this park differs from that of the other theme parks, although Hollywood Boulevard takes on the role of "Main Street, USA" with the purpose of directing guests toward the numerous attractions.

Over the past few years, Walt Disney World has successfully expanded the scope and magnitude of the park's attractions, building some of the finest in Orlando. With scores of tourists lining up for the rides and shows, arriving early is the key to avoid waiting for long periods in line. It is also worth bearing in mind that some of the attractions might be particularly intense and can frighten young children.

The entertainment schedule changes frequently and streets can be closed off for either celebrity visits or in case of a live filming session. Although events such as these usually take place in winter, it's a good idea to find out about times, locations, and shows as soon as you enter the park from Guest Services, which is located on the left of the main entrance.

At about 3:30pm, the park holds its afternoon parade, usually based on one of Disney's recently animated movies. Be aware that, due to the open plan of the park, the heat can become quite uncomfortable for guests.

Fantasmic! takes place at night – once a night during the slow season and twice during peak periods. Despite seating about 10,000 people at a time, you may need to turn up quite early – up to two hours ahead of time – during peak periods to ensure a seat.

HOLLYWOOD BOULEVARD

Delightful Art Deco styled buildings vie with a replica of Grauman's Chinese Theater to present an image of Hollywood that never was. It's here that your picture will be taken and you might see

Visitors heading for the Rock 'n' Roller® Coaster starring Aerosmith ride

The famous Hollywood Brown Derby Restaurant, Hollywood Boulevard

TOP 10 ATTRACTIONS

1. THE TWILIGHT ZONE TOWER OF TERROR™
2. FANTASMIC!
3. ROCK 'N' ROLLER® COASTER STARRING AEROSMITH
4. MUPPET* VISION 3-D
5. STAR TOURS
6. INDIANA JONES™ EPIC STUNT SPECTACULAR!
7. BEAUTY AND THE BEAST – LIVE ON STAGE
8. VOYAGE OF THE LITTLE MERMAID
9. THE GREAT MOVIE RIDE
10. THE MAGIC OF DISNEY ANIMATION

some of the cast members, acting as reporters or police, chasing celebrities. Moreover, it is on the boulevard that the cast members will try to direct you to Echo Lake's Indiana Jones Epic Stunt Spectacular! – a live action show featuring stunts from the Indiana Jones films.

Halfway up the boulevard, a street breaks off to the right. This is known as Sunset Boulevard, and is home to two of Disney's Hollywood Studios' most popular rides: The Twilight Zone Tower of Terror and the Rock 'n' Roller Coaster starring Aerosmith.

At the junction of Sunset and Hollywood boulevards lies an enormous canopy that is shaped like Mickey's hat from *The Sorcerer's Apprentice*. This is a combination store, shady spot, and pin station *(see p42)*, where budding traders can ambush the cast and swap badges.

At the top of Hollywood Boulevard lies the Central Plaza, which is dominated by the replica of Grauman's Chinese Theater. Here you can experience **The Great Movie Ride**, a trip through movie history that features every film genre, ranging from musicals to horror films to gangster movies. Huge ride vehicles carrying 60 guests apiece track silently past the largest movie sets ever built for a Disney ride. As always, Disney's vast experience in the movie industry has led to the creation of some superb sets. Memorable cinematic moments, such as Gene Kelly singing in the rain and Dorothy going down the Yellow Brick Road on her way to Oz, are re-created with the help of highly realistic Audio-Animatronic figures. Combined with old film clips, special effects, and some fun live action sequences, this is an enjoyable 25-minute ride that ends on a very upbeat and optimistic note. The American Idol Experience offers the opportunity to perform, watch, and vote for the singers.

1 DAY ITINERARY

1. *Upon entering the park, immediately get a Fastpass to* ***The Twilight Zone Tower of Terror****.*
2. *Stroll back up Sunset Boulevard and get in line for* ***The American Idol Experience****.*
3. *As you exit, head for Animation Courtyard and take in the various shows (which usually have minimal wait times) –* ***The Magic of Disney Animation, Voyage of the Little Mermaid, Playhouse Disney – Live on Stage*** *and* ***Walt Disney: One Man's Dream****.*
4. *If your time window for the Tower of Terror has arrived, go back down Sunset to ride it. Wait in line for the* ***Rock 'n' Roller Coaster starring Aerosmith*** *after you ride the Tower (if the wait time is less than one hour; otherwise come back to it later).*
5. *Enjoy lunch in the large restaurant area on Sunset, or take in the* ***Beauty and the Beast – Live on Stage*** *show.*
6. *Walk down to the southeast end of the park and get a Fastpass for* ***Star Tours****. Head to the* ***Muppet Vision 3-D*** *show and walk down New York Street after you're done there.*
7. *Just before heading into Star Tours, get a Fastpass for the* ***Indiana Jones Epic Stunt Spectacular!***
8. *Dine at your pre-reserved restaurant.*
9. *Head for your scheduled Indiana Jones show, then walk across the park for your last chance to re-ride either Tower of Terror or Rock 'n' Roller Coaster if the wait times have fallen to under one hour. Time this so that you emerge from the ride about 90 minutes to one hour prior to the start of* ***Fantasmic!***
10. *As darkness descends on the park, head for the Amphitheater to catch Fantasmic! and end the day on a perfect note.*

SUNSET BOULEVARD

Like Hollywood Boulevard, Sunset Boulevard is a rose-tinted evocation of the famous Hollywood street in the 1940s. Theaters and storefronts – some real, some fake – have been re-created with characteristic attention to detail. The Hollywood Tower Hotel lies at one end of the boulevard. This decrepit, lightning-ravaged hotel is home to one of Orlando's scariest rides – **The Twilight Zone Tower of Terror**™. The ride straps you into a runaway service elevator for a voyage inspired by the 1950s TV show *The Twilight Zone*. The pre-show area is a library into which you are ushered by a melancholic bellhop. From here you enter what appears to be the boiler room of the hotel and you walk through to board the freight elevators fitted with plank seats. The elevator doors sometimes open to allow glimpses of ghostly corridors. As you reach the 13th floor, the elevator actually trundles horizontally across the hotel. But it's hard to concentrate on anything other than the ghastly 13-story plunge that everyone knows will come – but not exactly when. The original single drop has now been increased to seven and, during the first drop, enormously powerful engines actually pull you down faster than free fall. Terrifyingly brilliant, this ride is a technological masterpiece. You can also enjoy a brief, fleeting view of the whole park, and indeed outside the park – a break with Disney tradition – before you begin the scary descent. The Tower of Terror ride is not to everyone's taste, but diehard enthusiasts and novices alike pack this ride from the outset.

An indoor extravaganza, the **Rock 'n' Roller® Coaster starring Aerosmith** ride accelerates from 0 to 60 mph (96 km/h) in just 2.8 seconds. Strapped into "stretch limos," guests experience 5G pulls as they hurl through the twists and turns. Replete with loops,

steep drops, and corkscrew spins, the Rock 'n' Roller Coaster employs a fully synchronized and very loud soundtrack as it hurls you toward the neon-lit equivalent of oblivion. Those who enjoy sitting in the front can get to the seats via the lower ramp. The pre-show is a rather tame affair and presents a recording session of the popular American band, Aerosmith.

The boulevard also features two outdoor arenas for shows. The **Theater of the Stars** is a huge, covered amphitheater with 1,500 seats. The **Beauty and the Beast – Live on Stage** show is performed several times throughout the day here. The production is about 30 minutes long and has beautifully choreographed scenes adapted from the movie of the same title. The exquisitely detailed sets, and costumes are works of art. Since the show is extremely popular, go early to get a good seat. The gigantic **Hollywood Hills Amphitheater** is home to the spectacular and dazzling show, **Fantasmic!**

TOP TIPS

• *Fastpasses to the top rides – the Tower of Terror and the Rock 'n' Roller Coaster – are usually gone by early afternoon. If you do not arrive early at the park, your only chance to ride these rides will be to either wait in the "standby" line for up to two hours each, or stay in the park until it's nearly closing time, when the line wait times drop to around 45 minutes.*

• *In the boiler room of the Tower of Terror, take any open gateway to the lifts – don't worry if the other guests do not do the same. You'll get a better seat and a better view.*

• *Many people leave the park during bad weather or as night approaches, but this is in fact the best time to head for the Tower of Terror ride.*

Sunset Boulevard also offers a large seating area, where guests can choose from a wide range of food stands and restaurants. Visitors can opt for a quick snack, a light meal, or a full lunch. There is something to suit every budget.

FANTASMIC!

Each of the Disney parks aim to bring down the curtain with a spectacular show, but Disney's Hollywood Studios' Fantasmic! extravaganza outdoes them all. It is, quite simply, the finest event of its kind in Florida. Combining lasers, fan fountain projection, animation, and a cast of more than 50 actors and dancers, Fantasmic! manages to choreograph the entire event with split second accuracy to music, fireworks, and lighting. Set on an island in a lagoon meant to represent Mickey Mouse's imagination, the "story," such as it is, cleverly weaves elements of all the classic Disney films into a single battle between good and evil.

Illuminated boats, flying floats, and a lake that bursts into flames are but some of the remarkable features of this enchanting event. Playing to audiences of 10,000 per showing, Fantasmic! completely mesmerizes adults as well as children with incredible special effects and their interaction with live performers. The wide array of famous characters represented will bring squeals of recognition and delight from all ages.

As expected, the show is exceptionally popular with most visitors as a finale for the evening, which means that arriving early is a must if you want to sit near the front – be aware that you may get wet in the first few rows. Seating opens approximately two hours before showtime, and the earlier show tends to fill up faster than the final performance. Even in the quietest time of the off-peak season, all 10,000 places are taken up to 30 minutes before the show starts. However, this truly is one event you would never forgive yourself for missing.

◁ **The sinister exterior of The Twilight Zone Tower of Terror**™**, Disney's Hollywood Studios**

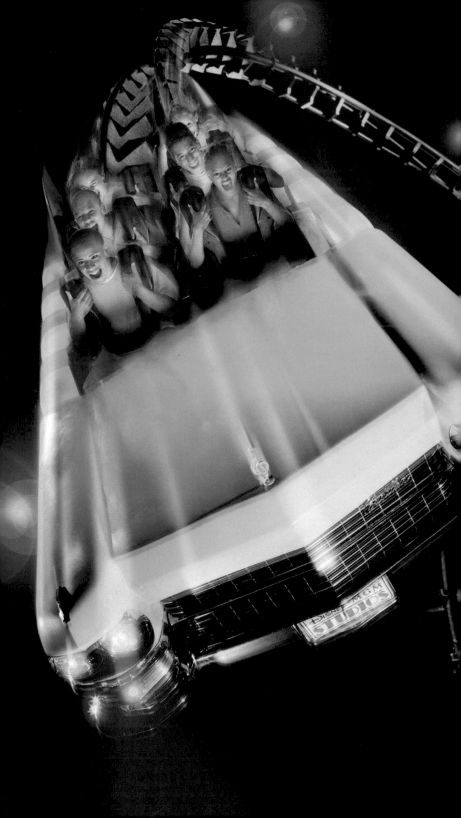

A giant ant at the "Honey, I Shrunk the Kids" Movie Set Adventure

ANIMATION COURTYARD

The original idea behind Animation Courtyard was not just to give visitors an inside look into the history and process of animation, but also a glimpse at all forthcoming Disney animated films as they were being made. With the shutting down of Disney's animation unit in January 2004, this area of the park is now less popular, but still has features worth visiting.

The **Magic of Disney Animation**, which used to be a tour of the working spaces in the Animation Department, is now a guided visit with a sole Disney artist and some films exploring Disney's rich history in animated films. The artist does live sketches on the spot and answers questions about how films are made. The "tour" concludes with the audience – mostly children – sitting at tables and working with the artist to create their own Disney character. For adults, the. most interesting aspect of this attraction are the sketches from Disney classics, along with copies of the Academy awards the unit has won over the years.

The **Voyage of the Little Mermaid** show is enacted by cartoon, live, and Audio-Animatronic characters. Special effects use lasers and water to create the feel of an underwater grotto. It is one of the most popular shows in the park, though young children sometimes find the lightning storm scary.

Disney Junior – Live on Stage! is also geared toward youngsters and features singing and dancing Disney Channel characters from shows such as Mickey Mouse Clubhouse, Handy Manny, and Little Einsteins. This 20-minute show encourages audience participation. Don't miss it.

Walt Disney: One Man's Dream could be dismissed as propaganda, but it is difficult not to admire Walt's great vision and risk-taking ability. A fascinating "museum" features collections of early Disney memorabilia, multi-media appearances of the man himself, and plenty of scale models and historical props from the parks. Wind your way to the cinema to see a film on Walt Disney. Despite the title, the film and photos make it pretty clear that Walt Disney received extensive help from his family – particularly brother Roy, who worked arduously to complete and expand Walt Disney World after his brother's death in 1966. Especially admirable is Walt's enthusiasm for the expansion of his dream – the plans for Disney World® and his dream project, Epcot®. However, Walt would probably be fairly shocked at the size, scope and appeal of the company these days, having humbly said: "Never forget, it started because of a mouse."

SHOPPING

Most of the best shops are on Hollywood Boulevard, which stays open half an hour after the rest of the theme park has closed. Mickey's of Hollywood is the big emporium for general Disney merchandise. Celebrity 5 & 10 has a range of affordable movie souvenirs, such as clapper boards and Oscars®, as well as books and posters. More expensive is Sid Cahuenga's One-Of-A-Kind, where you can buy rare film and TV memorabilia such as genuine autographed photographs – of Boris Karloff and Greta Garbo, for example – or famous actors' clothes. Limited-edition "cels" in Animation Gallery in Animation Courtyard are also very expensive and will make an even bigger dent in your wallet; the same shop sells Disney posters and books too.

◁ **The electrifying Rock 'n' Roller® Coaster starring Aerosmith ride, Disney's Hollywood Studios®**

Some of the characters from **Journey into Narnia: Prince Caspian** are brought to life in an attraction offering an in-depth and unique look into the making of the movie. Guests have the option of a meet and greet with Prince Caspian himself against a backdrop of the Dancing Lawn, the location where the Narnians first confront Prince Caspian in the movie. Audio and visual effects with multiple surround screens immerse guests into the movie like never before. Also on display are authentic props from the movie set.

STREETS OF AMERICA

In this area the streets of New York, San Francisco, Chicago, and various other cities are recreated by movie sets. The bricks and stone are painted on plastic and fiberglass, and the buildings' facades are propped up with girders. The sets are used for filming, but visitors can wander freely.

Nearby is the **Lights, Motors, Action!® Extreme Stunt Show®**, in which visual thrills are supplied for 33 minutes, several times a day, by special cars and motorcycles, showing how stunts are performed in Hollywood action films.

Toy Story Pizza Planet Arcade is a trumped up arcade made to resemble Andy's favorite hangout. It is packed full of video games.

Muppet™ Vision 3-D is a highly enjoyable, slapstick 3-D movie, starring the Muppets. The 25-minute show is a favorite with kids. Trombones, cars, and rocks launch themselves at you out of the screen; they are so realistic that children often grasp the air expecting to touch something. A full Muppet orchestra plays music in a pit. Audio-Animatronic characters and the excellent special effects, such as a cannon blowing holes in the walls of the theater, enhance the show's impact. The 12-minute pre-show is pure Muppet mischief. Here you will see Kermit and Miss Piggy at their best. In addition, the actual 3-D movie – hosted by Audio-Animatronic Statler and Waldorf – is full of playful comedy for all ages.

If you've got young children, don't miss the imaginative **"Honey, I Shrunk the Kids"**

Movie Set Adventure. Everything is larger than life in this playground that is specifically designed for the younger set to burn off their excess energy. As you enter, you are surrounded by 30-ft (9-m) high blades of grass, a slide made from a roll of film, and an ant the size of a pony. The huge tunnels, slides, giant spiders, and other props keep children amused for hours. Since the area is not very large, the playground can get very crowded, and it's a good idea to head for it early. Due to its popularity, parents find it difficult to get kids to leave.

Although it never fails to be entertaining, the half-hour **Studio Backlot Tour** best comes to life when a film is actually being shot. The tour begins with a show explaining how the effects of controlling the weather and the forces of nature – such as the sea – are accomplished on film. Members of the audience are also roped in for some of the demonstrations.

Precision driving skills at the Lights, Motors, Action!® Extreme Stunt Show®

Action-packed explosive thrills at the Indiana Jones™ Epic Stunt Spectacular!

A 200-seat tram then takes you through various departments – you pass through the production bungalows, the wardrobe department (where you can see costumers at work), the scenery shop, and so on. You also get to look in on three sound stages, where, if you're lucky, a TV show, commercial, or movie might be being filmed. If any actual television or film production happens to be taking place, the audience is usually allowed to walk onto the sound stage and observe the work in progress.

The tram then travels on through the **Boneyard®**. This is an outside area that holds vehicles which have featured in various films, including bone cages from *Pirates of the Caribbean: Dead Man's Chest*, ships from the *Star Wars* series, trucks from the *Indiana Jones* films, and cars from the *Herbie the Lovebug* films.

The most memorable part of the tour takes place in the area known as **Castastrophe Canyon**. Set in the American Southwest, this provides a highly realistic, terrifying, and entertaining journey through floods, explosions, earthquakes, and various other disasters. On leaving the canyon, you are taken behind the set and are able to get a quick glimpse of the equipment used to create all these effects.

The last part of the tour involves walking through the exhibits of the **American Film Institute Showcase**. Here themed exhibitions, which change from time to time, relate to such subjects as special effects or greatest film villains, and include props and life-sized figures in costume. There's also an AFI shop where you can buy movie- and TV-related souvenirs and memorabilia.

ECHO LAKE

The interest here is focused on three shows and one thrill ride. The shows reveal the tricks of the film and TV trade.

The audio portion of Hollywood's "magic" is given its due with the whimsical film **Sounds Dangerous – with Drew Carey**. Comedian/actor Drew Carey is a police detective who goes undercover with a hidden camera that keeps losing its picture, but never its sound. In an innovative twist, part of the film takes place in complete darkness, leaving the audience with only the headphones to help them imagine what is going on.

Nearby, the **Academy of Television Arts and Sciences Hall of Fame** features the likenesses of many television legends, who have been honored for their achievements either in front of or behind the camera.

The storyline of the sensational ride **Star Tours** is based on the *Star Wars* films. Your spaceship, a flight simulator similar to those used to train astronauts, takes a wrong turn and then has to evade meteors and fight in an inter-galactic battle. The large-scale show **Indiana Jones™ Epic Stunt Spectacular!** re-creates well-known scenes from the *Indiana Jones* movies to deliver lots of big bangs as

Dinosaur Gertie at the entrance to Echo Lake

well as daredevil feats to thrill the audience. Death-defying stuntmen leap between buildings as they avoid sniper fire, explosions, and traps. As an educational sideline, the stunt director and real stunt doubles demonstrate how some of the action sequences are realized.

Surrounding Echo Lake are many eating spots that have been designed to look like sets from films.

PIXAR PLACE

The main attraction here is **Toy Story Mania!** This is a high-energy 4-D adventure where enormous toys and props make guests feel as if they have been shrunk to the size of Woody or Buzz Lightyear – just the right size to participate in the interactive games that have been set up, midway-style, under the bed in Andy's room.

EATING & DRINKING

It is definitely worth going to the trouble of making a reservation at one of the full-service restaurants at Disney's Hollywood Studios®, though more for their atmosphere than their food. You can reserve a table by calling (see p77), or by going directly to the Dining Reservation Booth, at the crossroads of Hollywood and Sunset boulevards, or to the restaurants themselves.

The exclusive and costly Hollywood Brown Derby replicates the Original Brown Derby in Hollywood, where the stars met in the 1930s – right down to the celebrities' caricatures on the walls and the house specialties of Cobb Salad and grapefruit cake. Kids usually prefer the Sci-Fi Dine-In Theater Restaurant, a 1950s drive-in where customers sit in mini-Cadillacs to watch old science-fiction movies, while munching on popcorn, burgers, and sandwiches. In the 50's Prime Time Café, you are served in 1950s kitchens with the TV tuned to period sitcoms; the food – which includes items such as meatloaf, pot roast, fried chicken, and milk shakes – is homey. Adults in search of beverages can visit the Tune-In Lounge next door.

The best place to eat without a reservation is the self-service Art Deco-themed cafeteria Hollywood & Vine, where you can choose from a buffet that includes pasta, salads, seafood, ribs, and steaks. It also has an excellent selection of desserts. Mama Melrose's Ristorante Italiano serves pizza, pasta, and seafood in a typical Italian diner environment.

RIDES, SHOWS & TOURS CHECKLIST

This chart is designed to help you plan what to visit at Disney's Hollywood Studios®. Sights are listed within each area.

		WAITING TIME	HEIGHT/AGE RESTRICTION	BEST TIME TO RIDE /ATTEND	FASTPASS	MAY CAUSE MOTION SICKNESS	OVERALL RATING
HOLLYWOOD BOULEVARD							
R	THE GREAT MOVIE RIDE	O		Any			◆
S	AMERICAN IDOL EXPERIENCE	◗					▼
SUNSET BOULEVARD							
R	ROCK 'N' ROLLER® COASTER STARRING AEROSMITH	●	4 ft	►11	➡	✓	◆
R	THE TWILIGHT ZONE TOWER OF TERROR™	●	3 ft 4 in	►11	➡	✓	★
S	BEAUTY AND THE BEAST – LIVE ON STAGE	◗					◆
S	FANTASMIC!	●					◆
ANIMATION COURTYARD							
S	DISNEY JUNIOR – LIVE ON STAGE!	◗		Any			▼
S	VOYAGE OF THE LITTLE MERMAID	●		Any	➡		◆
T	MAGIC OF DISNEY ANIMATION	◗		Any			◆
S	WALT DISNEY: ONE MAN'S DREAM	◗		Any			▼
S	JOURNEY INTO NARNIA: PRINCE CASPIAN	◗		Any			▼
STREETS OF AMERICA							
S	MUPPET™ VISION 3-D	●		Any			★
S	LIGHTS, MOTORS, ACTION!® – EXTREME STUNT SHOW®	●		►11	➡		★
T	STUDIO BACKLOT TOUR	O		Any			★
ECHO LAKE							
R	STAR TOURS	◗	3 ft 4 in	►11	➡	✓	★
S	INDIANA JONES™ EPIC STUNT SPECTACULAR!	●		Any			◆
S	SOUNDS DANGEROUS – STARRING DREW CAREY	◗		Any			▼
PIXAR PLACE							
R	TOY STORY MANIA!	◗		Any			◆

Key: Ride – R Show – S Tour – T; Waiting Times Short – O Average – ◗ Long – ●; Overall Rating Good – ▼ Excellent – ◆ Outstanding – ★; Time to Ride: Anytime – Any Before 11am – ►11

Disney's Animal Kingdom® ❹

While the other Disney theme parks host a healthy collection of fish, birds, and other examples of nature, Disney's Animal Kingdom practically overflows with life and nature in all its forms. Quixotically, it is both the largest of the theme parks – five times the size of Magic Kingdom – and yet the easiest to cover, since a large portion of that extra space is accessible only by safari tour. Children and adults find great delight in the never-ending array of animals and exotic landscapes and architecture, both real and mythical, but teens and other thrill seekers have tended to find the rides too few and far-between for their tastes. To make the park a more enticing prospect for this group of visitors, it features an exciting attraction, Expedition Everest – Legend of the Forbidden Mountain, which opened in 2006. A thrilling high-speed train adventure, set in a reproduction of the mighty Himalayas, it offers thrills galore.

Carvings on the bark of The Tree of Life in Discovery Island®

TACKLING THE PARK

The park is divided into seven Lands: The Oasis, Discovery Island, Dinoland USA, Camp Minnie-Mickey, Africa, Asia, and Rafiki's Planet Watch. Navigation within the park is quite different from other parks. When you first pass through the turnstiles, you enter **The Oasis** – a foliage-festooned area offering several routes to the park's central hub, Safari Village. The Oasis contains many little surprises, most of which are missed by visitors who race through to reach the attractions. Time spent waiting quietly at the various habitats will be well-rewarded. The park has a strong emphasis on leisurely walks – with dozens of semi-hidden nature paths and byways filled with scenic views – and shows rather than rides, but

the rides Animal Kingdom does have are all outstanding and get very crowded.

There's plenty for young children to enjoy as well, with three areas of the park more or less dedicated to the little ones. If you love animals or are interested in conservation issues, this park is a heaven on earth, but time is needed to really absorb the experience – this is not a place for hurried tourists seeking quick excitement. Keep your camera charged and loaded – you'll want to take lots of stunning pictures.

DISCOVERY ISLAND®

As you emerge into the open space of the village, **The Tree of Life** looms – this is a massive, 14-story structure

that is the signature landmark of the park. It holds sway over a pageant of brightly colored shop fronts and a multitude of pools and gardens, each holding a variety of wildlife. The main shops, baby care, and first aid post all face The Tree of Life. Embedded in the tree and of endless fascination and

The It's Tough to be a Bug® show in Discovery Island®

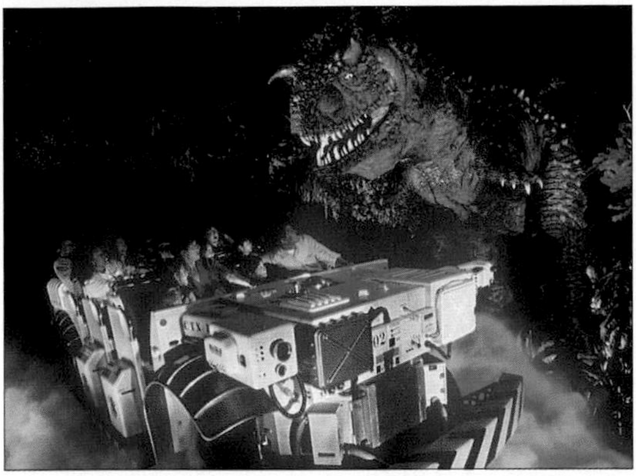

The popular DINOSAUR ride, which brings dinosaurs back to life

delight to visitors are over 325 carvings or other images of various animals. While waiting in line for the shows or character greetings, children in particular spend time trying to identify them all. Under its branches lie the bridges that cross to the other Lands and within the trunk itself is the **It's Tough to be a Bug®** show. Held in a stunningly detailed "underground" theater, this 3-D film and sensory experience is one of the finest in the whole of Walt Disney World and not to be missed. Hosted by Flik and featuring many of the characters from Disney and Pixar's hit film *A Bug's Life* the show combines animatronics and sensory enhancement to heighten the realism of the computer-animated 3-D. The show cleverly plays on our natural fear of insects and the audience is generally kept alternating between laughter and repulsion; the delightfully creepy finale keeps the crowd laughing right out the door.

DINOLAND USA®

This land is a mixed bag of children's play areas, rides, and serious exhibits of dinosaur artifacts. Fans of dinosaur lore will enjoy the actual dinosaur skeletons that lead you to the popular ride **DINOSAUR**, in which guests board a mobile motion simulator that travels back in time and bucks and weaves violently, trying to avoid carnivorous dinosaurs. Very young children may find the ride, which is mostly in the dark, quite scary. The pre-show is an excellent opportunity to educate yourself on Earth's past. The recreated layers of sedimentary soil and rock provide an insight into the history of the planet, and is accompanied by occasional narration from science entertainer Bill Nye.

Younger children will get a lot more fun, and dizziness, out of the carnival atmosphere of the outdoor rides, including the **Primeval Whirl®** and the **TriceraTop Spin**, a roller coaster with spinning cars. There's also **The Boneyard**, a playground where children can dig for dinosaur bones. For all-round family entertainment, the featured show in Dinoland USA is **Finding Nemo – The Musical**. The 30-minute show is a dazzling production that combines puppets, dancers, aerialists, and animated backdrops. The theme park's Theater in the Wild becomes a magical undersea setting with the help of innovative lighting, sound, special effects, and amazing theatrical puppetry of Michael Curry (co-designer of the Broadway version of *The Lion King*).

TOP 10 ATTRACTIONS

1. KILIMANJARO SAFARIS®
2. FESTIVAL OF THE LION KING
3. IT'S TOUGH TO BE A BUG®
4. KALI RIVER RAPIDS®
5. DINOSAUR
6. FINDING NEMO – THE MUSICAL
7. FLIGHTS OF WONDER
8. PRIMEVAL WHIRL®
9. TRICERATOP SPIN
10. EXPEDITION EVEREST – LEGEND OF THE FORBIDDEN MOUNTAIN

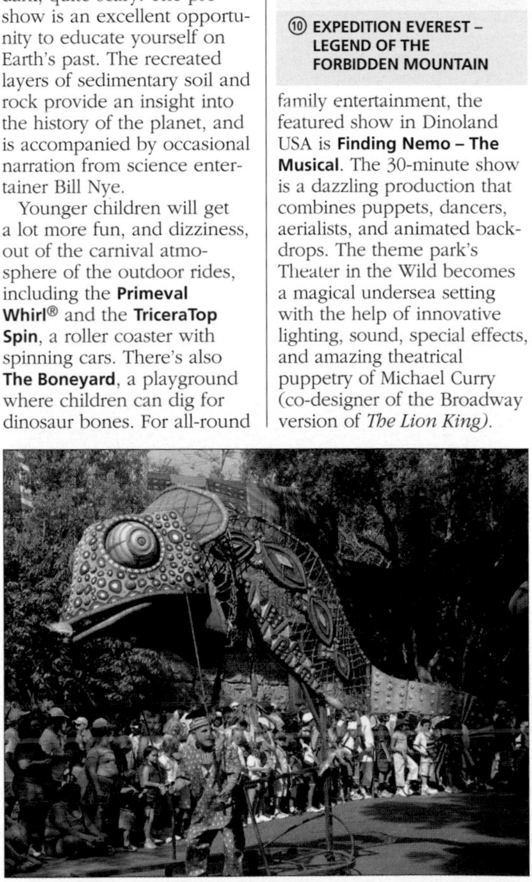

An Iguana puppet, being paraded through the park at Animal Kingdom®

TOP TIPS

• *Check the start times of the Festival of the Lion King and Flights of Wonder – the times vary. See the attractions that run continuously after you check out these scheduled shows.*

• *The Wildlife Express Train is a great way to get between Africa (on the northwest side of the park) and Rafiki's Planet Watch (on the northeast side). This ride is very relaxing in the hotter hours of the day.*

CAMP MINNIE-MICKEY

Designed primarily for guests to meet Disney characters, this Land also has one of the park's two live stage productions. Lines for the **Camp Minnie-Mickey Greeting Trails** – at the end of which the youngsters get to meet with the characters – can, predictably, become very long and sometimes become entwined with the lines for the stage shows.

A very popular show, and hands-down the finest live-action show in the whole of Walt Disney World, the 30-minute **Festival of the Lion King** encourages cheering and singing like no other. Exceptionally well-choreographed and costumed, this colorful spectacle is one of the most elaborate shows to be performed outside Broadway. Particularly now that the theater is fully enclosed and

air conditioned, it's a must-not-miss attraction that is best seen at the beginning or the end of the day. Each performance seats an audience of 1,000, but line-ups continue through the day. Be prepared for wait times that are exceptionally long and for standing in outside lines in unshaded, poorly ventilated areas.

Mickey's Jammin' Jungle Parade is a daily parade that winds through the park about one hour before closing. It brings a menagerie of abstract animal images to life in the form of towering animated puppets in fun costumes, accompanied by Mickey, Minnie, Donald, Goofy, and The Lion King's Rafiki. Elaborate rickshaw taxis put selected guests in the middle of the parade, while party patrols of "animals" interact with guests and invite them to sing along with the music.

AFRICA

Entered through the village of Harambe, Africa is the largest of the Lands. The architecture is closely modelled on a Kenyan village and conceals Disney cleanliness behind a façade of simple, run-down buildings and wobbly telegraph poles.

The **Kilimanjaro Safaris®** is the park's busiest attraction, though it gets quieter in the afternoon. Guests board open sided trucks driven into an astonishing replica of the East

Lions and rhinos, to be glimpsed on Kilimanjaro Safaris®

African landscape. During this 20-minute drive over mud holes and creaking bridges you have the opportunity to see many African animals including hippos, rhinos, lions, and elephants, all roaming apparently free and undisturbed. It isn't unusual for a white rhino to get close enough to sniff the truck.

Affording an excellent opportunity to see gorillas close up, the **Pangani Forest Exploration Trail®** leads visitors into a world of streams and splashing waterfalls. It can get rather congested with guests exiting the safaris. The trail gets less busy in the late afternoon and you can actually spend some time watching the animals. The pleasant Wildlife Express, a re-creation of the African train system, takes you to **Rafiki's Planet**

Visitors savoring the sights of a re-created East African landscape on Kilimanjaro Safaris®

EATING & DRINKING

Disney's Animal Kingdom® has few full-service restaurants. The Rainforest Café® is near the entrance of the park, so reservations are a must. Character dining takes place at the amusing Restaurantosaurus, an all-you-can-eat buffet. Restaurantosaurus also features a full McDonald's. On opposite sides of Discovery Island® are Pizzafari and the Flame Tree Barbecue lunch restaurants, while Africa boasts the Tusker House Restaurant. Asia offers only snack stands which are also located throughout the other areas of the park. Feeding the animals or throwing coins in the water supplies is strongly discouraged.

The swirling water adventure ride, Kali River Rapids®

Watch, which features two educational programs, Conservation Station and Habitat Habit, and Affection Section, a shaded petting yard.

ASIA

This land features gibbons, exotic birds, and tigers set in a re-creation of post-Colonial Indian ruins. **Kali River Rapids®** offers you a chance to get completely drenched. This short ride presents some of the most striking and detailed surroundings in the park, which you may miss as yet another wave saturates the parts still merely damp. Tapirs, Komodo dragons, and giant fruit bats can be found on the **Maharaja Jungle Trek®**, the climax of which is undoubtedly the magnificent Bengal tiger roaming the palace ruins. Through glazed walled sections of the palace, you can get close to the tigers.

A campy, funny show with an unexpected amount of thrills, the **Flights of Wonder** showcases beautiful birds demonstrating natural behavior with polished trainers and a clever "story." Be aware that the birds fly extremely low and so graze the tops of the audience's heads, but ducking down just causes the birds to fly even lower.

Expedition Everest™ – Legend of the Forbidden Mountain involves a high-speed train bound for Mount Everest, taking passengers on a daring ride over rugged terrain and along icy slopes and contains both roller coaster thrills and yeti mystique.

RIDES, SHOWS & TOURS CHECKLIST

This chart is designed to help you plan what to visit at Animal Kingdom. The major rides, shows, and tours are listed within each area.

		WAITING TIME	HEIGHT /AGE RESTRICTION	BEST TIME TO RIDE /ATTEND	FASTPASS	MAY CAUSE MOTION SICKNESS	OVERALL RATING
	DISCOVERY ISLAND®						
S	**IT'S TOUGH TO BE A BUG®**	O		Any	➡		◆
	DINOLAND USA®						
R	**DINOSAUR**	◗	3 ft 4 in	Any	➡	✓	▼
R	**PRIMEVAL WHIRL®**	●	4 ft	►11	➡	✓	◆
R	**TRICERATOP SPIN**	●		►11		✓	★
S	**FINDING NEMO: THE MUSICAL**	◗		Any			◆
	AFRICA						
R	**KILIMANJARO SAFARIS®**	●		Any	➡	✓	★
T	**PANGANI FOREST EXPLORATION TRAIL®**	●		Any			◆
	ASIA						
R	**KALI RIVER RAPIDS®**	◗	3 ft 2 in	Any	➡	✓	★
S	**FLIGHTS OF WONDER**	◗		Any			★
T	**MAHARAJA JUNGLE TREK®**	●		Any			◆
T	**EXPEDITION EVEREST™**	●	3 ft 8 in	11►	➡	✓	★
	CAMP MINNIE-MICKEY						
S	**CAMP MINNIE-MICKEY GREETING TRAILS**	●		Any			◆
S	**FESTIVAL OF THE LION KING**	◗		Any			★
S	**MICKEY'S JAMMIN' JUNGLE PARADE**						▼

Key: Ride – R Show – S Tour – T; Waiting Time Short – O Average – ◗ Long – ●; Time to Ride: Anytime – Any Before 11am – ►11; Overall Rating Good – ▼ Excellent – ◆ Outstanding – ★

Water Parks

Walt Disney World® features two of the best water parks in the world, including the second-largest on record. While playing second fiddle to the major theme parks of the resort, the water parks manage to attract huge numbers of visitors, particularly during the hot summer months.

Typhoon Lagoon bears only a pretense of a theme, a whimsical pirate/nautical motif that features everything from thrilling slides to winding rapids to gentle rivers. Apart from the chance to snorkel with real sharks and other fish, it's a normal water park, only Disney-fied. On the other hand, Disney's Blizzard Beach is winter fun all year round with a wonderful working "flooded ski resort" that throws visitors into a "failed" winter wonderland and substitutes flumes and slides for skis and toboggans. This truly clever idea keeps the area covered in "snow" but with nice warm water throughout the year.

Sliding down Mount Gushmore at Blizzard Beach

BLIZZARD BEACH ❺

During a "freak" winter storm – or so the legend goes – an entire section of the Disney property was buried under a pile of powdery snow. Disney Imagineers quickly set to work, building Florida's first ski resort, complete with ski lifts, toboggan runs, and a breathtaking ski slope. However, the snow started to melt quickly, and the Disney people thought all was lost until they spotted an alligator snowboarding himself down the mountainside. In a flash, they reinvented the ski resort as a water/ski park, Blizzard Beach; they turned luge runs into slides and the mountain into the world's longest and highest flume, and created creeks for inner-tube enthusiasts to paddle around in.

The centerpiece of Blizzard Beach is the 120-ft (36-m) high **Summit Plummet**, which rockets particularly brave visitors at speeds of over 60 mph (96 km/h). Incredibly popular with teens, it's too intense for children – you must be at least 4 ft (1.2 m) tall to ride it. The Slush Gusher and Toboggan Racer are similar, but less frightening, water slides. Two firm family favorites are the Downhill Double Dipper, which features two side-by-side, 50-ft (15-m) high racing slides that pit you against a competitor while sliding on an inner tube, and Snow Stormers, taking kids down one of three 350-ft (110-m) long, twisting and turning flumes while lying on toboggan mats. The thrills continue with the **Teamboat Springs** whitewater raft ride, a rollicking race through choppy waters that lasts far longer than you'd expect but leaves you wanting more anyway. The Runoff Rapids is another speedy trip through harrowing waterways, this time in an inner tube.

For those with a more relaxed agenda, there is the lovely chair lift to carry you up the side of **Mount Gushmore**, where you can go rock-climbing or hiking. Or you may choose to lazily float around the entire park by tubing down Cross Country Creek, enjoy the pool area called Melt-Away Bay. Kids' areas include the Blizzard Beach Ski Patrol Training Camp, aimed at older children, and Tike's Peak for the little ones.

During high season, Blizzard Beach fills up very quickly, and can actually close its gates when at full capacity. Either arrive a half-hour before opening, or wait until after 2pm, when fewer people are in the park, for best access to rides and rental lockers.

TOP TIPS

• Blizzard Beach and Typhoon Lagoon have their own, free, parking lots; Winter Summerland shares the Blizzard Beach lot. You don't need to wait for Disney transportation if you've got a vehicle – you can drive to the water parks and park right there.

Swimmers head almost straight down Summit Plummet

◁ **Snorkeling amid colorful fish at Shark Reef, Typhoon Lagoon**

TYPHOON LAGOON ⑥

This water park offers less in the way of man-made thrills and more natural excitement, though it features some traditional water park favorites as well. Where Blizzard Beach trades on its novelty, Typhoon Lagoon revels in natural beauty and sealife encounters, and boasts a surf pool that is one of the world's largest, at 650,000 cu ft (18,406 cu m). The motif of this park is that of a shipwreck – the "Miss Tilly" which got caught in a storm so severe it landed on the peak of **Mount Mayday** – in a tropical paradise.

At the top of Mount Mayday are three whitewater raft rides of varying intensity – the thrilling Gang Plank Falls, the incredibly high and wild Mayday Falls, or the relatively tame Keelhaul Falls.

Also on Mount Mayday are the body-slide rides known collectively as Humunga-Kowabunga, which require riders to be at least 4 ft (1.2m) tall. Great fun but highly intimidating, these rides involve falls of roughly 50 ft (15 m) at speeds of 30 mph (48 km/h) almost straight down. The Storm Slides offer three flumes that twist and turn inside the mountain itself.

The newest addition to Typhoon Lagoon is **Crush 'n' Gusher**, in which torrents of gushing water take the most daring of raft riders on a

The Wave Pool, with "Miss Tilly" in the backgound

gravity-defying adventure through twisting caverns.

More relaxing is the powerful **Wave Pool** which offers 6-ft (1.8-m) high waves alternating with gentler periods. The other peaceful attraction is the meandering, relaxing, and stunningly beautiful **Castaway Creek**, where you can inner-tube your troubles away for what seems like forever. Children

can spend many happy hours at the aquatic playground, Ketchakiddee Creek, and the smaller wave pools. Of special note is the **Shark Reef**, where visitors can either observe tropical fish and live, small sharks from an "overturned freighter" or grab a snorkel and mask and swim with them. It is perfectly safe and offers lovely views of incredibly colorful sealife.

Getting up close and personal with sealife at Shark Reef

WINTER SUMMERLAND

Although Fantasia Gardens, on Buena Vista Drive, was the first themed mini-golf park on Disney property, Winter Summerland is unique in that it continues the motifs of the neighboring water parks, Blizzard Beach and Typhoon Lagoon, but adds a Christmas twist, with two elaborately-designed 18-hole courses – the Winter and Summer courses. The two courses were supposedly built by St. Nick's elves, who were divided into two camps – those who missed the North Pole and those who preferred the Florida heat.

Both courses feature plenty of interactive elements and are surprisingly challenging. Generally the most popular, the Winter Course is widely perceived as being slightly easier, with "snow" and holiday elements abounding. A few of the holes on each course are identical except for the substitution of sand for snow on the Summer holes. The Summer Course features surfboards, water sprays, and other tropical obstacles, including a sand-buried snoozing Santa. The two courses converge for the final two holes in a log cabin-style lodge.

Disney Cruise Line®

With a cruise line that offers two gorgeous, larger-than-average ships, private destinations, and an all-inclusive fare, Disney World, in 1998, extended its reach to the high seas of the Caribbean. In addition to the popular three- and four-night trips, there are now extended itineraries available to passengers, which offer more island ports and longer duration cruises. Disney's Cruise Line has a pair of powerful incentives no other cruise line can match: apart from its outstanding reputation for quality and comfort, it offers vacations that include stays at Walt Disney World as part of the total package.

A Disney Cruise Line® ship docked at a pier

A Disney Cruise Line® ship at Castaway Cay

THE SHIPS & THE DESTINATION

The two Disney cruise ships, the **Disney Magic** and the **Disney Wonder**, have staterooms that are around 25 percent larger than those of most other cruise ships. Two ships, the **Disney Dream** and the **Disney Fantasy**, joined the fleet in 2011 and 2012. The usual modern styling of most other ships is replaced with the stately elegance of European vessels of

Dining in style at Palo restaurant aboard a Disney ship

old, with an Art Deco theme for the Magic and Art Nouveau for the Wonder. Both ships offer theater, restaurants, spas, and fitness centers among several other amenities. **Castaway Cay**, Disney's own private island, is the end point of every Disney cruise, and is very much a tropical extension of Walt Disney World's hotels and resorts. There are uncrowded beaches, snorkeling, bicycling, glass-bottom boat tours, watersports, and much more on offer. In addition, there is always plenty to do for children on board and off – so much so that you may see very little of them during your trip.

THE SHORT (THREE–FIVE-NIGHT) CRUISES

The itinerary on the shorter cruises for both ships is the same – after arriving at Port Canaveral by charter bus and checking in, you cast off and arrive in Nassau in the Bahamas the next day. The following day you arrive at

Castaway Cay, and leave there in the evening to return to Canaveral at 9am the next morning. The four-night cruise adds a day at sea, while the five-night cruises spend an extra night at Castaway Cay or Key West before returning to Port Canaveral.

THE LONG (SEVEN–TEN-NIGHT) CRUISES

Disney offers both an Eastern Caribbean and a Western Caribbean tour for their longer cruises, which include stops in St. Maarten and St. Thomas in addition to Castaway Cay for the eastern cruise, or Grand Cayman and Cozumel along with Castaway Cay for the western cruise. Long European cruises are also available.

TOP TIPS

• Keep in mind that the all-inclusive fare does not include things such as tips for servers, stateroom hostess, assistant server, and head server. Other additional charges are for soft drinks at the pool, and alcoholic beverages. There is a $15 per person charge for eating in the adults-only specialty restaurant. Shore excursions are also extra significant charges – port charges as well as government taxes are added to the fee.

• It is a good idea to plan ahead for shore excursions to avoid waiting in a line to sign up for them once on the ship and taking a chance. You can log on to the website (see p77) to sign up for shore excursions.

Fort Wilderness Resort & Campground ❼

A campground would seem to be at odds with the provide-every-luxury mentality of most Disney World accommodations, but Fort Wilderness, which opened in 1971, still represents one of Walt Disney's aims – to foster an appreciation of nature and the outdoors. Located on Bay Lake in the Magic Kingdom® resort area, it has more than 750 shaded campsites and over 400 cabins to provide various levels of "roughing it." While wildlife is fairly sparse in this area, amenities and even entertainment are plentiful. The center of Fort Wilderness is Pioneer Hall, home to several restaurants and the hugely popular dinner show, Hoop-De-Do Musical Revue *(see p75)*. There is convenient boat transportation to Magic Kingdom® and motorcoach conveyance to all theme parks.

Riders enjoying a canter at Fort Wilderness Resort & Campground

A cabin at Disney's Fort Wilderness Resort & Campground

ACCOMMODATIONS & COMMUNITY AREAS

The campsites at Fort Wilderness are small but reasonably secluded, with electric and water "hookups" at all locations. All the cabins offer house-like comfort in confined quarters *(see p140)*.

There are 15 air-conditioned "comfort stations" all around the campground, with facilities such as laundries, showers, telephones, and even ice machines, open 24 hours a day. Two "trading posts" offer groceries and rent out recreational equipment.

RECREATION

There is plenty to keep visitors happily occupied at Fort Wilderness Resort. The **Tri-Circle D Ranch** has two heated pools, guided horseback tours, and pony rides. Other recreational facilities include tennis, volleyball, and basketball courts, bike and boat rentals, fishing, an exercise trail, nightly wagon rides, horseshoes and shuffleboard, carriage rides, a petting zoo, and video arcades. You can also opt for skiing, parasailing, and wakeboarding. Equipment is usually available for rental. Reservations are required for the guided tours on horseback or for fishing.

In addition, Fort Wilderness offers a **Campfire** program with singalongs and outdoor movies. Available to all Disney guests – and not just Fort Wilderness residents – the program features an hour of singalongs complete with toasted marshmallows and the American delicacy "smores" – melted marshmallow and chocolate on graham crackers. Hosted in part by the Disney chipmunks Chip 'n' Dale, the singalong leads into the screening of a Disney animated feature. An additional attraction is the nighttime **Electrical Water Pageant** *(see p75)*, which goes by Fort Wilderness Resort at about 10pm. There is a nice all-you-can-eat breakfast buffet at Pioneer Hall.

SPORTS AT WALT DISNEY WORLD

Besides Fort Wilderness, all Disney resorts have sports and fitness facilities, though available only for residents. In 1997, Disney's **ESPN Wide World of Sports®** complex was opened, primarily as a training camp and athletic haven for exhibition games, Olympic training, and other recreational activities *(see p178)*. While the DWWS experience is largely passive, the same cannot be said for what is Disney's most "hands-on" experience to date: **The Richard Petty Driving Experience** *(see p177)*, where visitors can train and become NASCAR-style race car drivers, actually driving real race cars at speeds in excess of 100 mph (161 km/h) around a race track. Unlike most Disney experiences, you are in full control of the vehicle. These cars boast over 600 horsepower engines so the thrill is most decidedly real. As might be expected, safety instruction takes top billing for this sport.

Downtown Disney® ➑

Shopping, fine dining, exciting shows, and concerts are on offer at Downtown Disney®, giving visitors plenty to do at Walt Disney World® Resort after the theme parks have closed. Downtown Disney® includes the Marketplace, a lovely outdoor mall with stores and restaurants and West Side, featuring stores, eateries, and concert venues. Pleasure Island was originally the ultimate party zone based around several themed night-clubs and shows, but it has been transformed into a family-friendly shopping and dining experience. Downtown Disney® offers free parking and free admission, though some venues, such as DisneyQuest®, a five-story "indoor interactive theme park," charge separate admission, unless you have the Ultimate Park Hopper and Premium Annual passes (*see p76*). Buses run continually to the on-property resort hotels. Downtown Disney® now has its own iconic attraction, a giant tethered balloon that takes guests 400 ft (122 m) into the air to view the amazing scenery of Walt Disney World® Resort and surrounding Orlando beyond.

spend approximately 10 minutes enjoying breath-taking 360-degree views of Walt Disney World® Resort and, depending on the weather, there are views of up to 10 miles (16 km) away. The balloon is the world's largest tethered gas balloon, and is attached to a gondola that can hold up to 29 guests and a pilot. Weather permitting, flights operate daily from 9am until midnight and are wheelchair accessible. Flights cost $18 per adult and $12 per child (aged 3–9 years).

WEST SIDE

Each store, restaurant, or business on Downtown Disney®'s West Side has a unique feel to it, making for a splendid evening's exploring. Among the do-not-miss shops are the **Magnetron** shop, with magnets and similar kitschy items; the **Magic Masters** trick shop, which features continuous live magic demonstrations; and the popular **Candy Cauldron** where sweets are made on the spot. There's also the state-of-the-art stadium-seating **AMC 24 Theatres**.

Full-service restaurants here include the popular Cuban and Latin fare of **Bongos Cuban Café** (which features a band and dancing), the gourmet entrées of the upstairs **Wolfgang Puck's Café**, the Southern US cuisine of the **House of Blues** restaurant, and the American food of movie-memorabilia-studded **Planet Hollywood**. Quick

Harley-Davidson store at Pleasure Island, Downtown Disney®

PLEASURE ISLAND

For more than 20 years Pleasure Island was centered around several nightclubs, live entertainment, and nightly firework displays. Today, it is filled with unique shopping venues and eateries. **Fuego by Sosa Cigars** combines an upscale lounge with a retail store for cigars and smoking accessories. The **Orlando Harley-Davidson** store offers a huge selection of men's, women's, and children's apparel, gifts, and collectibles. There are two Harley-Davidson motorcycles for guests to sit on, and you can even buy a Harley-Davidson cookbook. **Curl** is a high-end surf shop that offers

surfers a selection of fashion-able surfwear clothing and accessories, plus skateboards and surfboards, and there are many other stores besides.

Dining experiences range from the energetic **Raglan Road Irish Pub** or kid-friendly **T Rex Café**, to fine dining at **Fulton's Crab House** or casual Italian at **Portobello**.

CHARACTERS IN FLIGHT

Visitors can take to the skies from Downtown Disney® in an illuminated balloon with handpainted silhouettes of a dozen of Disney's famous "flying characters" such as Mary Poppins, Aladdin, and Dumbo. The giant balloon, operated by **Aérophile**, is tethered so there is no chance of floating away. Passengers

Downtown Disney® West Side glittering in the evening

Pirates of the Caribbean: Battle for Buccaneer Gold at DisneyQuest®

bites can be obtained from **Wetzel's Pretzels**, featuring hot pretzels and cold Häagen-Dazs ice cream, and the lower level of Wolfgang Puck's Café, which serves brick-oven pizzas and salads. The West Side has three special attractions that require separate admissions: the House of Blues concert hall (part of the national chain, which attracts major music acts), the breathtaking **Cirque du Soleil®** show **La Nouba™**, and the electronic funhouse called **DisneyQuest®**.

In addition to regular shows by national artists, with a side stage for smaller acts, the House of Blues offers a Sunday Gospel Brunch that features live gospel performers showing off their

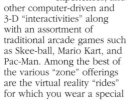

La Nouba™ show at Cirque du Soleil®

uniquely American religious singing. The Cirque du Soleil® show, which is a theatrical production based on a circus, is so popular that it is always sold out. This fabulous show has 64 performers on stage at the same time, performing a variety of gymnastic feats. Reservations are a must. DisneyQuest® is extremely popular with teens and younger kids and features state-of-the-art video arcades, virtual reality experiences, and other computer-driven and 3-D "interactivities" along with an assortment of traditional arcade games such as Skee-ball, Mario Kart, and Pac-Man. Among the best of the various "zone" offerings are the virtual reality "rides" for which you wear a special helmet with glasses, such as **Aladdin's Magic Carpet Ride**, **Ride the Comix**, and **Invasion!**, along with the two-man shooter rides such as **Pirates of the Caribbean: Battle for Buccaneer Gold**.

MARKETPLACE

An open-air mall with some excellent shops and a good variety of restaurants, the Marketplace makes for a relaxing walk when you're not pressed for time. Among the highlights, especially for children, is the **LEGO Imagination Center**, which features photo-op displays of wonderful LEGO constructions, from a spaceship to a dragon in the pond next to the store.

Also of interest to kids will be the **Once Upon a Toy** and **Disney's Days of Christmas** stores. Kids and adults alike will be awed by the sheer size of the **World of Disney** emporium, the largest Disney memorabilia store in the world and the "mother lode" for all Disney souvenirs.

Restaurants include the colorful **Rainforest Café**, **Fulton's Crab House** with its superb seafood and riverboat ambience, and **Ghirardelli's Soda Fountain & Chocolate Shop** with its malt-shop atmosphere. Quick bites can be found at **Cap'n Jack's** floating restaurant and the **McDonald's**, **Wolfgang Puck Express**, and **Earl of Sandwich** chain eateries.

AFTER DARK EVENTS

Apart from the Downtown Disney® attractions, other prime after-dark entertainment includes **dinner shows** and the **Electrical Water Pageant**. A floating parade that wanders around park resorts such as Polynesian and Contemporary, the Electrical Water Pageant is best viewed from the unobstructed beach in Fort Wilderness. This kids' favorite showcases 20 minutes of dazzling electrical animation – dolphins jumping out of the water, whales swimming by, even a fire-breathing dragon. Around since 1971, it often serves as an opening act or postscript for the Magic Kingdom® and Epcot® fireworks. Disney's two long-running dinner shows, Hoop-Dee-Doo Musical Revue and Disney's Spirit of Aloha, should not tempt visitors to leave the theme parks early but they are still enjoyable. The first is a popular Western comedy show at Fort Wilderness' Pioneer Hall; the second features authentic Polynesian music, dance, and food. Another show, Mickey's Backyard BBQ, provides country 'n' western fun.

The superbly constructed LEGO dragon at the Marketplace

Essential Information

Spread over a large area of 47 sq miles (121 sq km) and brimming with attractions, Walt Disney World® Resort can provide entertainment for the whole family for at least a week. Guests who do not have much holiday time need to plan carefully to make the most of their visit to this dream vacationland. The information here is geared toward aiding them in this task.

WHEN TO VISIT

The busiest times of the year are Christmas, the last week of February until Easter, and June to August. At these times, the parks begin to approach capacity – some 90,000 people a day in Magic Kingdom alone. All the rides will be operating and the parks are open for longer periods. During off-season, 10,000 guests a day might visit the Magic Kingdom, only one water park may be operating, and certain attractions may be closed for maintenance. The weather is also a factor – in July and August, hot and humid afternoons are regularly punctuated by torrential thunderstorms. Between October and March, however, the temperatures and humidity are both more comfortable and permit a more energetic touring schedule.

BUSIEST DAYS

Each of the theme parks is packed on certain days. The busiest days are as follows: Magic Kingdom: Monday, Thursday, and Saturday. Epcot: Tuesday, Friday, and Saturday. Disney's Hollywood Studios: Wednesday and Sunday. Note, however, that after a thunderstorm, the water parks are often almost empty – even at the peak times of the year.

OPENING HOURS

When the theme parks are busiest, opening hours are the longest, typically 9am to 10–11pm or midnight. In less busy periods, hours are usually 9am to 6–8pm. Call to check. The parks open at least 30 minutes early for pass holders and guests at any of the WDW hotels and resorts.

LENGTH OF VISIT

To enjoy Walt Disney World to the full, you may want to give Magic Kingdom and Epcot two full days – or one and half days, with half a day at a water park – each, leaving a day for Disney's Hollywood Studios and Animal Kingdom. Set aside three nights to see Fantasmic!, IllumiNations, and Wishes firework displays.

THE IDEAL SCHEDULE

To avoid the worst of the crowds and the heat:
• Arrive as early as possible and visit the most popular attractions first.
• Take a break in the early afternoon, when it's hottest and the parks are full.
• Return to the parks in the cool of the evening to see parades and fireworks.

TICKETS & TYPES OF PASSES

There are several types of passes available for visitors. You can buy one-day, one-park tickets, but if you're staying for more than three days consider the **Park Hopper Pass**. This offers you one-day admission to each theme park on any four or five days. For most, one of these multi-day park hopper passes will suffice.

The **Park Hopper Plus** offers unlimited access to the theme parks and water parks on any five, six, or seven days.

However, one of the best passes is the **Ultimate Park Hopper Pass**, which is exclusively available to guests staying in Disney hotels. It offers unlimited admission to theme parks, water parks, and the sports complex. Prices are determined by the length of your stay.

Non-Disney guests visiting for more than ten days should consider the **Annual Pass** or the **Premium Annual Pass**, which costs little more than a seven-day Park Hopper. Separate Annual Passes are offered by the water parks and DisneyQuest. Child ticket pricing applies to ages three through nine.

Passes are available at Disney stores, the airport, the Tourist Information Center on I-Drive, and the official Disney website. In addition, passes are sometimes included in package deals.

GETTING AROUND

An extensive, efficient transportation system handles an average of 200,000 guests each day. Even if you stay outside Walt Disney World Resort, many nearby hotels offer free shuttle services to and from the theme parks, but you can check this when you make your reservation.

The transportation hub of Walt Disney World is the **Ticket and Transportation Center (TTC)**. Connecting it to the Magic Kingdom are two monorail services. A third monorail links the TTC to Epcot. Ferries run from the TTC to the Magic Kingdom across the Seven Seas Lagoon.

Ferries connect the Magic Kingdom and Epcot with the resorts in their respective areas, while buses link everything in Walt Disney World, including direct links to the Magic Kingdom. All ticket holders can use the entire transportation system for free.

Although Disney transportation is efficient, you may wish to rent a car if you want to enjoy the entire area without inconvenience. The theme parks are spread out and, especially for visits to swimming attractions such as Blizzard Beach and Typhoon Lagoon, Disney transportation is not always the best option for children. Young children who are wet and tired from swimming will not welcome waiting in line for the Disney bus.

COPING WITH LINES

Lines tend to be shortest at the beginning and end of the day, and during parade and meal times. Lines for the rides move slowly, but the wait for a show is rarely longer than the show itself. The Fastpass *(see p34)* allows visitors to reserve time at 25 of the most popular attractions rather than wait in long lines. Disney parks fill rapidly after the first hour of opening. Until then, you can usually just walk onto rides for which you'll have to line up later.

DISABLED TRAVELERS

Wheelchairs can be borrowed at the park entrance and special bypass entrances allow disabled guests and carers to board rides without waiting in line. Staff, however, are not allowed to lift guests or assist with lifting for safety reasons.

VERY YOUNG CHILDREN

As Walt Disney World® can be physically and emotionally tiring for children, try to adapt your schedule accordingly. If you've come with preschool-age kids, focus on Magic Kingdom®.

The waiting and walking involved in a theme park visit can exhaust young children quickly so it's a good idea to rent a stroller, available at every park entrance. Each stroller is personalized when you rent it, but if it should go missing when you leave a ride, you can get a replacement with your rental receipt. Baby Care Centers for changing and feeding are located all around the parks.

In a system called "switching off," parents can enjoy a ride one at a time while the other parent stays with the child – without having to line up twice.

MEETING MICKEY

For many youngsters, the most exciting moment at WDW Resort is meeting the Disney characters. You will spot them in all the theme parks, but you can have more relaxed encounters in a number of restaurants, usually at breakfast. Each theme park and many of the resorts also offer "character dining," though you must call well ahead of time to make a reservation. Remember to bring an autograph book.

SAFETY

The resort's excellent safety record and first rate security force mean problems are rare and dealt with promptly. Cast members watch out for young unaccompanied children and escort them to lost children centers. Bags of all visitors are checked.

STAYING & DINING

Lodging in the Disney-run hotels and villa complexes is of a very high standard. However, even the lowest-priced places are more expensive than many hotels outside Walt Disney World®. But do keep in mind that, apart from Disney quality, your money also buys:
• Early entry into the theme parks (up to 60 minutes).
• Guaranteed admission to the theme parks even when the parks are otherwise full.
• The delivery of shopping purchases made anywhere in Walt Disney World® Resort.

For dining at any full-service restaurant in Walt Disney World®, especially in Epcot®, book a Priority Seating – the table booking equivalent of the Fastpass.

For more information, see pages 138–40 and 148–50.

PARKING

Visitors to Magic Kingdom® must park at the TTC and make their way by tram or foot; Epcot®, Disney's Hollywood Studios®, and Animal Kingdom® have their own parking lots. Parking is free for Disney resort residents – others must pay, but only once a day no matter how many times they move their vehicle. The lots are large, so remember the character name and row of the section where you are parked.

DIRECTORY

GENERAL

General Information
Tel (407) 824-4321.
http://disneyworld.
disney.go.com

Accommodation Information/ Reservation
Tel (407) 934-7639.

Dining Reservations (including Dinner Shows)
Tel (407) 939-3463.

Disney Tours
Tel (407) 939-8687.

Golf Reservations
Tel (407) 939-4653.

THEME PARKS & ATTRACTIONS

Blizzard Beach
Tel (407) 560-3400.

Disney Cruise Line®
Tel (888) 325-2500.
www.disneycruise.disney.
go.com

Disney's Hollywood Studios®
Tel (407) 824-4321.

Disney's Animal Kingdom®
Tel (407) 938-3000.

Downtown Disney®
Tel (407) 824-4321.

Epcot®
Tel (407) 824-4321.

ESPN Wide World of Sports®
Tel (407) 828-3267.

Fort Wilderness Resort & Campground
Tel (407) 824-2900.

Magic Kingdom®
Tel (407) 824-4321.

The Richard Petty Driving Experience
Tel (407) 939-0130.

Typhoon Lagoon
Tel (407) 824-4321.

ORLANDO'S OTHER THEME PARKS

With everything from roller coasters to performing killer whales, filmy fantasy to amazing shopping and dining experiences, the theme parks at Orlando provide endless entertainment options, and have catapulted the city into the ranks of the world's top vacation destinations. The pioneering effort was, of course, Walt Disney World® in 1971; other parks quickly followed.

SeaWorld®, which opened in 1973, has a range of educational and entertaining programs and brings visitors in close touch with whales, sea lions, manatees, and many other marine creatures. It also features sea-themed rides such as Kraken®, one of the world's tallest and fastest floorless roller coasters. Located across from SeaWorld®, Discovery Cove® is a tropical paradise where guests can swim with dolphins, snorkel with fish, and hand-feed exotic birds.

Universal Orlando® came onto the scene in 1990 with the opening of its park, Universal Studios Florida®. A lively entertainment venue, Universal CityWalk®, followed in 1998; then came a second Universal theme park, Islands of Adventure®. With its wildly exciting, high-tech rides and shows, based on blockbuster movies, Universal Orlando® has emerged as serious competition to Disney. Another popular attraction is Wet 'n Wild®, which boasts a variety of thrill rides.

The theme parks are constantly evolving, with exciting areas and new, jazzy rides being added at regular intervals. For instance, The Waterfront®, is a 5-acre (2-ha) village suffused with the festivity of the most vibrant cities by the sea, while Universal Orlando®'s showcases The Wizarding World of Harry Potter™.

Another popular waterpark from SeaWorld® is Aquatica, which combines rides and slides with a chance to see rare marine mammals close-up.

A mother-child pair of dolphins gamboling at Discovery Cove®

◁ The 150-ft (46-m) high monster roller coaster, Kraken®, at SeaWorld® Orlando

Exploring Orlando's Other Theme Parks

Conveniently located in the area around International Drive *(see pp110–11)*, Universal Orlando, SeaWorld, Discovery Cove, and Wet 'n Wild do not lag far behind Walt Disney World in the entertainment stakes. SeaWorld and Discovery Cove focus on the natural world with their beautifully re-created habitats that hold various creatures of the deep. SeaWorld's shows, such as Blue Horizons and Believe, and its world-class rides provide plenty of excitement. The other two major theme venues are geared more toward older childen and adults. The water park Wet 'n Wild is an out-and-out big-thrill rides experience, while Universal Orlando entices with two theme parks full of movie magic and amazing rides laden with special effects, as well as an exuberant entertainment district.

SIGHTS AT A GLANCE

Aquatica ❷
Discovery Cove ❸
SeaWorld® Orlando ❶
Universal Orlando ❹
Wet 'n Wild® ❺

Blue Horizons show at SeaWorld® Orlando

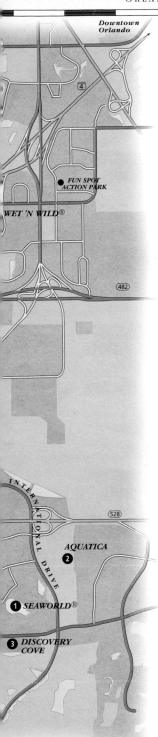

Universal Orlando®'s Revenge of the Mummy® – The Ride

SEE ALSO

- *Where to Stay* pp140–41

- *Where to Eat* pp150–51

GETTING AROUND

To the northeast of Walt Disney World®, Orlando's other major theme parks are connected to each other and to Disney by I-4, the crucial artery of the Orlando region. Universal Orlando® is at one end, situated off exits 74A and 75B from I-4. At the other end is Discovery Cove®, across the road from Sea-World®, which is located at the intersection of I-4 and the Beach Line Expressway. Wet 'n Wild® is situated off I-4, exit 75A.

Apart from the connections offered by the public bus service LYNX, there are private charters as well as free shuttle services provided by some hotels to the various theme parks. If you wish to cover a lot of ground in less time, the best option is to rent a car. However, keep in mind that I-4 is a high traffic zone. For more details, see pages 193–7.

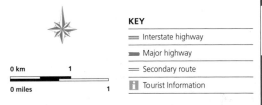

KEY

▬▬	Interstate highway
▬▬	Major highway
▬▬	Secondary route
🛈	Tourist Information

0 km   1

0 miles   1

A couple having fun at The Blast, a ride at Wet 'n Wild®

SeaWorld® Orlando ❶

In terms of scale and creativity, the world's most popular marine life adventure park is a match for any of Orlando's other theme parks. Opened in 1973, the park is home to thrilling rides as well as beautifully choreographed and flawlessly executed shows, including Believe and Blue Horizons. The park is also renowned for Shamu, SeaWorld®'s mascot killer whale, and his many friends. Some attractions even allow you to touch or feed the marine life – an experience of a lifetime. The park also provides a platform for the promotion of educational, research, and conservation programs. Each presentation at the park illustrates ways and means by which people can protect and safeguard the environment and the wildlife that occupies it.

TACKLING THE PARK

SeaWorld® is usually less crowded than Orlando's other theme parks. Its gentler pace means that a visit after 3pm affords a cooler and less crowded experience. Try to set aside at least an entire day to cover all the attractions the park has to offer. Pick up a map from Guest Services, and plan your day. You can use the 400-ft (122-m) high Sky Tower as a point of reference while navigating the park.

Most of the presentations are walk-through exhibits or sit-down stadium shows. The stadiums seat so many that finding a good spot is seldom a problem. Bear in mind that if you sit near the front you may get wet. It is also worth noting that the shows are timed so that it's all but impossible to leave one show just in time for another. This is done to reduce crowding, but it is possible to get a seat in the Clyde and Seamore (Sea Lion and Otter) show if you leave the Shamu stadium about four minutes early – while all the performers are taking their bows at the end of the show.

During peak season, head for the Wild Arctic®, Journey to Atlantis®, Shark Encounter, and Kraken® attractions early in the day as they get very crowded later on and form long lines. Young children enjoy meeting the actors in furry suits who play the parts of Shamu and the crew – a killer whale, a penguin, a pelican, a dolphin, and an otter. They are usually found near the park's exit around closing time. SeaWorld® also has several restaurants to choose from if you are hungry.

Tourists touching and feeding the friendly dolphins in a lagoon at Dolphin Cove®, Key West at SeaWorld®

Sea lions basking on the rocks at Pacific Point Preserve®

ANIMAL ATTRACTIONS

The meticulously designed habitats at SeaWorld® offer a rare look at marine creatures, such as dolphins, penguins, and sharks, as they would be in their natural settings.

Key West at SeaWorld®
One of the park's most visited animal attractions, Key West at SeaWorld® is a tropical paradise featuring animals of the Florida Keys. Spread over 5 acres (2 ha), the attraction's Dolphin Cove® and Stingray Lagoon® are home to several bottlenose dolphins and more than 200 stingrays. Guests can also experience the thrill of feeding and touching these animals. At Turtle Point®, various species of endangered and threatened sea turtles can be seen, and an underwater viewing area offers a peek at a beautiful coral reef.

Sunset Celebration, which takes place every night at Key West, is a colorful and festive affair abuzz with live music and entertainers.

Pacific Point Preserve®
Designed as a replica of the Northern Pacific coast, this 2.5 acre (1 ha) area has many beaches and rocky outcroppings. Visitors enjoy the antics of sea lions, harbor seals, and fur seals as they play, jump, and have a great time at this attraction. Don't miss the highly entertaining feeding sessions as the sea lions and other mammals dive around for food and swallow an entire fish in one gulp. Check at the information desk for timings.

Manatee Rescue
Named the country's best new zoological exhibit by the American Zoological Association, the attraction offers an up close and personal look at manatees. This highly educational exhibit includes a film show about the doleful and appealing herbivores. Injured manatees are brought to the park by an animal rescue team, and are released back into their habitat once they have recovered.

Penguin Encounter®
A re-creation of the polar regions, this glacial terrain is covered with snow and has a sub-zero temperature. Four

Rockhopper penguins on icy ledges at Penguin Encounter®

species of penguins – gentoo, rockhopper, chinstrap, and king – waddle along the rocky cliffs and swim gracefully in the icy waters, while puffins play close at hand. A 120-ft (35-m) long moving walkway passes through the habitat and gives guests a close view of the birds.

Summer Nights at SeaWorld®
During the summer months there are added experiences and adventures on offer at the park, including opportunities to feed dolphins, night shows such as Shamu Rocks and the Hawaiian-themed Makahiki Luau dinner show, and a nightly fireworks and fountains finale. After 6pm Summer Nights Central comes alive along the lake with food and drink, games and music, with live bands performing weekly. A VIP guided tour including front-of-the-line service is bookable in advance.

Shark Encounter
Walk through an underwater tunnel surrounded by hair-raising creatures such as poisonous fish, scary barracudas, creepy eels, and predatory sharks. The 60-ft (18-m) long tunnel is made up of acrylic panels – each weighing almost 5000 lbs (2268 kg) – and offers a close but safe look at these dangerous animals.

Those looking for a more thrilling experience can try the interactive Sharks Deep Dive program, which is a part of the Shark Encounter. Here, visitors wear special wetsuits and snorkel or scuba dive in a shark cage while more than 50 sharks swim around them. This two-hour program is expensive and permits only two guests at a time. Children below the age of ten are not allowed.

A'LURE
A'Lure – The Call of the Ocean is a circus-like show that combines spectacular acrobatics, giant puppets, and aerial tumbling techniques on a massive stage at the Nautilus Theater. An oversized projection screen backdrop displays images of schools of fish, graceful manta rays, and giant sea serpents while performers use music, comedy, colorful costumes, silk ropes, and gravity-defying techniques to tell the tale of the mythological Sea Sirens who lure sailors into their underwater lairs.

RIDES & SHOWS

Spectacular stunts, hilarious animal antics, and exhilarating thrills characterize SeaWorld®'s rides and shows.

Wild Arctic®
Journey to the North Pole in a highly realistic simulated helicopter flight through blizzards and avalanches. At the end of this perilous "flight," visitors embark on an exploration of the frozen landscape. They also meet the region's animal inhabitants, such as giant walruses, frisky harbor seals, beautiful beluga whales, and two playful polar bears called Snow and Klondike.

Journey to Atlantis®
Unpredictable drops, twists, and turns are what riders can expect from this high-speed part water and part roller coaster adventure ride – the most thrilling being a terrifying drop, almost straight down, from a height of 60 ft (18 m). Eight riders, aboard an old Greek fishing boat, are pitchforked into a battle for the lost city of Atlantis and face lugelike plunges and curves interlaced with amazing special effects as they fight their way through to safety.

Kraken®
Named after a giant mythical sea monster, the floorless roller coaster Kraken is one of the fastest coasters in Orlando.

SEAWORLD®'S SERIOUS SIDE

The buzzwords at SeaWorld® are Research, Rescue, and Rehabilitation – the "three Rs." SeaWorld®'s animal rescue team is on call 24 hours a day and has helped thousands of ill and injured whales, dolphins, manatees, birds, and turtles. In fact, the park's manatee rescue program is the largest in the world. The animals are nursed and, if necessary, operated on in SeaWorld®'s rehabilitation center. Those that recover sufficiently are released back into the wild. SeaWorld® also runs several educational tours, such as the Saving a Species tour, which offer a glimpse into their conservation programs.

SeaWorld®'s animal rescue team providing aid to a manatee calf

Riders are taken to a height of 149 ft (45.5 m) and then dropped 144 ft (44 m), while taking seven hair-raising loops that turn them upside down – all at an incredible speed of 65 mph (104 km/h). Adding to the thrill are the open-sided seats, offering only shouder restraints as support and leaving nothing for riders to hold on to as they are hurled through the air.

One Ocean
SeaWorld®'s Shamu show is a spectacular, multisensory celebration of life below the waves. The killer whales, of course, take centre stage, performing stunning choreography amid a setting of dancing fountains, brilliant displays of colored lighting, and underwater imagery capturing the below-surface motion of the performing creatures as well as windows onto the wider undersea world. A soundtrack of cont-emporary global music emphasizes the show's message of "one world, one ocean."

Shamu's Happy Harbor®
With its maze of cargo netting and slides, canvas mountains to climb, and inflatable rooms, this 3-acre (1.2-ha) play area is aimed at younger kids. There are small rides as well as the Shamu Express®, a kid-friendly coaster that's fast enough to thrill the whole family as it travels around the track at 26 mph (42 km/h).

Riders plummet down a sharp drop at the Journey to Atlantis® ride

SeaWorld's first kid-friendly roller coaster, the Shamu Express®

TOP 10 ATTRACTIONS

1. ONE OCEAN
2. BLUE HORIZONS
3. KRAKEN®
4. SHARK ENCOUNTER
5. JOURNEY TO ATLANTIS®
6. WILD ARCTIC®
7. PENGUIN ENCOUNTER®
8. CLYDE AND SEAMORE TAKE PIRATE ISLAND®
9. SHAMU'S HAPPY HARBOR®
10. MANTA®

Clyde & Seamore Take Pirate Island®
Held at the Sea Lion and Otter Stadium, this hilarious show features two sea lions – Clyde and Seamore – otters, and a walrus, who, along with their trainer, embark on a swashbuckling adventure filled with lost treasure, pirate ships, and comical mix-ups at sea.

A'Lure – The Call of the Ocean
SeaWorld's Nautilus Theater hosts this mystical, circus-like show, which tells the tale of the Sea Sirens whose hypnotic call lures fishermen into their underwater lairs. It features stunning special effects, acrobatic feats, tumblers, and silk yo-yo artists.

Pets Ahoy!
This amusing show has an all-star cast of animals such as cats, birds, dogs, pigs, skunks, and many others performing amazing tricks and funny skits. Almost all of the animals have been rescued from animal shelters. Guests are also given tips on training pets at home.

Manta®
Strapped into a giant manta ray-shaped roller coaster, guests soar through the air at speeds of almost 60 mph (96 km/h), simulating the graceful gliding and swooping flight of a manta ray through the sea. The coaster dips so close to the water that at times its wings skim the waves in this head-down, face-first thrilling ride.

Blue Horizons
The power of the sea and the elegance of flight are conveyed through the truly spectacular show at Blue Horizons, featuring dolphins, false killer whales, exotic birds, and a cast of world-class divers and aerialists.

Tours & Other Attractions
Smaller exhibits at SeaWorld® include Dolphin Nursery for new dolphin moms and their calves; and Clydesdale Hamlet, home to SeaWorld's famous Budweiser Clydesdales. The Polar Expedition Tour takes guests on a 60-minute educational exploration of the polar regions and a look at the Penguin Research Facility, while Adventure Express Tour offers reserved seats, guided tours of SeaWorld®, animal feeding opportunities, and backdoor access to rides.

EATING, DRINKING & SHOPPING

The Waterfront® at SeaWorld® is a world-class dining, entertainment, and shopping area spread over more than 5 acres (2 ha), which offers merchandise and foods from all over the world. Restaurants range from full-service to cafeteria-style and include Voyagers Smokehouse, which serves smoked and grilled meats; Seafire Inn, which offers stir fried dishes and hosts the Makahiki Luau show; the Sand Bar, which serves savory snacks and martinis; and Spice Mill Café, which features international cuisine. Dining outside The Waterfront® allows guests to eat alongside killer whales, while at Sharks Underwater Grill *(see p150)*, guests are served "Floribbean" fare as they eat just inches away from circling, menacing sharks. Spontaneous entertainment emerges around every corner as the Groove Chefs make music using kitchenware, and the Long Shoremen inspire laughter with their improvized comedy routines. The shops at The Waterfront® offer SeaWorld® memorabilia and an array of gifts.

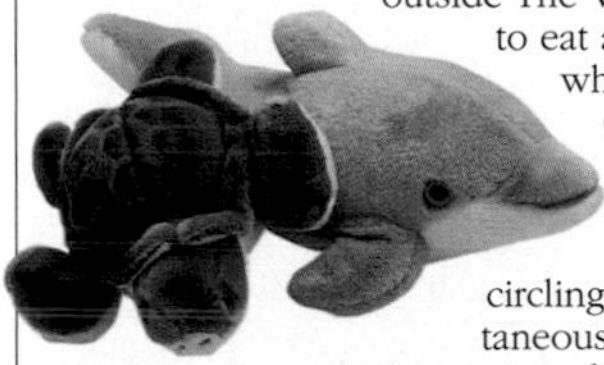

Stuffed turtle and dolphin toys from SeaWorld® shops

Aquatica ❷

The most recent addition to SeaWorld's trio of theme parks, Aquatica is home to some of the most thrilling water rides in Orlando. Inspired by the wildlife and landscapes of the South Seas, the park features dozens of slides, meandering rivers, lagoons, and white, sandy beaches. The biggest difference between Aquatica and Orlando's other water parks, such as Wet 'n Wild, is its marine life and unique animal encounters. There are stunning Commerson dolphins, giant anteaters, brilliantly colored parrots, and exotic fish. The park also has more than 100 species of tree and 250 varieties of shrubs, grasses, vines, and flowers.

VISITORS' CHECKLIST

Orange Co. 5800 Water Play Way. ***Tel*** *(407) 351-1280, 1-888-800-5447.* 🚌 *I-Trolley, Shuttle service from SeaWorld and Discovery Cove.* 🕘 *9am–10pm daily (call ahead: hours change depending on season and weather).* 💳 ♿ 🛍 🍴
www.aquaticabyseaworld.com

Taking the plunge into the Commerson dolphin habitat at Aquatica

TACKLING THE PARK

Come early as the park often reaches capacity by 10:30am and has to close admittance until mid-afternoon. Ticket prices compare favorably to some of Florida's other waterparks at $44.95 plus taxes for a single day ticket, and $99.95 plus taxes for combined entry to SeaWorld. Children aged three to nine can visit at a reduced rate and ages two and younger are allowed in for free.

As you enter the park, you will be introduced to Dolphin Plunge, the park's signature ride, which provides visitors with their first glimpse of the beautiful, black and white Commerson dolphins.

Private cabanas accommodating up to seven people are also available for rent and come with special amenities, however, they are an expensive option at $224.99 a day during peak season. Cabanas should be booked in advance as they are usually reserved by the time the park opens.

The Banana Beach Cookout offers the best value dining in the park. The all-day pass allows unlimited trips to the buffet. Single meals are also on offer. Prices are based on adult and child portions.

ATTRACTIONS

Aquatica offers a huge variety of rides, slides, animal encounters, and relaxing beaches suitable for all ages.

Dolphin Plunge

An exhilarating 250-ft (76-m) plunge through clear tubes into the park's amazing Commerson dolphin habitat. Riders must be over 48 in (122 cm) tall to share in this joyous adventure. Others can go to Dolphin Lookout and watch the excitement unfold as riders tumble down and dolphins swim past.

Taumata Racer

Older children and teens flock to the Taumata Racer, the biggest thrill ride at the park. Eight people compete against each other on specially designed mats in this high-velocity experience that includes a 300-ft (91-m) slide, and a final whirl around a 360-degree turn that speeds racers across the finish line.

Hooroo Run

Prepare yourself for a sense of weightlessness as you soar down this six story, 250-ft (76-m), triple-drop water ride. The flume takes rafts of up to four riders at a time. Guests must be 42 in (107 cm) tall.

Tassie Twister

Hang on tight as this fun flume twirls single or double inner tubes through tunnels and into a super bowl spin before dropping riders into Loggerhead Lane. Then sit back and enjoy the lazy river ride through the park's exotic landscapes where you can admire fish and bird habitats, and get an underwater view of the Commerson dolphins.

Walkabout Waters

Younger children will enjoy Walkabout Waters, an interactive water playground with slides, water cannons, and tunnels. Height restrictions vary by slide, but there are plenty of activities for children of all ages.

TOP 5 ATTRACTIONS

① DOLPHIN PLUNGE

② TAUMATA RACER

③ HOOROO RUN

④ TASSIE TWISTER

⑤ WALKABOUT WATERS

Discovery Cove® [3]

Located across the road from its big sister, SeaWorld®, Discovery Cove® is an enticing tropical paradise with beaches, reefs, and lagoons. Although the entry price is high, the park offers some exceptional experiences, the highlight being an opportunity to swim with Atlantic bottlenose dolphins. Forgoing the dolphin experience, however, can reduce the cost of a visit by almost half. Alternatively, for an extra fee you can take part in the "Trainer for a Day" program and see the park from behind the scenes. Unlike Florida's other theme parks, Discovery Cove® has a capacity of only 1,000 guests a day. As a result the service is good and crowds are limited, but you should make reservations well in advance.

TACKLING THE PARK

Make sure you set aside an entire day to cover the park's wide range of attractions. The price is steep at $289 plus taxes per person, ($189 without dolphin swim) with no reductions for children. It includes snorkeling gear, the use of beach amenities, breakfast, lunch, and snacks, and unlimited admission to SeaWorld® or the Busch Gardens® Tampa Bay for 14 consecutive days.

Visitors are greeted by a personal guide, given a photo ID card, and taken on a familiarization tour through the park. Cameras are allowed except at Dolphin Lagoon, and avoid wearing jewelry as it might be distracting for the animals. Guests with disabilities are welcome and outdoor wheelchairs are provided. Only the park's special "fish-friendly" sun-screen (included in the ticket price) may be worn at Discovery Cove®.

ATTRACTIONS

Discovery Cove® has five beautifully designed habitats all of which provide fun, interactive experiences with a variety of exotic birds and marine life.

Grand Reef

Here, visitors can swim and snorkel alongside exotic fish, encounter giant stingrays and explore grottos, colorful reefs, and the remains of an artificial shipwreck. A transparent partition separates you from large sharks and barracudas, but nevertheless creates the thrilling illusion of swimming with these predatory creatures.

The Aviary

Towering high above the rest of Discovery Cove®, this free-flight aviary is now home to more than 250 exotic birds. The small bird sanctuary is filled with several types of finch, hummingbirds, and honeycreepers, which you can feed by hand.

Aquamarine lagoons surrounded by lush foliage at Discovery Cove®

VISITORS' CHECKLIST

Orange Co. 6000 Discovery Cove Way. ***Tel** (877) 434-7268.*
🚌 *8, 42 from Orlando.* 🕐 *9am–5:30pm daily.* 💳 ♿ 🛍 🍴 **www.**discoverycove.com

Ray Lagoon

This large, secluded tropical pool is filled with several southern and cownose rays. Some of these rays are fairly large. However, they are harmless and gentle creatures. Guests can swim and snorkel alongside the rays and even reach out and touch them as they glide past.

Wind-Away River

Following a serpentine route through most of Discovery Cove®, one of the most popular stopovers on the river are the cascading waterfalls, where guests can cool off from the heat of the Florida sun. The river also features a specially designed underwater cave, which families can explore, as well as an underwater viewing window for a peek into Tropical Reef.

Dolphin Lagoon

Discovery Cove's most famous attraction offers visitors the opportunity to swim with Atlantic bottlenose dolphins. The experience begins with a 15-minute orientation program, which includes a film about the dolphins, explaining how to communicate with them using hand signals. This is followed by 30 unforgettable minutes spent playing with these gentle mammals under the watchful eyes of the trainers.

TOP 5 ATTRACTIONS

1. DOLPHIN LAGOON
2. GRAND REEF
3. RAY LAGOON
4. THE AVIARY
5. WIND-AWAY RIVER

Universal Orlando® ❹

Once a single movie park, competing with the other local attractions, Universal Orlando® has transformed into an expansive resort destination, which includes two theme parks, Universal Studios Florida® and the Islands of Adventure®; a 30-acre (12-ha) complex, Universal CityWalk®; and three resorts *(see pp140–41)*. Together, these diverse options present a formidable reason to spend time away from Disney. Located off exits 75A or 74B from I-4, Universal's car parking brings guests through CityWalk® on a series of moving walkways to a fork where they choose between the two parks.

VISITORS' CHECKLIST

Orange Co. 1000 Universal Studios Plaza, exits 75A or 75B on I-4. 🅵 *(407) 363-8000.* 🚌 *21, 37, 40 from Orlando.* ⏱ *minimum opening hours 9am–6pm daily; extended evening opening in summer & on public hols. CityWalk: 11am–2am daily.* 🎭 ♿ 🍴 🛍 **www.**universalorlando.com; **www.**citywalkorlando.com

TACKLING THE PARKS

The busiest times of the year at Universal Orlando® are the same as at Walt Disney World® *(see p76)*; the weekends are normally busier than the weekdays.

During peak season, the parks are open until late, and two full days are just about long enough to see everything at both of them. However, during off-season, they shut early, and you will need three to four days to cover all the attractions in the area.

Those staying for a longer duration can opt for any one of Universal's multi-day packages – such as 2 Parks/2 Days, 2-Park Unlimited, or 3-Park Unlimited – which offer cost-effective admissions to the parks and CityWalk, in addition to special discounts on hotel stays, food, and merchandise.

Universal Orlando® Resort logo

Lines at Universal can sometimes be even longer than those at Walt Disney World®, and you might have to wait a considerable time for the best rides. One way of combating the lines is by purchasing the Universal Express Plus pass, which allows visitors to skip the regular lines at participating rides and attractions. Moreover, guests staying at any of the Universal Orlando® properties can use their room keys as Universal Express passes on all rides – with no limit – and also as a credit card throughout the park, charging food, gift shop items, and other expenditures to their room. On a busy day, visitors might like to consider indulging in the five-hour guided VIP Tour. Accommodating up to 12 people at a time, the tour provides priority admission to at least eight attractions, access to

production facilities and sound stages, discounts, and a walk around backstage areas. At the end of the tour, guests also have Universal Express Pass access to the attractions.

Most rides are likely to be too intense for very young children and of course some have minimum height restrictions; the exception to this is ET Adventure. The attractions designed to appeal to youngsters can be found at Woody Woodpecker's Kid Zone, and include A Day in the Park with Barney, and Animal Actors on Location.

Universal Orlando® has made special provisions for families traveling with children, and for people with disabilities. Wheelchairs and strollers are available on rent near the entrance of both the parks. All the shopping and dining venues, and most of the attractions, are wheelchair friendly. The Family Service center also offers first aid and several restrooms with nursing and diaper-changing facilities.

The brightly illuminated world of Universal's Islands of Adventure®

Exploring Universal Studios Florida®

Everything in this motion picture theme park is designed to take visitors into the magical world of movie-making. Built with the help of Steven Spielberg as a creative consultant, the park opened in 1990 and is home to several state-of-the-art rides, shows, and attractions – all based on popular films and television shows. Even the streets, shops, and restaurants are reminiscent of Hollywood sets, and the life-size reconstructions of New York and San Francisco are unbelievably realistic. The park is divided into six main sections – Production Central, New York, Hollywood, Woody Woodpecker's Kid Zone, World Expo, and San Francisco/Amity.

A sheer vertical climb at the start of the Hollywood Rip Ride Rockit®

LIVE FILMING

While there is no guarantee that you will be able to see live filming on the day you visit Universal Studios Florida, there is a slim possibility that cameras may be rolling on the backlot of the theme park itself. However, there is a good chance, especially from September to December, that you could be in the audience for the taping of a TV show. Those interested can also call ahead and check to find out which shows are being filmed during their visit. Tickets for the shows are issued on a first-come-first-served basis – on the day of filming – and are available at the Studio Audience Center located near Guest Services. Go there as soon as you enter the park to pick some up.

FRONT LOT

The entrance to Universal Studios Park is known as Front Lot because it has been created to resemble the front lot of a working Hollywood film studio from the 1940s. However, the shooting schedule notice board near the turnstiles, with the details of shows being filmed, is real enough.

Just inside the park, the palm-lined Plaza of the Stars has several shops *(see p93)*, but do not linger here on arrival. Instead, you should immediately head off to the main attractions before the lines reach their peak.

PRODUCTION CENTRAL

Although this is the least aesthetic section of the park, two of Universal's most popular rides are located here. **Hollywood Rip Ride Rockit®** is a roller coaster that begins with a straight-up climb before launching into a series of plunging, twisting loops

Logo of the fun ride
Shrek 4-D™

taken at speeds of up to 65mph (105kph), on a track that towers – 17 stories above the park – the tallest in Orlando. The ride includes six heart-stopping near-miss moments and the world's first non-inverting loop. Riders choose their individual soundtrack from a list of 30 songs by various artists before they ride the coaster. Visitors can edit and buy a music video of their trip at the end. **Shrek 4-D™**, is a popular fun-packed attraction, that features a 13-minute 3-D movie, in which Shrek and his friends set out to rescue Princess Fiona who has been kidnapped. The motion-simulated effects and special "OgreVision" glasses enable you to see, hear, and almost feel the action right in your seat. Starring the voices of Eddie Murphy, Mike Myers, John Lithgow, and Cameron Diaz, the ride is both a sequel to the original film *Shrek* and a bridge to the next installments, *Shrek 2, Shrek the Third*, and beyond.

Amazing special effects enthrall the audience at Shrek 4-D™

Guests experiencing the forces of a tornado at Twister...Ride It Out®

NEW YORK

Universal's reproduction of the Big Apple is uncannily realistic and captures the minutest of details very effectively. The area is home to more than 60 life-size facades, some of which replicate actual buildings in the city of New York, and others which reproduce those that have appeared only on screen. Macy's, the well-known department store, can be found here, as can Louie's Italian Restaurant, which was the location for a shootout in the original *Godfather* movie. Cutouts of structures such as the New York Public Library and the famous Guggenheim Museum cleverly create an illusion of depth and distance.

The washed out storefronts, warehouses, and even the stained and somewhat cracked cobblestone streets have been specially treated by a process called "distressing" to make them appear old.

New York is also host to the virtual reality ride **Revenge of the Mummy® – The Ride**. This attraction replaced the popular King Kong ride, but you can still see reminders of Kong's presence: look for two giant ape hieroglyphs near the Anubis statue. Based on the phenomenally successful film, *The Mummy* and its equally popular sequel, *The Mummy Returns*, the ride combines extremely advanced special effects, such as space age robotics and high-speed roller coaster engineering, to take guests on a terrifying journey into the dark world of ancient Egypt. As they are swept through Egyptian tombs, passageways, and crumbling columns, riders have to face skeletal warriors and a giant animated figure of the menacing Mummy.

Another ride at New York is **Twister...Ride It Out®**, based on the movie *Twister*. Located inside a huge compound, the attraction pits visitors against Mother Nature at her most ferocious, as they stand just 20-ft (6-m) away from a graphically simulated tornado. Experience the overwhelming strength of the elements as cars, trucks, and even a cow are swirled up in the air by the ear-splitting, five story-high funnel of winds. This is a very loud ride, and can frighten young children.

Away from the rides, guests can also head down Delancey Street to take in **The Blues Brothers**, a 20-minute live music stage show, where Jake and Elwood perform a medley of their biggest hits. Relive moments from the original cult movie – starring John Belushi, Dan Aykroyd, Carrie Fisher, and Cab Calloway – as the brothers put on a show in an attempt to save their former school.

The huge, scary skeletal warriors at Revenge of the Mummy® – The Ride

Hollywood Boulevard, a fine example of the park's superbly created sets

HOLLYWOOD

Two of the most attractive sets at Universal Studios are the streets of Hollywood Boulevard and Rodeo Drive. While ignoring actual geography, these sets pay tribute to Hollywood's golden age from the 1920s to the 50s. The famous Mocambo nightclub, the luxurious Beverly Wilshire Hotel, the top beauty salon, Max Factor, and the movie palace, Pantages Theater, are just some notable examples of the wonderful re-creations lining these streets.

Shaped like a hat, the Brown Derby restaurant was once a fashionable eatery where the film glitterati used to congregate; Universal's own version is a fun hat shop. Schwab's Pharmacy, where hopefuls hung out sipping sodas and waiting to be discovered, is brought back to life as an old-fashioned ice cream parlor. The widely recognized Hollywood Walk of Fame, with the names of stars embedded in the sidewalk, just as in the real Hollywood Boulevard, has also been faithfully reproduced.

The top attraction in Hollywood is **Terminator 2®: 3-D**. Designed with the help of James Cameron, the director of the *Terminator* movies, this exciting ride uses the latest in 3-D film technology and robotics, along with explosive live stunts and giant screens, to catapult the audience into a battle with futuristic cyborgs. The fast-paced 3-D action film features the star of the original films, Arnold Schwarzenegger, and other cast members. A typical sequence has a Harley-Davidson "Fat Boy" dramatically bursting off the screen and onto the stage. Note that young children may find this ride a bit scary.

Lucy – A Tribute acknowledges the talent of Lucille Ball, the queen of comedy and one of the world's favorite stage and television stars. The museum showcases clips, scripts, costumes, props, and other memorabilia from the comedian's hit TV show, *I Love Lucy*. The set of the show has been meticulously replicated, and the tribute also features an interactive game for trivia buffs to test their Lucy knowledge. There is a gift shop where guests can pick up mementos.

Another fascinating exhibit at Hollywood is the **Universal Horror Make-Up Show**. The attraction offers a behind-the-scenes look at how movies use makeup to create scary monsters and creepy effects. Props from films, such as the wax head from *The Exorcist*, the chambers where a man was merged with a fly in *The Fly*, and several masks, are on display. In addition, trained workers demonstrate the substitutes that can be used to resemble blood and slime. This partly gory and partly entertaining show takes place in a theater-like setting. Universal grades this show as a PG 13, and clips from gory films are included, so it is not suitable for all.

TOP 10 ATTRACTIONS

1. **REVENGE OF THE MUMMY® – THE RIDE**
2. **MEN IN BLACK™ – ALIEN ATTACK™**
3. **TWISTER...RIDE IT OUT®**
4. **JAWS®**
5. **THE SIMPSONS RIDE™**
6. **SHREK 4-D™**
7. **TERMINATOR 2®:3-D**
8. **DISASTER!**
9. **HOLLYWOOD RIP RIDE ROCKIT®**
10. **ET ADVENTURE®**

The audience face a giant robot, Terminator 2®: 3-D

ET and his alien friends on their colorful home planet, ET Adventure®

WOODY WOODPECKER'S KID ZONE

As the name suggests, this area caters specifically to preschoolers and younger children. Rides, shows, and attractions here have been designed to provide loads of fun with a minimum amount of scare factor.

Based on Steven Spielberg's 1982 movie, **ET Adventure®** is an enchanting, if rather tame, ride. Riders board flying bicycles and embark on a mission to save ET's home planet. Soaring high above a twinkling cityscape and through space, they fly past policemen and FBI agents before arriving at a strange world inhabited by aliens.

A must-see for animal lovers, the **Animal Actors on Location**™ show features a talented troupe of dogs, cats, chimpanzees, birds, and other animals performing tricks and comical skits – some based on popular TV shows and movies. Animals playing the parts of canine superstars Beethoven and Lassie demonstrate how they are trained for film work. Audience participation and the antics of the animals make this an entertaining show.

A Day in the Park with Barney™ appeals only to very young children. A musical show set in a magical park, it features the lovable T-Rex Barney, who plays the lead in *Barney & Friends* – a top preschool-age TV show. The big purple dinosaur and his fun-loving friends, Baby Bop and BJ, sing, dance, and play with the children.

Inspired by the animated films *An American Tail* and *An American Tail: Fievel Goes West*, **Fievel's Playland®** features a playground as seen through the eyes of a mouse. Larger-than-life props, such as a cowboy hat, boots, glasses, cans, and a teacup have been used to construct tunnel slides, a 30-ft (9-m) spider web climbing area, and a 200-ft (61-m) twisting water slide.

Other attractions at Kid Zone are **Woody Woodpecker's Nuthouse Coaster®** – a gentle and child-friendly introduction to the world of roller coasters – and **Curious George Goes to Town** – a colorful playground with lots of water for kids to splash around in, as well as a ball area where they can play with hundreds of foam balls.

WORLD EXPO

Architecturally inspired by the Los Angeles 1984 Olympics Games and Expo '86 in Vancouver, World Expo has two major attractions.

Men in Black™ – **Alien Attack**™, based on the *Men in Black* films, is an addictive ride in which visitors join Agent J (as played by Will

Guests fending off an attack by bug-eyed monsters at the Men in Black™ – Alien Attack™ ride

Smith) in a simulator, battling aliens who have escaped after their shuttle crashed on Earth. This ride-through interactive video game is filled with 360-degree spins and lots of gunfire and infrared bullets, as well as plenty of noise. Each person has laser weapons and can earn bonus points by hitting certain aliens. The scores reflect the team's ability to destroy aliens.

The Simpson's Ride™ is an adventure starring the world's favorite animated family. The attraction begins with guests walking along the extended tongue of a 32-ft (9.7-m) high Krusty the Clown. They are then swept into Krustyland, a fantasy amusement park, for a giant, wrap-around cinematic experience. Kids will explore a side of Springfield previously unimagined, including the Simpson family characters.

SAN FRANCISCO/ AMITY

Most of this area is based on San Francisco, notably the city's Fisherman's Wharf district. For instance, the Chez Alcatraz snack bar is modeled to resemble the ticket booths for tours to Alcatraz Island. San Francisco's main draw is the amazing, interactive special effects ride, **Disaster! A Major Motion Picture Ride Starring...You!** Guests are asked to assist a studio that is going bankrupt by acting as extras for key insert scenes, thus becoming a part of the production of a major motion picture, *Mutha Nature*. This ride features high-tech virtual imagery

Visitors on a trip to Disaster! A Major Motion Picture Ride Starring...You!

technology along with a special appearance by actor Dwayne Johnson, "The Rock", who has appeared in blockbusters such as *The Mummy Returns*. The ride's big finale sequence involves an updated version of an earthquake simulator.

Amity, the other half of this corner of Universal Studios, is named after the fictional resort island in New England that was the setting for *Jaws*. The **JAWS®** ride begins as a serene cruise around the bay, but soon the deadly dorsal fin appears, and then a 32-ft (9.7-m) long mechanical great white shark is tearing through the water at a terrifying speed and lunging at your boat.

A tremendously popular attraction is **Fear Factor Live**, the first ever theme park experience based on a reality TV show. Casting takes place 75 minutes before the show, which tests the courage and strength of participants with a variety of stunts. Of more

Beetlejuice show's sign

limited appeal is **Beetlejuice's Graveyard Revue™**, a live rock 'n' roll dance concert featuring Beetlejuice, Dracula, and the Frankenstein monster, literally pounding out hit songs.

EATING, DRINKING & SHOPPING

The food at the restaurants in Universal Orlando's theme parks is generally good, and there are plenty of options. Advance reservations are advisable for Lombard's Seafood Grille, specializing in fish dishes, and the International Food and Film Festival, which offers Asian, Italian, and American cuisine. Mel's Drive-In is definitely the place to go for fast food and shakes; the wonderful 1950s diner is straight out of the 1973 movie American Graffiti.

Most of the shops at the parks stay open after official closing times, and offer a wide range of themed souvenirs. The Universal Studios Store in the Front Lot sells everything from fake Oscars to oven mitts bearing the Universal logo, and you can buy autographed, but extremely expensive, photographs of your favourite movie star at the On Location store. Most of Universal Orlando's attractions have their own store.

MEETING THE STARS

Actors in wonderful costumes can be seen all along the streets of Universal Studios, playing the likes of Jake and Elwood from *The Blues Brothers*, Shrek, Scooby Doo, Dora the Explorer, and the Simpsons, as well as legends of the silver screen such as Marilyn Monroe.

Guests can also eat with the stars at a Character Breakfast in the park an hour prior to the scheduled opening time. The stars chat with guests, pose for photos, and sign autographs. Space is limited so advance booking is advisable.

Exploring Islands of Adventure®

Logo of Islands of Adventure®

One of the world's most technologically advanced theme parks, Islands of Adventure® is home to some of the most thrilling roller coaster and water rides in Florida. Spread over an area almost as vast as Universal Studios Florida®, the park consists of five themed zones – Marvel Super Hero Island, Toon Lagoon, Jurassic Park, The Lost Continent, and Seuss Landing – all positioned around a central lagoon. Each Island has a creative and imaginative layout, which serves as an introduction to famous comic book, cartoon, and movie characters. Set aside an entire day to cover all the attractions on offer at Islands of Adventure®.

TOP 5 RIDES

① **AMAZING ADVENTURES OF SPIDER-MAN®**

② **INCREDIBLE HULK COASTER®**

③ **DRAGON CHALLENGE™**

④ **POPEYE & BLUTO'S BILGE-RAT BARGES®**

⑤ **JURASSIC PARK RIVER ADVENTURE®**

Incredible Hulk Coaster®

MARVEL SUPER HERO ISLAND®

Super heros and villains from the Marvel Comics' stable of characters are the inspiration behind this Island's four main attractions.

Arguably the best coaster in Florida, the **Incredible Hulk Coaster®** is a green leviathan that accelerates from zero to 40 mph (64 km/h) in just two seconds. Riders are taken 110 ft (33.5 m) in the air, turned upside down, and sent plummeting down a terrifying 105-ft (32-m) drop. With seven inversions and one drop, then a trip under a bridge, this stimulating ride is guaranteed to leave you breathless.

Highly advanced 3-D film technology, spectacular special effects, and motion simulated action makes the **Amazing Adventures of Spider-Man®** one of the most sought-after rides at the park. Guests are cast into a battle between Spider-man and villains, as the super hero leaps from tall buildings, saving guests from the villains. A scary 400-ft (122-m) simulated free fall is the highlight of this exciting, edge-of-your-seat ride. **Doctor Doom's Fearfall®** catapults its riders high into the air before plunging them down a 150-ft (46-m) fall. The ride also offers a great view of the entire park. **Storm Force Accelatron®** is a more intense version of the Mad Tea Party ride *(see p39)* at Disney.

TOON LAGOON®

Favorite cartoon characters come to life against this Island's colorful backdrop. The Comic Strip Lane, at the entrance, is lined with life-size images of toons such as Betty Boop, Olive Oyl, and Beetle Bailey.

Based on the Rocky and Bullwinkle cartoons, **Dudley Do-Right's Ripsaw Falls®** is a thoroughly drenching and enjoyable flume ride. Be prepared for the 15-ft (4.5-m) dive into a deep lagoon.

Popeye & Bluto's Bilge-Rat Barges® is a whitewater raft ride where visitors help Popeye save Olive Oyl from Bluto, and are squirted and splashed by water guns fired from the nearby shores and playgrounds.

Children love exploring **Me Ship, The Olive**, a three-level, interactive play area with bells, organs, ladders, tunnels, and whistles. The ship also overlooks the raft ride and offers water cannons to soak riders below.

JURASSIC PARK®

Step into a lush, tropical, and jungle-like setting as you enter this Island, where all the attractions are based on the *Jurassic Park* films. The **Jurassic Park River**

Fantastic special effects at the Amazing Adventures of Spider-Man®

◁ Tourists flocking to the entrance of Universal Studios Florida®

Visitors under attack at the Jurassic Park River Adventure®

tellers, and a talking fountain. An exciting stage show, **The Eighth Voyage of Sinbad® Stunt Show** is filled with stunts, flames, and explosions, as Sinbad embarks on a journey to find treasure. The best show, however, is **Poseidon's Fury®**, which features a battle between the King of the Seas and the King of the Gods. Visitors walk through a tunnel surrounded by a giant swirling whirlpool, while massive waves crash around them and the gods throw flaming fireballs at each other.

SEUSS LANDING™

Those with no experience of Dr. Seuss might find **The Cat in the Hat™** a somewhat bewildering and chaotic ride. A spinning and whirling couch takes you on a trip with the mischievous cat and characters such as Thing 1 and Thing 2. Some children may find the cat's sudden pounces at the corners scary.

Younger kids enjoy riding **One Fish, Two Fish, Red Fish, Blue Fish™** as they spin around on a remote controlled fish and try to avoid being squirted by water jets.

Caro-Seuss-El™ is a merry-go-round with lovable Dr. Seuss characters, such as Dog-alopes, Aqua-Mop Tops, cowfish, and elephant-birds among others, as the horses.

If I Ran The Zoo is another playground and the ideal place for kids to burn off energy.

The High in the Sky Seuss Trolley Train Ride™ runs high above Seuss Landing.

Adventure® starts out as a peaceful cruise along a river, where you encounter friendly dinosaurs before an accidental raptor breakout. Suddenly you are faced with a menacing T-Rex and the only escape route is a 85-ft (26-m) drop into a lagoon.

Jurassic Park Discovery Center® is an interactive exhibit, with realistic replicas of dinosaurs, a Beasaurus area, which allows visitors to see and hear things as dinosaurs did, and several games and quizzes. It also offers a virtual demonstration of a raptor egg hatching in the lab.

The remaining draws at the island are **Pteranodon Flyers®**, a slow sky ride over Jurassic Park and **Camp Jurassic®**, a playground with caves and buried fossils for kids, amber mines and dinosaur nets.

THE WIZARDING WORLD OF HARRY POTTER™

Opened in 2010, this themed land allows guests to visit Hogwarts, Hogsmeade Village, and other familiar locations from the Harry Potter books and films. Rides, attractions, shops, and restaurants all promote the Potter theme.

Dragon Challenge™ – part of Harry Potter and the Forbidden Journey™ – has two coasters, Fire and Ice, racing toward each other in a battle to see who will arrive back first. Riders come within inches of each other as the dragons go through several inversions and sharp corners. There is a separate, and longer, line for those who want to sit in the first car of the coasters.

THE LOST CONTINENT®

Enter a magical world that is inhabited by mythical creatures, mysterious fortune-

Riders miss each other by inches at the Dragon Challenge™ ride

Exploring Universal CityWalk®

Logo of Universal's CityWalk

The gateway to Universal Orlando's offerings, CityWalk is a 30-acre (12-ha) entertainment, dining, and shopping complex that allows visitors to continue their Universal experience long after the parks have closed – most of the places remain open from 11am to 2am. Restaurants, shops, concerts, nightclubs, and a movie theater present a range of options for an exciting night out. The banks of a sparkling lagoon running through CityWalk are perfect for an after-dinner stroll. While admission to the complex itself is free, some clubs have a cover charge. However, guests can visit select clubs for the price of one with Universal's CityWalk Party Pass.

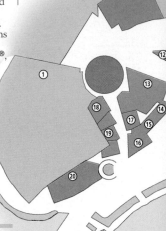

RESTAURANTS

Citywalk offers a delectable selection of international cuisines to choose from.

Award-winning chef Emeril Lagasse's **Emeril's® Restaurant Orlando** *(see p151)*, serves delicious, but expensive, New Orleans Creole-based cuisine. Those looking for excellent Caribbean, Cajun, and fresh Florida fare should visit **Jimmy Buffett's®; Margaritaville®** *(see p151)*, which also offers live entertainment every night.

Munch on tasty Hispanic food from 21 nations at **Latin Quarter**™, while a dance troupe performs the salsa. At the family-style **Pastamoré Ristoranté**, you can dine on superb Italian cuisine, with dishes such as grilled eggplant and chicken parmigiana as well as panini.

More than 1,000 pieces of rock memorabilia can be seen at the famous **Hard Rock Café® Orlando** *(see p150)*. The café serves up great

American food at reasonable prices. At **Bubba Gump Shrimp Co.**, shrimp is served in numerous ways, just as Forrest Gump would like it. The staff ask trivial questions about the movie.

The **NASCAR Sports Grille®**, an officially sanctioned NASCAR eatery, features authentic racing memorabilia along with a menu of steaks, BBQ, shrimp, chili, and salads. Voted Orlando's best theme restaurant, **NBA City** offers a large viewing area with screens, where basketball fans can watch games while enjoying burgers, steaks, pastas, and sandwiches.

ENTERTAINMENT

Live music, concerts, and hot dance floors fill the many clubs at CityWalk with energy and a sense of festivity.

Bob Marley – A Tribute to Freedom is a replica of the famous musician's Jamaican

home. Nightly performances by local and national reggae bands are the highlight here.

Take center stage at **City-Walk's Rising Star** karaoke club. Belt out your favorite songs as the lead singer of a live band, complete with back-up singers.

Some of the biggest bands in the music world perform at the **Hard Rock Live!® Orlando** concert hall – call ahead to find out which group will be playing during your visit. One of CityWalk's most popular dance clubs is **the groove**. The lively atmosphere offers a mixture of hip-hop, rock, and dance music.

Duplicating the famed New Orleans watering hole, **Pat O'Brien's®** is a much-celebrated bar, known for its specialty drinks, such as the Hurricane, and the "dueling piano" bar.

Catch a movie at any of the 20 theaters in the state-of-the-art **Universal Cineplex**. In addition, the outdoor stages and areas are settings for street performances.

Red Coconut Club is CityWalk's ultra-lounge. It is a two-story, trendy cocktail lounge offering exotic signature drinks and appetizers.

Hard Rock Café® and music venue, at CityWalk®

A live music concert in progress at Hard Rock Live!® Orlando

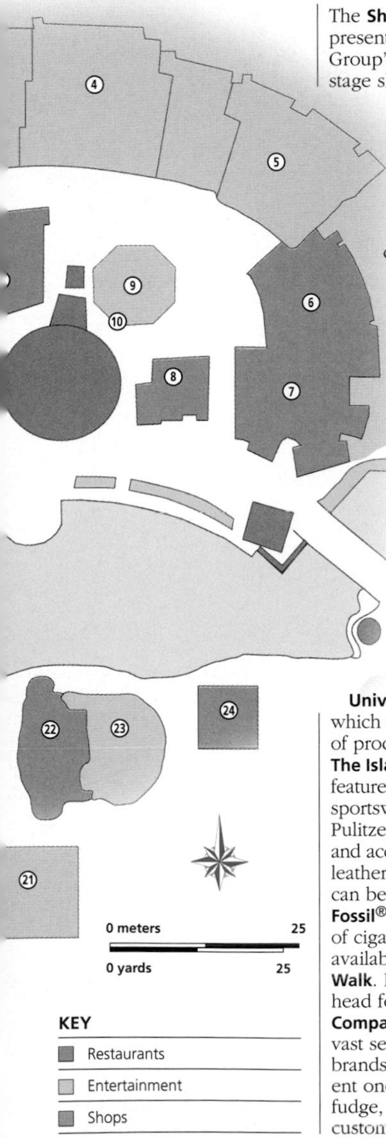
④
⑤
⑥
⑦
⑧
⑨
⑩
㉒
㉓
㉔
㉑
0 meters 25
0 yards 25
KEY
Restaurants
Entertainment
Shops

The **Sharp Aquos Theatre** presents the Blue Man Group's world-renowned live stage shows.

SHOPS

The central area features several stores with an extensive choice of merchandise *(see p161)*. Interesting stores include **Hart & Huntington**, which is not your typical tattoo studio, and **The Endangered Species Store®**, which has merchandise aimed at raising eco-awareness. **Fresh Produce®** sells apparel in bright vegetable and fruit dyes, and beach products, clothing, and accessories are available at **Quiet Flight® Surf Shop.** Souvenir hunters will also enjoy shopping at **Universal Studios Store®**, which offers a vast collection of products from the park. **The Island Clothing Store** features Tommy Bahama sportswear, LaCoste, Lilly Pulitzer, footwear, jewelry, and accessories, while watches, leather items, and sunglasses can be purchased at the **Fossil®** store. A superior range of cigars and accessories are available at **Cigarz at CityWalk**. If you want candy then head for **Katie's Candy Company**, where they have a vast selection from the usual brands (more than 100 different ones stocked) to fresh fudge, candy apples, and custom-made candies.

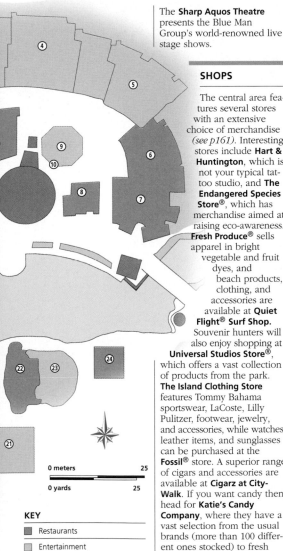

TOP 5 ATTRACTIONS

① HARD ROCK LIVE!® ORLANDO

② BOB MARLEY – A TRIBUTE TO FREEDOM

③ THE GROOVE

④ LATIN QUARTER™

⑤ JIMMY BUFFETT'S®; MARGARITAVILLE®

CITYWALK VENUES

Bob Marley – A Tribute to Freedom ③
Bubba Gump Shrimp Co. ②
Cigarz at CityWalk ⑱
CityWalk's Rising Star ⑨
Emeril's® Restaurant Orlando ⑧
The Endangered Species Store ⑫
Fossil® ⑭
Fresh Produce® ⑮
Hard Rock Café® Orlando ㉒
Hard Rock Live!® Orlando ㉓
Hart & Hartington ⑰
The Island Clothing Store ⑯
Jimmy Buffett's®; Margaritaville® ⑦
Katie's Candy Company ⑲
Latin Quarter™ ⑥
NASCAR Sports Grille® ⑳
NBACity ㉔
Pastamoré Ristoranté ⑪
Pat O'Brien's® ④
Quiet Flight® Surf Shop ⑬
Red Coconut Club ②
the groove ⑤
Sharp Aquos Theatre ㉑
Universal Cineplex ①
Universal Studios Store® ⑩

The well-stocked sports store at NBA City

Wet 'n Wild® [5]

Wet 'n Wild® logo

One of Central Florida's top attractions, Wet 'n Wild® opened in 1977. It focuses on rides of the hair-raising variety, boasting an awesome collection of high-velocity rides – multi-passenger as well as solo, on toboggans, rafts, or inner tubes, down slides and chutes or through tubes. There are activities for smaller kids as well, with miniature versions of the park's popular adult attractions on offer at Kids' Park. A range of family activities and a beach party atmosphere add to Wet 'n Wild®'s appeal. Several outlets offer fast food; visitors can also bring in their own picnic hamper.

Wakezone
Skim across the water on a kneeboard across this cable-operated, half-mile (0.8-km) course of lake. You can also wakeskate at the lake.

The Black Hole™: The Next Generation
Experience pulsating lights and dynamic effects as your two-person raft is propelled forward.

The Flyer
Four-seater toboggans descend from a height of 40 ft (12 m), plowing through 450 ft (137 m) of banked curves and racing straight runs in this exhilarating watery ride.

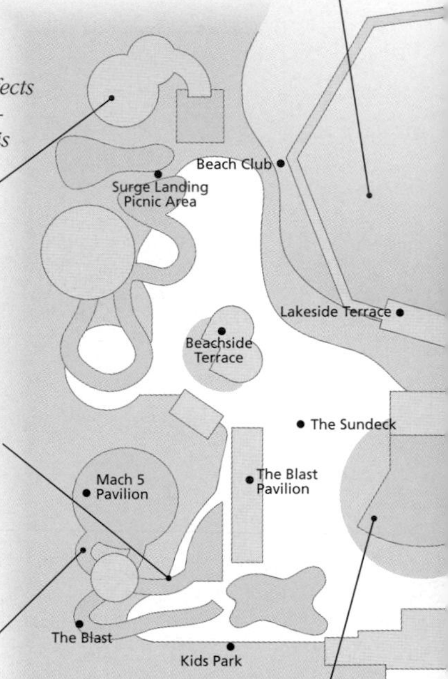
Beach Club
Surge Landing
Picnic Area
Lakeside Terrace
Beachside
Terrace
The Sundeck
Mach 5
Pavilion
The Blast
Pavilion
The Blast
Kids Park

Surf Lagoon, a 17,000-sq ft (1,580-sq m) wave pool, features 4-ft (1.2-m) high waves and a waterfall.

Mach 5
Riders navigate this solo flume ride on a foam mat. On tight turns, ride the flowing water as far up the wall as possible. You can choose from three different twisting-and-turning flumes.

TOP TIPS

- *Steps to the rides and asphalt walkways can get very hot. Wear non-slip footwear as protection.*
- *High-speed rides can leave you uncovered. Ladies should avoid wearing bikinis or consider adding a T-shirt.*
- *Rides have a 36-inch (91-cm) minimum height requirement for kids riding solo.*
- *Be sure to carry sunscreen.*

Brain Wash™
This six-story extreme tube ride involves a vertical drop into a 65-ft (16-m) domed funnel. Guests are surrounded by lights and sounds as they make the thrilling journey to the bottom, where they spin around at speed before splashing out of the ride.

VISITORS' CHECKLIST

6200 International Dr, Universal Blvd, off I-4 at Exit 74A, less than 2 miles (3 km) from Universal Orlando® & SeaWorld®. *Tel* (800) 992-9453, (407) 351-1800. 21, 38 from Downtown Orlando. 10am–5pm daily. Best to call as hours change with the seasons and weather. (free for children under 3; afternoon discounts available). www.wetnwildorlando.com

Bomb Bay
A six-story plunge down a nearly vertical slide from a bomb-like capsule, this is one of Wet 'n Wild®'s most sensational rides. Der Stuka is a slightly less scary version.

Knee Ski
Dock

Bubba Tub
Pavilion

Lazy River
Picnic Pavilion

Cabanas
Relax in a luxurious cabana, set in a lush, tropical oasis on an island surrounded by the Lazy River.

International
Pavilion

Lazy River®, a mile-long (1.6-km) circular waterway, lets you swim or float gently past swaying palms, orange groves, and waterfalls – a lovely re-creation of Old Florida.

Bubba Tub®
A raft large enough to hold five is the just the thing for watery splashes and fun for the family as it hurtles down a six-story slide with three big drops.

The Storm
Plummet down a chute with mist, thunder, and – at night – lightning effects, then drop into a huge open bowl, to swirl out with a splash into a lower pool in this exciting ride.

ORLANDO & CENTRAL FLORIDA

The thrills available at the numerous theme parks attract the majority of visitors to Orlando but the city and its surrounding region have much more to offer the discerning tourist, from beautiful beaches – quiet, unspoilt havens as well as bustling spots – to lush forests and serene lakes, to the space-related attractions at Cape Canaveral and a plethora of cultural activities.

As late as the first half of the 20th century, Orlando and neighboring towns such as Kissimmee were small, sleepy places dependent on cattle and the citrus crop. Everything changed with the arrival of Disney World. Its booming entertainment industry, which has spawned several new and exciting entertainment venues, has made Orlando one of the country's fastest growing areas. But quieter pleasures are still available within Orlando, in its numerous museums and leafy suburbs. Outside Orlando, the landscape becomes more bucolic, with huge agricultural fields interspersed between the highways. The charming towns of Sanford and Mount Dora to the north provide a glimpse of Central Florida of a few decades ago. West of the St. Johns River lies the wooded expanse of the Ocala National Forest and,

farther west, the world's largest artesian spring, Silver Springs. Along the Atlantic Coast, broad white sandy beaches flank the popular resort of Daytona Beach, which has been synonymous with car racing ever since the likes of Henry Ford and Louis Chevrolet raced automobiles on the beach during their winter vacations. Farther down, Cocoa Beach is another lively beach, famous for surfing. In between, along the Space Coast, the barrier islands across the broad Indian River boast 72 miles (116 km) of stunning sandy beaches, and there are two enormous nature preserves rich in bird life. Amid all this, set in a preserved marshy vastness beneath giant skies and in surprising harmony with nature, is the Kennedy Space Center, from where rockets are launched dramatically out of the earth's atmosphere.

The busy beach north of Main Street Pier, Daytona Beach

◁ Silver Glen Springs, Ocala National Forest

Exploring Orlando & Central Florida

The primary reason thousands of vacationers come to Central Florida is its theme parks, but the region has many other options for enjoyment. Smaller entertainment venues abound, and Orlando itself has 35 museums which house a diverse range of art. A wealth of retail stores and boutiques will satisfy the most discriminating shopper. Beaches in Central Florida range from empty, wild sands to the action-packed Daytona Beach and the buzzing surfing mecca of Cocoa Beach. Inland, the Ocala National Forest offers dozens of hiking trails, boating, and fishing; snorkeling and diving are also popular pursuits in crystal-clear springs. Kennedy Space Center, on the Space Coast, competes sharply with Orlando's attractions for excitement.

Sign for the town of Sanford

KEY

=== Highway

=== Major road

— Secondary route

=== Minor road

=== Main railway

SIGHTS AT A GLANCE

Blue Spring State Park **4**
Canaveral National Seashore **23**
Cassadaga Spiritualist Camp **5**
Cocoa **20**
Cocoa Beach **19**
Daytona Beach **7**
DeLeon Springs State Park **6**
Dinosaur World **15**
Fantasy of Flight **13**
Florida Southern College **14**
Gatorland **10**
Historic Bok Sanctuary **17**
Kennedy Space Center **25**
Kissimmee **11**
LEGOLAND® **16**
Merritt Island National
 Wildlife Refuge **24**
Mount Dora **3**
Ocala National Forest **8**
Orlando **1**
Sanford **2**
Silver Springs **9**
US Astronaut Hall of Fame **22**
Valiant Air Command
 Warbird Museum **21**
Yeehaw Junction **18**
A World of Orchids **12**

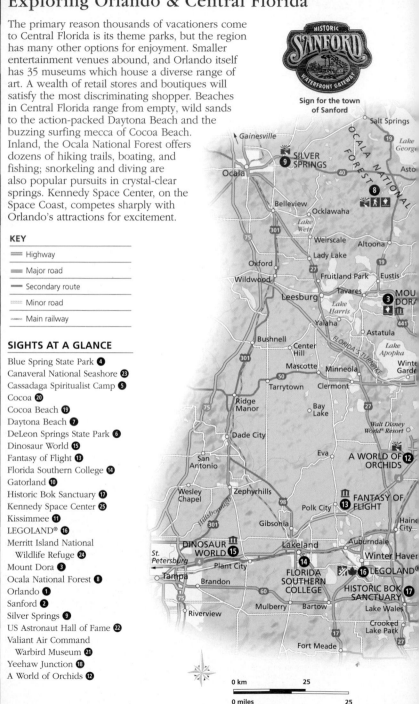

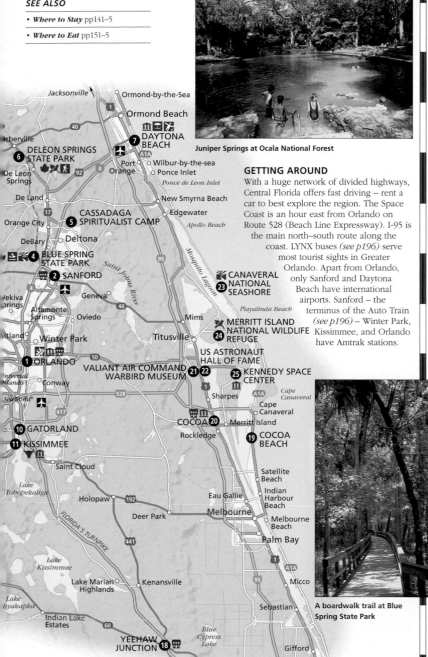

Juniper Springs at Ocala National Forest

GETTING AROUND

With a huge network of divided highways, Central Florida offers fast driving – rent a car to best explore the region. The Space Coast is an hour east from Orlando on Route 528 (Beach Line Expressway). I-95 is the main north–south route along the coast. LYNX buses *(see p196)* serve most tourist sights in Greater Orlando. Apart from Orlando, only Sanford and Daytona Beach have international airports. Sanford – the terminus of the Auto Train *(see p196)* – Winter Park, Kissimmee, and Orlando have Amtrak stations.

Jacksonville

Ormond-by-the-Sea

Ormond Beach

1

DAYTONA BEACH 7

Port Orange Wilbur-by-the-sea

Ponce Inlet

Ponce de Leon Inlet

New Smyrna Beach

Edgewater

Apollo Beach

rberville

DELEON SPRINGS STATE PARK 6

De Leon Springs

De Land

Orange City

CASSADAGA SPIRITUALIST CAMP 5

DeBary

Deltona

BLUE SPRING STATE PARK 4

SANFORD 2

Saint Johns River

Geneva

Altamonte Springs

Oviedo

ekiva rings

Winter Park

itland

ORLANDO 1

niversal rlando

Conway

SeaWorld

GATORLAND 10

KISSIMMEE 11

Saint Cloud

Lake Tohopekaliga

Holopaw

Deer Park

Lake Kissimmee

FLORIDA'S TURNPIKE

Lake Marian Highlands

Kenansville

Lake hyakapka

Indian Lake Estates

YEEHAW JUNCTION 18

West Palm Beach

Mosquito Lagoon

CANAVERAL NATIONAL SEASHORE 23

Playalinda Beach

Mims

Titusville

MERRITT ISLAND NATIONAL WILDLIFE REFUGE 24

US ASTRONAUT HALL OF FAME

VALIANT AIR COMMAND WARBIRD MUSEUM 21 22

Sharpes

KENNEDY SPACE CENTER 25

Cape Canaveral

Cape Canaveral

COCOA 20 Merritt Island

Rockledge

COCOA BEACH 19

Satellite Beach

Indian Harbour Beach

Eau Gallie

Melbourne

Melbourne Beach

Palm Bay

Micco

Sebastian

Blue Cypress Lake

Gifford

Vero Beach

West Palm Beach

A boardwalk trail at Blue Spring State Park

Orlando ●

Not much more than a sleepy provincial town until the 1950s, Orlando's fortunes were transformed by its proximity to Cape Canaveral and the theme parks. Downtown Orlando's glass-sided high-rises mark a busy business district; it also has a burgeoning arts and culture scene. In the evening, Orange Avenue, Orlando's main street, pulsates with an exciting nightclub scene. Another bustling street is International Drive, with its many attractions, plenty of shopping opportunities, and excellent restaurants. Winter Park, an elegant city just north of Orlando, boasts a bevy of cultural attractions from art museums to scenic boat tours; the nearby towns of Eatonville and Maitland feature quiet attractions, which make a pleasant change from the thrills and spills of the theme parks.

VISITORS' CHECKLIST

Orange Co. 🏠 180,000. ✈ Orlando International Airport, 1 Airport Blvd, 9 miles (14 km) SE of Downtown. 🚉 Amtrak Station, 1400 Sligh Blvd. 🚌 Greyhound Lines, 555 N John Parkway. ℹ 8723 International Dr, Suite 101, (800) 551-0181.

Charles Hosmer Morse Museum of American Art *in Winter Park features a lovely collection of glass by famed designer Louis Comfort Tiffany (see p112).*

Zora Neale Hurston National Museum of Fine Arts *in Eatonville exhibits the works of contemporary African-American artists. It is named after African-American writer Zora Neale Hurston, who grew up in Eatonville (see p113).*

Winter Park, Eatonville & Maitland
(see pp112–13)

0 km   30
0 miles   20

Downtown Orlando
(see pp107–109)

I-Drive
(see pp110–11)

Ripley's Believe It Or Not! Orlando Odditorium, *with its fantastic collection of the world's strangest odditites collected by Robert Ripley during his travels around the globe, is a major attraction on International Drive (see p111).*

Lake Eola Park, *a quiet haven in Downtown Orlando, has an ornate fountain set in the center of a picturesque lake (see p108).*

Exploring Downtown Orlando

The city's first designated historic district, Downtown Orlando encompasses eight square blocks and more than 80 buildings constructed between 1880 and 1940, which offer visitors a window into the city's past. Today, these buildings house offices, restaurants, and trendy galleries and boutiques. The crown jewel of Downtown Orlando, Lake Eola Park, separates the historic downtown district from Thornton Park, Orlando's center of new urbanism, with its collection of eclectic shops. The broader downtown area, especially the natural and cultural retreat Loch Haven Park to the north, features several unique and top-quality visual and performing arts centers and museums.

Sculpture at the Mennello Museum of American Folk Art

🏛 Orlando Science Center

777 E Princeton St, Loch Haven Park. *Tel* *(407) 514-2000.* ⬜ *10am–5pm Sun–Fri, 10am–10pm Sat.* 🎥 💻 📷 ♿ www.osc.org

Originally called the Central Florida Museum when it was opened in 1960, the museum acquired its current name in 1984. Covering 207,000 sq ft (19,200 sq m) of floor space, the present building was opened in February 1997.

The aim of the center is to provide a stimulating environment for experiential science learning, which it achieves by presenting a huge array of exciting, state-of-the-art interactive exhibits, designed to introduce kids of all ages to the wonders of science. The center's four floors are divided into ten themed zones dealing with subjects that range from mechanics to math, health and fitness to lasers. The Body Zone, for

instance, allows guests to explore the intimate workings of the human body. Other fascinating attractions include the DinoDigs exhibit with its collection of dinosaur fossils, which is very popular with children, as is the ShowBiz Science exhibit, which reveals some of the effects and tricks used in the movie business.

The gigantic Dr. Phillips CineDome surrounds visitors with amazing images and films on a range of topics such as Egyptian treasures and ocean life; it is also a planetarium with live shows by experts.

🏛 Orlando Museum of Art

2416 N Mills Ave, Loch Haven Park. *Tel* *(407) 896-4231.* ⬜ *10am–4pm Tue–Fri, noon–4pm Sat & Sun.* ⬤ *public hols.* 🎥 📷 ♿ www.omart.org

One of Southeastern USA's finest arts museums, the Orlando Museum of Art has a

superb permanent collection that includes pre-Columbian artifacts, with figurines from Nazca in Peru; African art; and American paintings of the 19th and 20th centuries. These are supplemented by traveling exhibitions from major metropolitan museums, and smaller shows of regional or local significance. Music, food, and the works of local artists are on offer at a lively get-together on the first Thursday evening of every month.

🎭 Orlando Shakespeare Theater

812 E Rollins St, Loch Haven Park. *Tel* *(407) 447-1700.* **www**.orlandoshakes.org

Spread over 50,000 sq ft (4,645 sq m), the elegant Shakespeare Center features the 324-seat Margeson Theater and three other, smaller theaters. The state-of-the-art venue mounts a varied program of high-quality Shakespearean productions, original plays, and innovative educational experiences throughout the year. It is also the home of Playfest, a 10-day spring festival of new plays, workshops, readings, and special guests.

🏛 Mennello Museum of American Folk Art

900 E Princeton St, Loch Haven Park. *Tel* *(407) 246-4278.* ⬜ *10:30am–4:30pm Tue–Sat, noon–4:30pm Sun.* ⬤ *major hols.* 🎥 ♿ **www**.mennellomuseum.com

This small, lakeside museum houses an unusual collection of paintings by curio-shop owner and Floridian folk artist, Earl Cunningham (1893–1977), and traveling exhibitions of the works of other folk artists. Quirky sculptures are scattered throughout the grounds.

The sparkling exterior of the Orlando Science Center

A bridge across a rocky stream at Harry P. Leu Gardens

♣ Harry P. Leu Gardens

1920 N Forest Ave. *Tel (407) 246-2620.* ○ 9am–5pm daily. ● Dec 25. ♿🅿🏠&
www.leugardens.org

The Harry P. Leu Gardens offer 50 acres (20 ha) of serene, beautiful greenery to stroll in. Features such as Florida's largest rose garden are formal while, elsewhere in the park, there are mature woods of spectacular live oaks, maples, and bald cypresses, festooned with Spanish moss; in winter, seek out the mass of blooming camellias. Other attractions are a herb garden and one filled with plants that attract butterflies. Visitors can also tour the early 20th-century Leu House and its gardens, which local businessman Harry P. Leu donated to the city of Orlando in 1961.

♣ Ivanhoe Row

N Orange Ave.
Shops *10am–5pm Mon–Sat.*
Stretching from Colonial Drive to Lake Ivanhoe, this row of antiques shops features an interesting mix of the old and the unconventional. Vintage linens, clothing, jewelry, and various collectibles are on offer here, as is also period furniture ranging from Victorian to Art Deco. The Wildlife Gallery

Sign for Ivanhoe Row

sells original paintings and sculptures of animals, while Art's Premium Cigars offers a range of cigars and smoking paraphernalia. The prices are on the high side, but you might find some unusual treasures here.

♣ Thornton Park

E of Lake Eola.
Close to the city's business center, hip and artsy Thornton Park offers a blend of trendy cafés, unique boutiques, stylish eateries such as HUE Restaurant, which serves world-class cuisine, and pretty B&Bs. Most active after 6pm, it is a popular neighborhood for locals to unwind in after work. One of the area's most happening hangouts is Dexter's of Thornton Park *(see p152)*, with its chrome vinyl stools, terrazzo floors, contemporary art, and gourmet food. Other attractions include art shows, and a bar, and Marie-France, a chic jewelry boutique.

♣ Lake Eola Park

N Rosalind Ave & E Washington St.
Tel (407) 246-2827. ○ 5am–sunset daily. &
Orlando's most visited park, Lake Eola Park is spread over 43 acres (17 ha) and is encircled by a 0.9-mile (1.4-km) pedestrian-only path. This charming park in the heart of the city is planted with beautiful flower beds and offers a lovely view of the downtown skyline. Cruise the lake in an electric gondola or in a two-person swan-shaped paddle boat, or feed the real swans as they drift along in the lake's shallow water.
The park hosts several annual and seasonal events, including the Fourth of July fireworks show and music performed against the stunning backdrop of the Walt Disney Amphitheater, a band shell with excellent acoustics. The Terrace in the Park restaurant serves fine cuisine, not the usual park fare.

SIGHTS AT A GLANCE

KEY

━━ Interstate highway

━━ Major highway

═══ Highway

─── Railroad

0 km   1

0 miles   1

A scene in progress from Les Liaisons Dangereuses, Mad Cow Theatre

Mad Cow Theatre

54 W Church St. *Tel (407) 297-8788*. www.madcowtheatre.com

Started in late 1997 as a simple project between a band of actors and some directors in a former blueprint studio in Maitland, this theatrical group has developed a reputation for outstanding productions performed at different settings for several years. In 2011, it acquired its current home on historic Church Street.

Attracting talented actors, designers, and directors, the Mad Cow Theatre presents a quality range of classics, musicals, and original works, and produces an annual Orlando Cabaret in July. Past productions have ranged from Chekhov and T.S. Eliot to Neil Simon. The group also offers educational shows and workshops.

Orange County Regional History Center

65 E Central Blvd. *Tel (407) 836-8500, (800) 965-2030*. 10am–5pm Mon–Sat, noon–5pm Sun. www.thehistorycenter.org

Housed in the former Orange County Courthouse, the Orange County Regional History Center sits on nearly 2 acres (0.8 ha) of land in Heritage Square, the old town center. It has four floors of exhibits and interactive areas for visitors of all ages, offering a glimpse into the history and environment of Central Florida. Everything, from wildlife, and the first

Native Americans in the area, to Walt Disney and the space program, is covered here. Highlights include replicas of a Seminole settlement and an early Florida Pioneer Cracker home. Visitors can also wander though a re-created Timucuan village. The museum has an interesting exhibition on the training of aviators, from World War II pilots to NASA astronauts. The center also offers several educational programs and school field trips for children, and organizes get-togethers such as concerts on a regular basis.

Wells' Built Museum of African American History & Culture

511 W South St. *Tel (407) 245-7535*. 9am–5pm Mon–Fri. www.pastinc.org

The Wells' Built Hotel was constructed in 1912 by Orlando's first African-American physician, Dr. William Monroe Wells, as a lodging for performers on the Chitlin' Circuit, a network of locations throughout southern United States where African Americans stayed and performed music. Many of the day's top black entertainers, including Billie Holiday, Ray Charles, Benny Carter, and Duke Ellington, have stayed here. The building was converted into a museum in 1999. The museum contains some original furniture, as well as artifacts, photographs, and exhibits relating to Orlando's African-American communities, focusing on locals who were the first African Americans to attain positions of prominence in their professions and the community. There is a photo display of the Chitlin' Circuit.

SAK Comedy Lab

29 S Orange Ave. *Tel (407) 648-0001*. www.sak.com

One of the best places for live comedy in Orlando, SAK Comedy Lab stages two hilarious shows per night. The later show is slightly racier, but obscene material is strictly avoided, and the high-energy improvization comedy is a great option for families looking for laughs. Especially popular are the series shows, such as *Duel of Fools*. The 200 seats of the theater are wrapped around the stage, giving all members of the audience a good view. Comedians who have performed here include Wayne Brady – one of the stars on the *Whose Line is it Anyway?* TV show.

Wells' Built Museum of African American History & Culture

Exploring International Drive

Garish and glittering International Drive, generally known as I-Drive, is a 3-mile (5-km) ribbon of innumerable attractions, including five major theme parks *(see pp78–101)*. Several of the entertainment venues are open day and night, making the area a zone of frenetic activity 'til late at night. I-Drive brims with hotels and restaurants catering to all budgets, and shopping malls and stores where tourists can pick up souvenirs as well as go in for serious discount shopping. Also located here is Orlando's excellent Official Visitor Information Center, which has coupons for many of the city's attractions, hotels, and restaurants. The most convenient way to take in I-Drive's sights is to hop onto the I-Ride Trolley *(see p197)*.

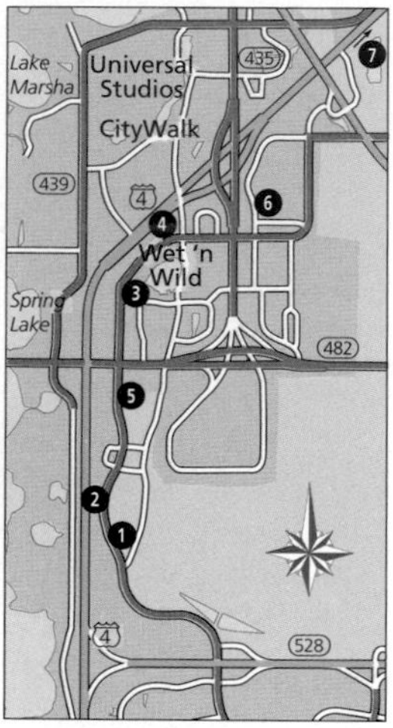

SIGHTS AT A GLANCE

Air Florida Helicopters [2]
Holy Land Experience [7]
iFly Orlando [4]
Magical Midway Park [3]
Ripley's Believe It Or Not!® Orlando Odditorium [5]
Fun Spot Action Park [6]
WonderWorks [1]

KEY

Interstate highway
Major highway
Highway

0 km 2
0 miles 2

🏛 WonderWorks

Pointe Orlando, 9067 International Dr. ***Tel*** *(407) 351-8800.* 🕒 *9am–midnight daily.* 🎟 ☕ 🛍 ♿
www.wonderworksonline.com

One of the most striking buildings on International Drive, WonderWorks looks as though a three-story tall, Neo-Classical building has landed upside down atop a 1930s brick warehouse. This interactive entertainment center boasts numerous hands-on exhibits – some incorporating virtual reality – and demonstrations that the whole family can enjoy. Visitors can experience hurricane-force winds and an earthquake, land the Discovery space shuttle, or even play basketball with a very tall simulated opponent. Other favorites include the Wonder-Coaster, where guests can design and ride their own roller coaster in a simulator.

The upside down façade of WonderWorks

✱ Air Florida Helicopters

8990 International Dr.
Tel *(407) 354-1400.* 🕒 *10am–5:30pm daily.* 🎟
www.airfloridahelicopters.com

Get a bird's-eye view of Sea World, Discovery Cove and other theme parks with Air Florida Helicopters. They operate a fleet of Robinson R44s which offer exceptional visibility and panoramic views for all passengers. The pilot narrates each tour and there are nine to choose from. Tours can also be designed to meet personal requests. Flights start at $20 with a minimum of two passengers per flight. The most expensive tour takes tourists over local celebrity mansions and to Lake Apopka where alligators, osprey and bald eagles can be seen.

The entrance to the Fun Spot arcade and amusement park

🏎 Fun Spot Action Park

5551 Del Verde Way. ***Tel*** *(407) 363-3867.* 🕒 *10am–11pm daily.* 🎟 *for rides and games (minimum age for solo go-karting is 10 years).* ☕
www.fun-spot.com

This arcade and amusement park really has something to offer for everyone, especially to those with a little bit of child in them. The park has four go-kart tracks, with exciting and challenging corkscrew and banked turns, 30-degree descents, bridges, multiple levels of overpasses and underpasses, and lots more. In addition to the go-karting there are bumper boats as well as the usual bumper cars, a 100-ft (30-m) Ferris wheel, 100 arcade

games on two floors (the largest arcade in central Florida), and a kid zone that has swings, a train, a traditional carousel, spinning tea cups, and flying bears. They also have a snack bar and café.

iFly Orlando
6805 Visitors Circle. *Tel (407) 903-1150.* 11:30am–9pm Sun–Thu, 11:30am–10pm Fri & Sat.
www.iflyorlando.com
Soar like a bird on a column of air moving at 120 mph (80 kmph). iFly Orlando's vertical wind tunnel opened in 1998 and since then more than 100,000 visitors have enjoyed the high adventure of skydiving without having to pack a parachute or jump out of a plane. The hour-long session includes a training class and two one-minute jumps which are more than enough to exhaust a novice. Kids as young as three can fly although there are some weight restrictions. It is possible for visitors who do not wish to jump to watch participants floating and spinning, and usually grinning.

Ripley's Believe It Or Not!® Orlando Odditorium
8201 International Drive. *Tel (407) 363-4418.* 9:30am–midnight daily.
www.ripleysorlando.com
Showcasing the bizarre and the extraordinary, Ripley's worldwide chain of attractions displays the fantastic odditities discovered by Robert Ripley (1893–1949) in the course of his travels. Housed in a building that appears to be sinking, the Orlando branch is one of the best of the 30 Ripley's, with 16

Holy Land Experience, a reconstruction of biblical Jerusalem

galleries of the unusual. Highlights include a 1907 Silver Ghost Rolls Royce – with moving engine parts – that was made from 63 pints of glue and 1,016,711 ordinary matchsticks, a version of the *Mona Lisa* made out of toast, and a holographic 1,069-lb (485-kg) man. The replicas of human and animal odditites on display may make some cringe. There is also a gift shop with collectibles for visitors who wish to take some unusual souvenirs home.

Magical Midway Park
7001 International Drive. *Tel (407) 370-5353.* 2pm–10pm Mon–Fri, 10am–midnight Sat & Sun.
www.magicalmidway.com
Magical Midway Park is a carnival-style midway with two elevated go-kart tracks, a fast track, thrill rides, and a collection of classic sideshow rides. This park promises lots of thrills, as you whip around cork-screw turns and feel jolts at high speeds. There is also a state-of-the-art arcade area, where it's possible to play a

game of air hockey, ride Harley-Davidson motorcycles, race in the Daytona USA or shoot a few hoops.

Another attraction is the StarFlyer thrill ride, in which a chair-like swing reaches heights of over 230 ft (70 m) in the air at 54 mph (87 kph). It is the only ride of its kind in the USA.

The squirting bumper boats and bumper cars are fun for all the family.

Holy Land Experience
4655 Vineland Rd. *Tel (407) 872-2272.* 10am–5pm Mon–Sat. Thanksgiving, Dec 25.
www.holylandexperience.com
This biblical history museum, which spreads over 15 acres, (6 ha) re-creates in elaborate and authentic detail the city of Jerusalem and its religious importance between the years 1450 BC and AD 66. Guides dressed in period costume, dramatic enactments of stories from the Old and New Testaments, and high-tech presentations bring Jerusalem to life in this religious theme park. Among the highlights of Holy Land Experience are reconstructions of Jesus's tomb and the limestone caves where the Dead Sea Scrolls were discovered. There are also displays of rare Bibles and biblical manuscripts. While the museum makes no bones about being a Christ-centric institution, visitors of all faiths can enjoy its very evocative journey back in time. A Middle-Eastern-style café serves "Goliath burgers."

The dramatic sinking home of Ripley's Believe It Or Not!® Odditorium

Exploring Winter Park, Eatonville & Maitland

Winter Park, Greater Orlando's most refined city, took off in the 1880s, when wealthy northerners came south and began to build lavish winter retreats along the area's waterways. Excellent stores and classy cafés afford ample opportunities for strolling and window-shopping, and there are several intriguing museums. Nearby Eatonville, the first incorporated African-American municipality in the USA, has an interesting museum on African-American culture, while Maitland, to the north, has beautiful homes and gardens and boasts an excellent art center.

SIGHTS AT A GLANCE

Albin Polasek Museum & Sculpture Gardens ④
Audubon Center for Birds of Prey ⑦
Central Park ②
Charles Hosmer Morse Museum of American Art ①
Cornell Fine Arts Museum ③
Holocaust Memorial Resource & Education Center of Central Florida ⑨
Maitland Art Center ⑧

Winter Park Scenic Boat Tour ⑤
Zora Neale Hurston National Museum of Fine Arts ⑥

0 km   2

0 miles   2

KEY

═══ Interstate highway

▬▬▬ Major highway

═══ Highway

backdrop to concerts on Sunday evenings by the Orlando Philharmonic. Other events include jazz concerts, the Winter Park Sidewalk Art Festival in March, screening of film classics, month-long Christmas festivities, and school activities. Many carry their own blankets and even chairs to enjoy the various musical events. Sculptor Albin Polasek designed the beautiful fountain called "Emily." Benches are scattered throughout and parking is free at the two lots adjacent to the park.

🏛 Cornell Fine Arts Museum

1000 Holt Ave. ☐ 10am–5pm Tue–Sat, 1–5pm Sun. **Tel** (407) 646-2526. **www**.rollins.edu/cfam
Located on the scenic Rollins College campus, this small but elegant museum houses Florida's oldest art collection. The diverse and distinguished collection features European and American paintings, sculptures, and decorative arts from the Renaissance to the 20th century, including the works of artists such as Cosimo Roselli, Henry Moore, William Merritt Chase, and Louis Sonntag.

🏛 Albin Polasek Museum & Sculpture Gardens

633 Osceola Ave, Winter Park. **Tel** (407) 647-6294. ☐ 10am–4pm Tue–Sat, 1–4pm Sun. ● public hols, July & Aug. 🅿️ 🔊 **www**.polasek.org
Listed on the National Register of Historic Places, the home of Czech-American sculptor Albin Polasek (1879–1965) is a beautifully maintained, serene spot spread over 3 acres (1 ha). The house and its lovely gardens showcase

Albin Polasek Museum & Sculpture Gardens

🏛 Charles Hosmer Morse Museum of American Art

445 N Park Ave. **Tel** (407) 645-5311. ☐ 9:30am–4pm Tue–Sat, 1–4pm Sun. ● public hols. 🅿️ (Sep–May: 4–8pm Fri free) 🔊 🔊 **www**.morsemuseum.org
The imposing, windowless walls of this museum rather ironically contain an outstanding collection of beautiful stained-glass windows and objects by the American designer, Louis Comfort Tiffany (1848–1933). Other highlights include American ceramics and representative collections

of the late 19th- and early 20th-century American and European paintings, graphics, decorative arts, furniture, and jewelry.

🌿 Central Park

Downtown Winter Park. **Tel** (407) 599-3334. ☐ daily. 🔊
Located alongside Winter Park's main street, Park Avenue, Central Park is a lovely shaded area that hosts numerous events throughout the year. Tall oaks, pretty fountains, and a splendid rose garden provide a scenic

Winter Park Scenic Boat Tour, along Winter Park's waterways

works spanning the career of the artist who specialized in the European figurative technique. The four galleries within the house also feature works by some other artists.

🚤 Winter Park Scenic Boat Tour
E end of Morse Blvd, Lake Osceola. *Tel (407) 644-4056.* ⬚ *tours depart on the hour 10am–4pm daily.* ● *public hols.* 📷
www.scenicboattours.com
Spend a very pleasant hour cruising along Winter Park's lovely lakes overhung with hibiscus and bamboo on this narrated pontoon boat ride. Running since 1938, this part-nature trip and part-local history lesson takes in landmarks such as Rollins College and huge lakeside mansions with green sweeping lawns, as well as cypress swamps where nature lovers can take a gander at birds such as herons and ospreys.

🏛 Zora Neale Hurston National Museum of Fine Arts
227 E Kennedy Blvd, Eatonville. *Tel (407) 647-3307.* ⬚ *9am–4pm Mon–Fri, 11am–1pm Sat.* ● *public hols.* 📷 ⬚ **www**.
zoranealehurstonmuseum.org
One of the brightest stars of the Harlem Renaissance of the 1920s and 30s, writer, anthropologist, and folklorist Zora Neale Hurston, born in 1891, grew up in Eatonville. Many of her most famous writings – including the 1937 novel, *Their Eyes Were Watching God* – reflected life in her hometown. This modest museum keeps her memory alive, offering maps for a self-guided walking tour

to the remaining literary landmarks of her neighborhood. Exhibitions center on Hurston and the Eatonville of days gone by. The museum also has rotating exhibits of works by contemporary African-American artists.

🦅 Audubon Center for Birds of Prey
1101 Audubon Way, Maitland. *Tel (407) 644-0190.* ⬚ *10am–4pm Tue–Sun.* ● *public hols.* 📷 *(donation requested).* ⬚
www.fl.audubon.org
One of the largest bird rehabilitation centers in Southeastern US, this sanctuary for birds, created by Florida Audubon Society, is a great place to get up close and personal with eagles, owls, hawks, vultures, and other raptors. The center takes in about 700 birds annually and releases about 40 percent of them. Guests are not allowed to witness the rehabilitation process. Those birds that cannot survive being released into the wild are kept here, living a pampered existence in this

Audubon Center for Birds of Prey

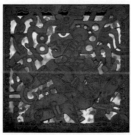
Decoration inspired by the Aztecs, at the Maitland Art Center

lovely lakeside location, while helping to educate visitors about wildlife issues and conservation. Guided tours are available for groups, and there is a wide-ranging volunteer program.

🏛 Maitland Art Center
231 W Packwood Ave, 6 miles (9.6 km) north of Downtown Orlando. *Tel (407) 539-2181.* ⬚ *11am–4pm Tue–Sun.* ● *public hols.* 📷 *(donation requested).* ⬚ 🏠
www.maitlandartcenter.org
Founded in the 1930s by artist André Smith, this was originally an artists' colony, with studios and living quarters. It is now an art museum and teaching center managed by the Maitland Historical Society. The studios are still used by working artists, and there are exhibitions of contemporary American arts and crafts as well as art classes taught by professional artists. Set around courtyards and gardens, the buildings are interesting, with murals and carvings that make abundant use of Mayan and Aztec motifs.

🏛 Holocaust Memorial Resource & Education Center of Central Florida
851 N Maitland Ave, Maitland. *Tel (407) 628-0555.* ⬚ *9am–4pm Mon–Thu, 9am–1pm Fri, 1–4pm Sun.* ● *public & Jewish hols.* 📷 ⬚
www.holocaustedu.org
Set up with the aim of preventing the oppression of minority groups in future by learning from the Holocaust, this small museum's permanent exhibit has 12 segments, each introducing a major theme of the Holocaust. The museum features multimedia displays on the history of the Holocaust as well as photographs and artifacts.

There is also an extensive library on the subject, with more than 5,000 volumes and 500 videotapes, some of which contain oral histories of survivors of the Holocaust. The library also stocks a selection of juvenile books on this tragic event.

S-32—Park Avenue and Municipal Zoo from the Band Shell on Lake Monroe, Sanford, Fla.

A postcard of Sanford, showing Lake Monroe

Sanford ❷

Seminole Co. 🏛 45,000. 🚂 🚌
ℹ 400 E 1st St, (407) 322-2212.
www.sanfordchamber.com

Located to the north of Orlando and on the southern shores of Lake Monroe, Sanford was founded in the 1870s by Henry S. Sanford, near Fort Mellon, the US Army post built during the Seminole Wars *(see p14)*. The construction of a railway station thereafter added to Sanford's prosperity and the thriving town soon became a major inland port

Sanford town sign

thanks to the commercial steamboat services, which also brought the city's early tourists.
Restored downtown Sanford dates from the 1880s, which was the height of the steamboat era. Several of the lovely old red brick buildings – a rarity in Florida – are home to antiques shops, and the area can easily be explored on foot in a couple of hours. Today's visitors are more likely to arrive on the Auto Train *(see p196)* than by river, but short pleasure cruises are also available.

Mount Dora ❸

Lake Co. 🏛 11,000. 🚂
ℹ 341 Alexander St, (352) 383-2165. **www.**mountdora.com

Set among the citrus groves of Lake County, this town is one of the prettiest Victorian settlements left in the state.

Its name comes from both its relatively high elevation of 184 ft (56 m) and the small lake on which it sits. Mount Dora was originally known as Royellou, after Roy, Ella, and Louis, the three children of the first postmaster.
Mount Dora's attractive tree-lined streets are laid out on a bluff above the lakeshore.
Visitors can refer to the 3-mile (5-km) historic tour map, which is available at the town's chamber of commerce.
The tour takes a scenic route around the quiet neighborhoods of late 19th-century clapboard homes and the wonderfully restored downtown historic district, which has an array of stores and antiques shops.
On Donnelly Street, you will find the grand **Donnelly House**, now a Masonic Hall. A notable example of ornate "steamboat architecture," the building is aesthetically decorated with pinnacles and a

cupola. Nearby, the small **Mount Dora History Museum** showcases local history exhibits. Water sports and fishing are on offer at Lake Dora.

🏛 **Mount Dora History Museum**
450 Royellou Lane. **Tel** (352) 383-0006. ◯ 1–5pm Thu–Sun. ● Jan 1, Thanksgiving, Dec 25. ♿ limited.

Blue Spring State Park ❹

Volusia Co. 2100 W French Ave, Orange City. **Tel** (386) 775-3663. ◯ 8am–sundown daily. 🅿 ♿
www.floridastateparks.org/bluespring

One of the country's largest first-magnitude artesian springs, Blue Spring pours out around 100 million gallons (450 million liters) of water a day. The temperature of the water is at a constant 73°F (24°C), and consequently the park is a favorite winter refuge for manatees. From November to March, when the manatees escape from the cooler waters of the St. Johns River, you can see them from the park's elevated boardwalks. Activities such as snorkeling and scuba diving are available in the turquoise waters of the spring head, as is canoeing on St. Johns. **Thursby House**, atop one of the park's ancient shell mounds, was built in the late 19th century.

Environs

Just about 2 miles (3 km) north as the crow flies is wooded **Hontoon Island State Park**. Reached by a free passenger

Shingles and gingerbread decoration on Donnelly House, Mount Dora

Children playing in front of Thursby House, Blue Spring State Park

ferry from Hontoon Landing, the island has an 80-ft (24-m) observation tower, picnic and camping areas, and a nature trail. Fishing skiffs and canoes can also be rented.

The original inhabitants of the park were the Timucua Indians. In 1955, a rare wooden owl totem was found here.

Hontoon Island State Park
2309 River Ridge Rd, DeLand. *Tel* (386) 736-5309. 8am–sundown daily. *www*.floridastateparks. org/hontoonisland

Cassadaga Spiritualist Camp ❺

1325 Stevens St, Cassadaga. *Tel* (386) 228-3171. 10am–6pm Mon–Sat, 11:30am–6pm Sun. *www*.cassadaga.org

Founded by a group of spiritualists in 1894 to study the philosophy, science, and religion of Spiritualism in

greater depth, the Cassadaga Spiritualist Camp is one of the oldest active religious communities in the United States. In 1991, the center was earmarked as a Historic District by the National Registry of Historic Places.

Spread over 57 acres (23 ha), the community is home to numerous certified and practicing healers, clairvoyants, mediums, and psychics, who offer healing sessions to those suffering from ailments of the body and the spirit. Visitors can arrange a session with any of the spiritual counselors for a specified fee. Accommodation is available on the premises. The center also organizes activities and classes on aspects of Spiritualism.

The Cassadaga Spiritualist Bookstore and Information Center has a vast collection of spiritual reading matter, CDs, and tapes, as well as gift articles such as crystals, jewelry, and ethnic artifacts.

DeLeon Springs State Park ❻

601 Ponce DeLeon Blvd. DeLeon Springs. *Tel* (386) 985-4212. 8am–sundown daily. *www*.floridastateparks.org/deleonsprings

The springs at this State Park were once believed to be the legendary fountain of youth. Today, they provide a pristine setting for various forms of outdoor recreation.

Swimming is one of the most popular activities here, with the springs being dammed to create a fine bathing area where the water remains at a pleasant 72°F (22°C). Numerous nature and hiking trails take visitors through beautiful, thickly wooded areas, and there are lovely picnic spots and pavilions. Fishing, boating, kayaking, and canoeing are permitted – you can rent kayaks and canoes or take a guided eco-tour on a pontoon boat. At the **Old Spanish Sugar Mill** restaurant, guests can cook their own pancakes.

Adjoining the park is **Lake Woodruff National Wildlife Refuge**, a preserve for endangered birds and animals. Explore the lakes and marshes of the refuge in a canoe.

Lake Woodruff National Wildlife Refuge
2045 Mud Lake Rd, DeLeon Springs. *Tel* (386) 985-4673. daylight hours daily.

The Old Spanish Sugar Mill amid the lush greenery and lakes of the DeLeon Springs State Park

Daytona Beach ❼

Volusia Co. 🏘 *64,000*. 🛬 🚆
ℹ *126 E Orange Ave*, *(386) 255-0415*. **www**.daytonabeach.com

Noisy Daytona Beach calls itself the "World's Most Famous Beach." This 23-mile (37-km) long beach is one of the few in Florida where cars are allowed on the sands, a hangover from the days when motor enthusiasts raced on the beaches: the first timed automobile runs took place just north of Daytona Beach, on the sands at Ormond Beach – the official "Birthplace of Speed" – in 1903.

Daytona is still a mecca for motorsports fans. The nearby **Daytona International Speedway** draws huge crowds, especially during the Speedweeks in February and the motorcycle racing events in March and October. Eight major racing weekends are held annually at the track, which can hold more than 110,000 spectators. The speed-way hosts NASCAR (National Association for Stock Car Auto Racing) meets – the Daytona 500 being the most famous – and sports car, motorcycle, and go-karting races. Events include charity bike-a-thons, vintage car rallies, superbike spectaculars, and production car tests. A tram tour around the speed-way track is available on days

The Daytona 500, held each February at Daytona International Speedway

A race car at Daytona International Speedway

when no races take place. Tickets for each Daytona 500 are usually sold out a year in advance, but visitors can relive the experience at DAYTONA USA, a popular attraction at the visitor center. One of the main exhibits is a film featuring spectacular in-car camera shots and behind-the-scenes action from a recent Daytona 500 race.

The beach, lined with hotels, bustles with frenzied activity. On offer are jet skiing, "banana-boat" rides, windsurfing, buggy rides, and gondola sky-rides above Ocean Pier. There are also more sedate and relaxing scenic excursions on a riverboat.

Downtown Daytona, known simply as "Mainland," lies across the Halifax River from the beach. The restored downtown area is home to the **Halifax Historical Society**

Museum. Located in a 1910 bank building, the museum is decorated with fancy pilasters and murals. Local history displays include a model of the boardwalk as it was in 1938.

Close by, **Jackie Robinson Ballpark and Museum** – named after the baseball legend – is the home field of the Daytona Cubs.

West of downtown, the excellent **Museum of Arts & Sciences** has exhibits that cover a range of subjects, from Florida prehistory to fine and decorative arts from 1640–1920. There is a notable Cuban and African art collection. The 1907 **Gamble Place**, run by the same museum, is a hunting lodge with period furnishings. Tours of the house require reservations, and also include the Snow White House – built in 1938 and an exact copy of the one in the 1937 Disney classic.

Daytona International Speedway
1801 W International Speedway Blvd. **Tel** 866-761-7223. ⬤ *daily*. ⬤ *Dec 25*. 📷 ✓ ♿ **www**.daytonainternationalspeedway.com

🏛 **Halifax Historical Society Museum**
252 S Beach St. **Tel** *(386) 255-6976*. ⬤ *10:30am–4:30pm Tue–Fri*, *10am–4pm Sat* ⬤ *public hols*. 📷 ♿ **www**.halifaxhistorical.org

Jackie Robinson Ballpark and Museum
105 E Orange Ave. **Tel** *(386) 257-3172*. **www**.daytonacubs.com

🏛 **Museum of Arts & Sciences**
1040 Museum Blvd. **Tel** *(386) 255-0285*. ⬤ *9am–5pm Tue–Sat*, *11am–5pm Sun*. ⬤ *Thanksgiving*, *Dec 24, Dec 25*. 📷 ♿ **www**.moas.org

Cars cruising the hard-packed sands of Daytona Beach

Beaches of the East Coast

The wide, sun-soaked sandy beaches of Central Florida's Atlantic Coast, with their warm waters and an average daytime temperature of 73°F (23°C), attract millions of visitors annually. The 72 miles (116 km) of the Space Coast feature lovely beaches, several being contiguous with lush nature preserves. Most are on barrier islands, and range from the pristine white beaches of the Canaveral National Seashore and the Indian River, to boisterous resorts such as Cocoa Beach. To the north of the Space Coast are Ormond Beach and the highly popular Daytona Beach, both associated with automobile racing. Most of the East Coast beaches are family-friendly, with picnic areas and restrooms, and also offer a wide range of water sports.

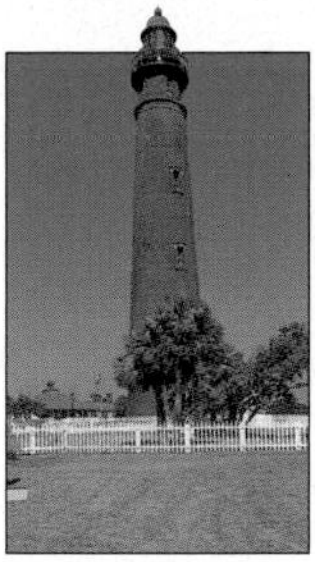

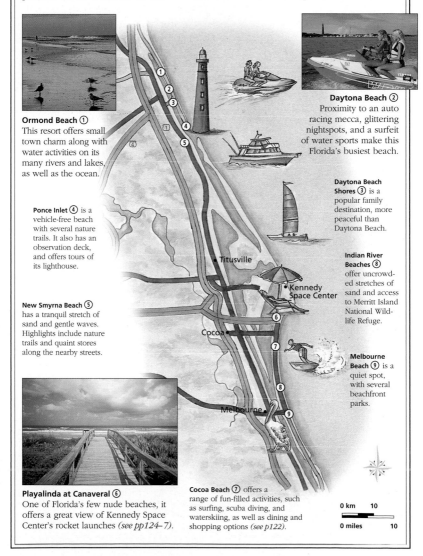

Ponce de Leon Inlet lighthouse

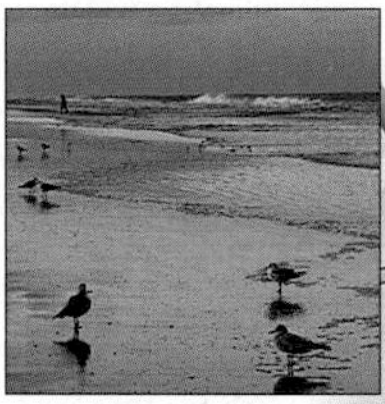

Ormond Beach [1]
This resort offers small town charm along with water activities on its many rivers and lakes, as well as the ocean.

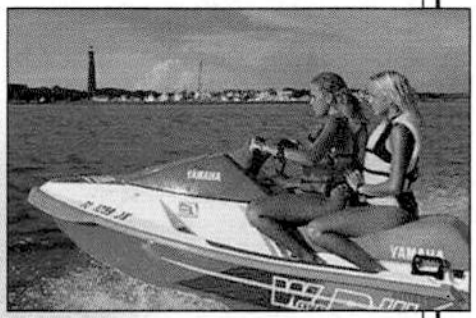

Daytona Beach [2]
Proximity to an auto racing mecca, glittering nightspots, and a surfeit of water sports make this Florida's busiest beach.

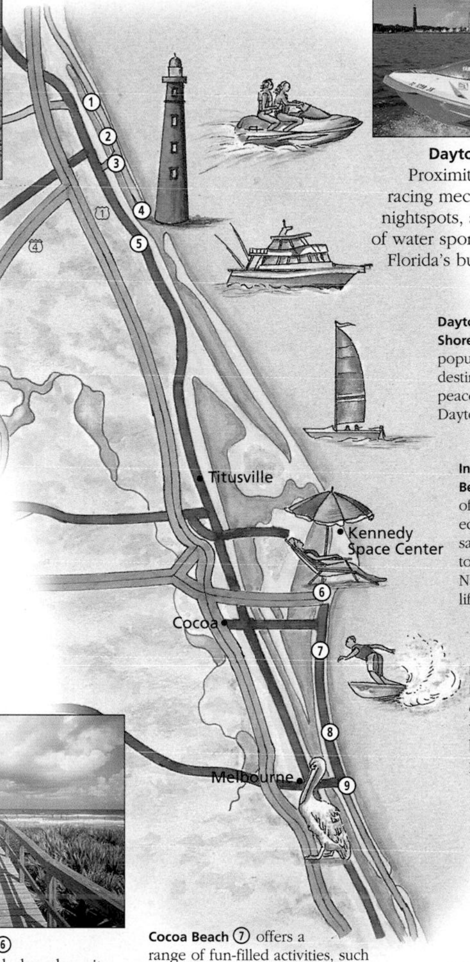

Daytona Beach Shores [3] is a popular family destination, more peaceful than Daytona Beach.

Ponce Inlet [4] is a vehicle-free beach with several nature trails. It also has an observation deck, and offers tours of its lighthouse.

Indian River Beaches [8] offer uncrowded stretches of sand and access to Merritt Island National Wildlife Refuge.

New Smyrna Beach [5] has a tranquil stretch of sand and gentle waves. Highlights include nature trails and quaint stores along the nearby streets.

Melbourne Beach [9] is a quiet spot, with several beachfront parks.

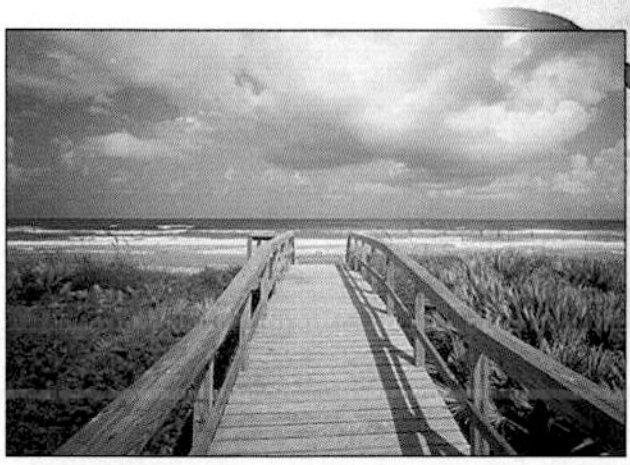

Playalinda at Canaveral [6]
One of Florida's few nude beaches, it offers a great view of Kennedy Space Center's rocket launches *(see pp124–7)*.

Cocoa Beach [7] offers a range of fun-filled activities, such as surfing, scuba diving, and waterskiing, as well as dining and shopping options *(see p122)*.

Ocala National Forest ❽

Lake Co/Marion Co. ℹ️ *3199 NE Co. Rd, (352) 236-0288.* ◯ *8am–sunset daily.* 🚻 *to campsite & swimming areas.* ♿ 🅰️ **Juniper Springs canoe rental** *Tel (352) 625-2808.* www. ocalacc.com/visitor-center/forestry.asp

Located between Ocala city and the St. Johns River, this is the world's largest pine forest, covering an area of 366,000 acres (148,000 ha). The forest is crisscrossed by spring-fed rivers and dozens of hiking trails. One of the last refuges of the endangered Florida black bear, it is also home to many more common animals such as deer and otter. Several birds, including barred owls, bald eagles, ospreys, the non-native wild turkey, and various species of waders – which frequent the river swamp areas – can all be spotted here.

The numerous hiking trails in the forest vary in length from boardwalks to short loop trails of under a mile (1.6 km) to a 66-mile (106-km) stretch of the cross-state National Scenic Trail. Bass fishing is popular on the many lakes scattered through the forest, and there are swimming holes, picnic areas, and campgrounds at recreation areas such as Salt Springs, Fore Lake, and Alexander Springs.

Canoes are easily available for rental. The 7-mile (11-km) canoe run down Juniper

The Jungle Cruise, one of the many attractions at Silver Springs

Creek from the **Juniper Springs Recreation Area** is one of the finest in the state. Book in advance as it is an extremely popular tourist destination. The Salt Springs Trail provides an excellent vantage point for bird-watching, and wood ducks congregate on Lake Dorr.

You can pick up guides and information at the main visitor center on the western edge of the forest, or at the smaller centers at Salt Springs and Lake Dorr, both on Route 19.

FLORIDA'S BUBBLING SPRINGS

Most of Florida's 320 known springs are located in the upper half of the state. The majority are artesian springs, formed by waters forced up through deep fissures from underground aquifers (rock deposits containing water). Those that gush over 100 cu ft (3 cu m) per second are known as first-magnitude springs.

Filtered through the rock, the water is extremely pure and sometimes high in salts and minerals. These properties, plus the sheer beauty of the springs, have long attracted visitors for recreational and health purposes.

Juniper Springs in Ocala National Forest, adapted for swimmers in the 1930s

Silver Springs ❾

Marion Co. *5656 E Silver Springs Blvd.* **Tel** *(352) 236-2121.* ◯ *10am–5pm daily.* 🚻 ♿ *limited.* **www**.silversprings.com

Glass-bottomed boat trips at Silver Springs have been revealing the natural wonders of the world's largest artesian spring since 1878. Today, Florida's oldest commercial tourist attraction offers not only the famous glass-bottomed boat rides but also jeep safaris and jungle cruises, which take you on a trip through the Florida out-back. The early Tarzan movies starring Johnny Weismuller were filmed here.

Another popular attraction here is the Alligator & Crocodile Encounter at Cypress Island: this 5-acre (2-ha) area is home to 13 of the 23 species of alligators and crocodiles. Nearby, Wild Waters is a lively, family-oriented water park.

Environs

The **Silver River State Park**, 2 miles (3 km) southeast, offers a lovely walk through a hardwood forest and cypress swamp area, leading to a swimming hole in a bend of the crystal-clear river.

The gaping jaws of an alligator marking the entrance to Gatorland

Silver River State Park

1425 NE 58th Ave, Ocala. *Tel (352) 236-7148.* 8am–sunset daily. www.floridastateparks.org/silverriver

Gatorland ⑩

Orange Co. 14501 S Orange Blossom Trail, Orlando. (800) 393-5297. Orlando. Orlando. 9am–6pm daily. www.gatorland.com

Spread over an area of 110 acres (44 ha), this park opened in the 1950s as a huge working farm, and has a special license to raise alligators for their hides and meat. Gatorland's breeding pens, nurseries, and rearing ponds are home to thousands of alligators that range in size from infants that fit into the palm of your hand to 12-ft (4-m) monsters. They can be observed from a boardwalk and tower as they bask in the shallows of a cypress swamp.

On sale at Gatorland

The shows are somewhat contrived but still fun. They include alligator wrestling and the Gator Jumparoo, in which huge alligators leap out of the water to grab chunks of chicken from the hands of the trainers. In addition, the park features close encounters and handling demonstrations of Florida's poisonous snakes.

One of Gatorland's popular attractions is a water park, Gator Gully Splash Park. The park's other highlights include an aviary, a bird breeding marsh, and a petting zoo.

Kissimmee ⑪

Osceola Co. 41,000. 1925 E Irlo Bronson Memorial Hwy, (407) 847-5000. www.floridakiss.com Old Town 5770 W Irlo Bronson Memorial Hwy. *Tel (407) 396-4888.* www.old-town.com

This cattle boom town, whose name means "Heaven's Place" in the language of the Calusa Indians, had cows freely roaming its streets in the early 1900s. Now the only livestock visitors are likely to encounter are those that appear in the twice-yearly **Silver Spurs Rodeo**, which was founded in 1944 *(see p179)* and is held in the state-of-the-art, climate-controlled, 8,300-seater **Silver Spurs Arena**. Most visitors headed for Walt Disney World® often stop at Kissimmee for the many inexpensive motels on the busy, traffic-ridden US 192.

One of the typically offbeat shops in Kissimmee's Old Town

Kissimmee's **Old Town** is a re-created pedestrian street of early 20th-century buildings with some unusual and eccentric shops, offering psychic readings, tattoos, Irish linen, candles, and so forth. There is also an entertaining haunted house and a small fairground with antique equipment.

Warbird Adventures, by the Kissimmee municipal airport, gives visitors the unforgettable opportunity to fly in an original World War II advanced T-6 navy trainer or a classic MASH helicopter. Whether you want a thrilling acrobatic adventure or a smooth sightseeing flight, visitors can take the controls and learn about flying one of these historical aircraft from an experienced instructor.

Silver Spurs Rodeo/Silver Spurs Arena

1875 Silver Spur Lane. *Tel (407) 677-6336.* contact for events. www.silverspursrodeo.com

Warbird Adventures

Tel (407) 870-7366. 9am–5pm daily. www.warbirdadventures.com

A World of Orchids ⑫

Orange Co. 2501 Old Lake Wilson Rd, Kissimmee. *Tel (407) 396-1887.* 9:30am–4:30pm Mon–Sat. Sun & public hols. www.aworldoforchids.com

Varieties of gorgeous orchids bloom through-out the year in this huge conservatory – complete with streams and waterfalls – spread over 3,000 sq ft (279 sq m). Also showcased here are several species of tropical plants, including palms and bamboo, as well as exotic birds and small animals, such as Asian squirrels and chameleons. Rare species of colorful fish are on display in beautifully set-up aquaria. Visitors can enjoy nature walks and guided tours, and stop at the gift shop to carry home a couple of these spectacular plants. Plan to spend at least an hour in this lovely setting.

Fantasy of Flight 13

Polk Co. 1400 Broadway Blvd SE, Polk City. ☎ *(863) 984-3500.* 🚆 *Winter Haven.* 🚌 *Winter Haven.* 🕐 *10am–5pm daily.* ● *Thanksgiving, Dec 25.* 🍴 ♿ **www**.fantasyofflight.com

This aviation center gains an advantage over similar attractions in Florida by being the only one to provide the very sensations of flying. The Fightertown section, for instance, allows visitors to ride in a World War II fighter aircraft simulator in a dogfight over the Pacific. Firstly, you receive a pre-flight briefing, and then once you are in the cockpit the control tower advises you about takeoff, landing, and the presence of enemy aircraft.

Other attractions include a series of vivid walk-through exhibits, which take you into a World War II B-17 Flying Fortress during a bombing mission, and into World War I trenches in the middle of an air raid. A hangar holds an impressive collection of vintage airplanes in mint condition, such as the first widely used airliner in the US, the 1929 Ford Tri-Motor, which appeared in the film *Indiana Jones and the Temple of Doom*, and the Roadair 1, a combined plane and car that flew just once, in 1959.

Florida Southern College 14

Polk Co. 111 Lake Hollingsworth Dr, Lakeland. ***Tel*** *(863) 680-4111.* 🚆 *Lakeland.* 🚌 *Lakeland.* 🕐 *daily.* ● *Jan 1, Jul 4, Thanksgiving, Dec 25.* **Visitor Center** 🕐 *10am–4pm Mon–Fri, 10am–2pm Sat.* ♿

Located in the picturesque town of Lakeland, Florida Southern College has the world's largest collection of buildings designed by Frank Lloyd Wright, one of America's most eminent architects. Amazingly, the college president managed to persuade Wright to design the campus with the promise of little more than the opportunity to express his ideas, and payment when the money could be raised. Work began in 1938 on what Wright, already famous as the founder of organic architecture, termed his "child of the sun." His aim of blending the buildings with their natural surroundings was achieved by using glass to bring outdoor light to the interiors. The original plan was for 18 structures, but only seven had been completed by the time Wright died in 1959; five were finished or added later.

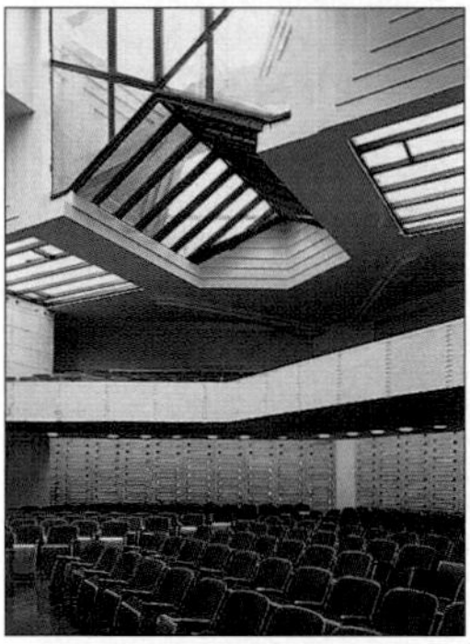

The light and spacious interior of the Annie Pfeiffer Chapel

The **Annie Pfeiffer Chapel** is a particularly fine expression of his ideas. Stained-glass windows break the monotony of the building blocks, and the entire edifice is topped by a spectacular tower in place of the traditional steeple. Wright called this tower a "jewel box."

On the whole, the campus has the light and airy feel that Wright sought to achieve. The buildings are linked to each other by the Esplanades – a covered walkway, stretching for 1.5-miles (2 km), in which light, shade, and variations in height draw attention from one building to the next.

You can wander around the campus at any time, but the interiors can be explored only during the week. The Frank Lloyd Wright visitor center at **Thad Buckner Building** has examples of Wright's drawings and furniture.

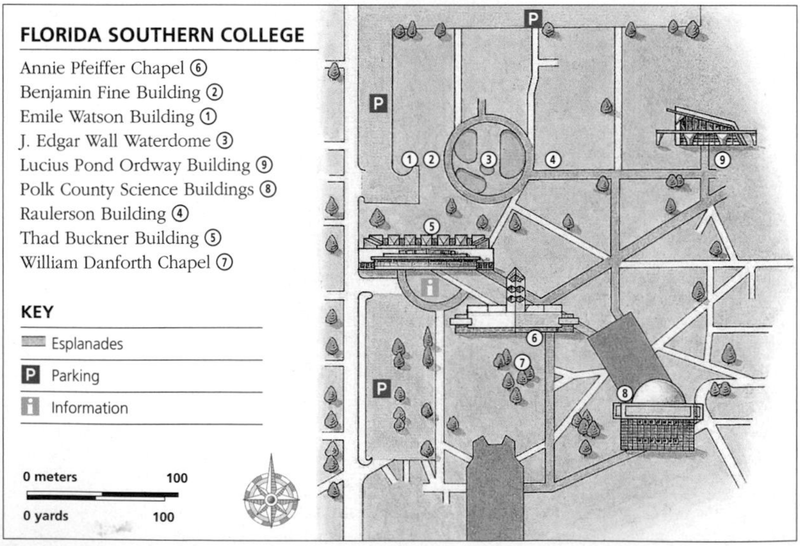
FLORIDA SOUTHERN COLLEGE
Annie Pfeiffer Chapel 6
Benjamin Fine Building 2
Emile Watson Building 1
J. Edgar Wall Waterdome 3
Lucius Pond Ordway Building 9
Polk County Science Buildings 8
Raulerson Building 4
Thad Buckner Building 5
William Danforth Chapel 7
KEY
Esplanades
P Parking
i Information
0 meters 100
0 yards 100
P
P
P
1
2
3
4
5
6
7
8
9

Dinosaur World ⓰

Hillsboro Co. 5145 Harvey Tew Rd,
Plant City. *Tel (813) 717-9865.*
◯ *9am–6pm daily.* 🅿 ☕ ♿
www.dinosaurworld.com

Tyrannosaurus rex and
around 150 other life-size
dinosaurs tower over vegetation in the lush park setting
of this outdoor museum.
Made of styrofoam and metal,
these realistic-looking and
scientifically accurate models
of prehistoric creatures are
arranged in a chronological
order throughout the park.
A museum displays fossils
and other dinosaur-related
objects. Other highlights
include a film on the world
of dinosaurs and a display
that explains the elaborate
process used by the park to
create its dinosaurs.
Dinosaur World offers many
hands-on activities for kids: at
a fossil dig, they can use little
shovels or dip their hands in
the sand to come up with tiny
treasures that are dinosaur
related; at the Boneyard, they
can hunt for dinosaur bones.
Picnic areas abound, and
there is a gift shop with fun
but pricey products.

LEGOLAND® ⓰

One LEGOLAND Way, Winter Haven.
Tel (877) 350-LEGO. 🚉 Winter
Haven. ◯ *10am–5pm daily.* 🅿 ♿
http://florida-legoland.com

One of Florida's interactive
theme parks, LEGOLAND® is
a 45-minute drive southwest
of the other theme parks
and downtown Tampa.
Specifically geared to cater
for families with children
aged between 2 and 12, it
offers family rides, interactive
attractions, 4-D movies, shows,
restaurants, and shopping
amid attractive landscaping.
At the heart of the park is
Miniland USA, with themed
areas including Washington,
D.C., New York City, Las
Vegas, and Daytona, as well as
Florida itself and the Kennedy
Space Center. **Castle Hill** takes
guests back to medieval
times, with a plethora of
knights, damsels, and dragons.

Millions of bricks are used to create the LEGOLAND® Miniland USA

Popular with toddlers is
DUPLO® Village where they
can fly a plane, drive a car,
and explore a whole town,
all scaled down to their
height. Life-sized LEGO
TECHNIC® vehicles can be
raced along a roller coaster
track by older children at the
LEGO TECHNIC® Test Track.
AQUAZONE® Wave Riders is
a water carousel ride in which
riders have to dodge water
blasters as they zip in and out
of the waves.

Historic Bok Sanctuary ⓱

Polk Co. 1151 Tower Blvd, Lake Wales.
Tel (863) 676-1408. 🚉 Lake Wales.
🚉 Winter Haven. ◯ *8am–5pm*
daily. 🅿 ♿ www.boksanctuary.org

Edward W. Bok arrived in the
US from Holland in 1870
at the age of six, and subse-
quently became an influential

The striking pink marble Singing
Tower at Historic Bok Sanctuary

publisher. Shortly before his
death in 1930, he presented
128 acres (52 ha) of beautiful
woodland gardens to the
American public "for the
success they had given him."
Sitting at the highest spot in
peninsular Florida – at 298 ft
(91 m) above sea level – the
gardens are spread over 250
acres (102 ha) around the
Singing Tower that soars
above the treetops. Bok's
grave is at its base. Visitors
are not allowed to climb the
tower; but try to attend its 45-
minute live carillon concert,
which is rung daily at 3pm.

Yeehaw Junction ⓲

Osceola Co. Desert Inn, 5570
S Kenansville Rd, Yeehaw Junction.
Tel (407) 436-1054. ◯ *daily.* ♿
www.desertinnrestaurant.com

Located at the crossroads of
US 60 and the Florida
Turnpike, quaintly named
Yeehaw Junction harks back
to the Florida of a couple of
centuries ago. It is known
for its motel and restaurant,
Desert Inn, which served as a
watering hole for lumbermen
and cowboys driving herds of
cattle from the center of the
state to the reservations and
plantations on the coast. Now
listed on the National Registry
of Historical Places, the 1880s
wooden building offers a
fascinating look into the
history of Cracker Country.
The restaurant serves gator-
and turtle-burgers, and also
has a large outdoor area for
festivals – mostly bluegrass
music – and barbecues.

The grand Porcher House, on the edge of Cocoa's leafy historic district

Cocoa Beach 19

Brevard Co. **ℹ** *400 Fortenberry Rd, Merritt Island.* **Tel** *(321) 459-2200.* 🏃 *14,000.* 🚊 *Merritt Island.* **www.** cocoabeachchamber.com

Located on a barrier island adjoining the Atlantic Ocean, this is one of the most popular beaches on the Space Coast. Known as the East Coast's surfing capital, bustling Cocoa Beach hosts several surfing festivals during Easter and the Labor Day weekends. Motels, chain restaurants, and the odd strip joint characterize the main throughfare. The best-known attraction here is the **Ron Jon Surf Shop**, a neon palace-like store with a huge T-shirt collection and surfboards *(see p163)*. Tour the Banana River Lagoon fringing Cocoa Beach to see marine and bird species. Or go fishing at the dock at Ramp Road Park, one of the state's best fishing spots.

🛒 **Ron Jon Surf Shop**
4151 N Atlantic Ave. **Tel** *(321) 799-8820.* 🕐 *24 hrs daily.* ♿
www.ronjons. com

Cocoa 20

Brevard Co. 🏃 *20,000.* 🚊 **ℹ** *400 Fortenberry Rd, Merritt Island, (321) 459- 2200.*

The most appealing of the sprawling communities along the Space Coast mainland, the vibrant town of Cocoa is located close to the Indian River. Its historic district, Cocoa Village, has buildings dating from the 1880s, replica gas streetlamps, and brick sidewalks. On Delannoy Avenue, on the eastern edge of the village, is the Classical Revival **Porcher House**, built of coquina stone in 1916 by a leading citrus plantation owner. Another not-to-miss site is the **Brevard Museum of History & Science**, which has nature trails that represent different ecosystems – pine sandhill, freshwater marsh, or hardwood hammock.

🏛 **Brevard Museum of History & Science**
2201 Michigan Ave. **Tel** *(321) 632-1830.* 🕐 *10am–4pm Mon– Sat, noon–4pm Sun.* ♿
www.brevardmuseum. com

Valiant Air Command Warbird Museum 21

Brevard Co. 6600 Tico Rd, Titusville. **Tel** *(321) 268-1941.* 🚊 *Titusville.* 🕐 *10am–6pm daily.* ● *Jan 1, Thanksgiving, Dec 25.* 🎟 ♿
www.vacwarbirds.org

This museum is home to an enormous hangar that features an impressive collection of military aircraft from World War II and later, all restored to flying condition. The pride of the collection is a Douglas C-47 called Tico Belle, which became the official carrier for the Danish royal family at the end of the war. An air show is held in March each year.

Tico Belle, the prize exhibit at the Warbird Air Museum

US Astronaut Hall of Fame® 22

Brevard Co. Junction of Rte 405 & US 1. **Tel** *(321) 269-6101.* 🚊 *Titusville.* 🕐 *9am–6:30pm daily.* ● *Dec 25.* 🎟 ♿ **www**. kennedyspacecenter. com/visitKSC/ attractions/fame. asp

Set up to commemorate the country's astronauts, the facility showcases a fascinating collection of their personal memorabilia and other related artifacts. The center also offers

The Ron Jon Surf Shop in Cocoa Beach, with everything for the surfing or beach enthusiast

interactive experiences in the form of a simulated ride in a mock space shuttle. On the same site, the Camp Kennedy Space Center offers some courses for children interested in learning about space.

Canaveral National Seashore ㉓

Brevard Co. Rte A1A, 20 miles (32 km) N of Titusville or Rte 402, 10 miles (16 km) E of Titusville. *Tel (321) 267-1110.* 🚌 *Titusville.* ⬤ *Beaches 6am–8pm Apr–Oct, 6am–6pm Nov–Mar.* ⬤ *for shuttle launches.* ♿ www.nps.gov/cana

Spread over an area of 57,000 acres (23,000 ha), Canaveral National Seashore located on a barrier island, features an astounding range of fauna and a wide range of habitats, including marshes, saltwater estuaries, hardwood hammocks, and pine flatwoods. The bird life makes the greatest visual impact.

The park incorporates Florida's largest undeveloped barrier island beach – a magnificent 24-mile (39-km) stretch backed by barrier dunes. Apollo Beach, at the northern end, is accessible along Route A1A, while Playalinda Beach is reached from the south, along Route 402. Note that this is a popular spot for nude bathing.

An alligator in the wild

Behind Apollo Beach, the Turtle Mound is a 40-ft (12-m) high midden of oyster shells created by Timucua Indians.

Merritt Island National Wildlife Refuge ㉔

Brevard Co. Route 406, 4 miles (6.5 km) E of Titusville. *Tel (321) 861-0667.* 🚌 ⬤ *sunrise–sunset daily.* ⬤ *for shuttle launches.* www.fws.gov/merrittisland

Experience an incredible variety of marine and wild-life at this expansive nature preserve adjoining Canaveral

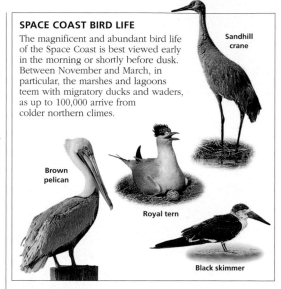

SPACE COAST BIRD LIFE

The magnificent and abundant bird life of the Space Coast is best viewed early in the morning or shortly before dusk. Between November and March, in particular, the marshes and lagoons teem with migratory ducks and waders, as up to 100,000 arrive from colder northern climes.

Sandhill crane

Brown pelican

Royal tern

Black skimmer

National Seashore. Covering an area of 140,000 acres (56,656 ha), the Merritt Island National Wildlife Refuge is a seaside haven for several endangered and threatened species of animals and birds, including manatees, sea turtles, Eastern indigo snakes, American alligators, otters, falcons, terns, ospreys, woodpeckers, owls, and many more. The refuge also provides sanctuary for thousands of plant species typical of Florida's ecosystems and habitats. By far the best way to explore the local wildlife is to follow the 7-mile (11-km) Black Point Wildlife Drive – a self guided tour through salt- and freshwater marshes. An excellent leaflet, available at the track's start near the junction of

Routes 402 and 406, explains such matters as how dikes help control local mosquito populations – although it is a good idea to come armed with insect repellent in summer. Halfway along the drive, you can stretch your legs by following the 5-mile (8-km) Cruickshank Trail, which starts nearby and has an observation tower.

East along Route 402, toward Playalinda Beach, the Merritt Island Visitor Information Center offers educational displays and a short film about the refuge. A mile (1.6 km) farther east, the Oak Hammock and Palm Hammock trails have short boardwalks across the marshland for bird-watching and photography.

A large part of the refuge lies within Kennedy Space Center (*see pp124–7*) and is out of bounds to the public.

Scenic view from Black Point Drive, Merritt Island National Wildlife Refuge

Kennedy Space Center ㉕

NASA insignia

Situated on Merritt Island Wildlife Refuge, just an hour's drive east of Orlando, the Kennedy Space Center is the only place in the Western Hemisphere from where humans are launched into space. It was from here, with the launch of *Apollo 11* in July 1969, that President Kennedy's dream of landing a man on the moon was realized. The center is the home of NASA (National Aeronautics and Space Administration), whose space shuttles *(see pp22–3)* once lifted off here, until the last mission in 2011. The Shuttle Launch Experience is an exhilarating launch simulation, with all the authentic sights, sounds, and sensations of a flight into orbit.

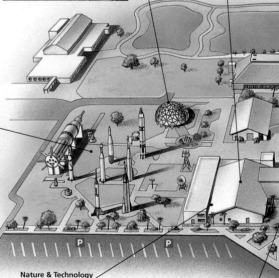

★ Apollo/Saturn V Center
A Saturn V rocket, of the kind used by the Apollo missions, is the showpiece here. There is also a reconstructed control room where visitors experience a simulated launch (see p127).

Lunch with an Astronaut
These sessions offer a unique opportunity to meet a veteran NASA astronaut, hear their space story, and get their autograph while enjoying a buffet lunch.

Astronaut Encounter

Children's Play Dome

★ Rocket Garden
You can walk through a group of towering rockets, each of which represents a different period of space flight's history.

Nature & Technology
Universe Theater

Entrance

STAR FEATURES

★ Apollo/Saturn V Center

★ Rocket Garden

★ KSC Bus Tours

★ IMAX® Theater

VISITOR COMPLEX

Each year more than 1.5 million visitors from around the world experience their own space adventure by visiting the site of America's space exploration program. Built in 1967, the Visitor Complex remains a popular destination.

★ KSC Bus Tours

A bus tour makes a circuit of the center's launch pads, passing the Vehicle Assembly Building and the "crawlerway," along which the shuttle is slowly maneuvered into position.

VISITORS' CHECKLIST

Brevard Co. Off Rte 405, 6 miles (9.5 km) E of Titusville. 🚌 *Titusville.* **Tel** *(321) 449-4444. Schedule of launches: (321) 867-4636.* ⬛ *9am–6pm daily.* ⬛ *Dec 25. The center closes occasionally due to operational requirements. Always call ahead to check.* 🖼 🍴 📷 ♿ *all the exhibits are accessible; wheelchairs & strollers are available at Information Central.* **www**.ksc.nasa.gov; **www**.kennedyspacecenter.com

★ IMAX® Theater

The IMAX® Theater runs films about space exploration. Footage from the shuttle missions offers some breathtaking views of Earth from space (see p126).

Shuttle Launch Experience
Hold on tight to enjoy an all-too-real simulation of a space shuttle launch.

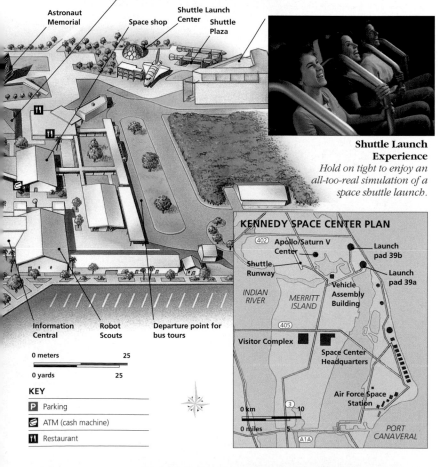

Astronaut Memorial

Space shop

Shuttle Launch Center

Shuttle Plaza

Information Central

Robot Scouts

Departure point for bus tours

0 meters — 25

0 yards — 25

KEY

🅿 Parking

💳 ATM (cash machine)

🍴 Restaurant

KENNEDY SPACE CENTER PLAN

(402) Apollo/Saturn V Center

Launch pad 39b

Shuttle Runway

Launch pad 39a

INDIAN RIVER

MERRITT ISLAND

Vehicle Assembly Building

(405)

Visitor Complex

Space Center Headquarters

Air Force Space Station

0 km — 10

0 miles — 5

(3)

(A1A)

PORT CANAVERAL

Exploring the Kennedy Space Center

Built in 1967 for astronauts and their families to view space center operations, today the Visitor Complex is host to more than 1.5 million tourists each year. The 131-sq-mile (340-sq-km) facility offers guests a full-day, comprehensive space experience, including excellent IMAX® films at the Visitor Complex, live-action shows, astronaut encounters, and the Apollo/Saturn V Center – the climax of the narrated, video-enhanced bus tour. The go-at-your-own-pace tour enables visitors to stop and explore each of the major destinations. One all-inclusive admission ticket takes visitors on the KSC Tour, both IMAX® space films, and all exhibits.

Kids enjoy the Robot Scouts at the Imax® Theater

VISITOR COMPLEX

The place where everyone heads first is the **IMAX® Theater**, where two back-to-back IMAX® theaters put on stunning films on screens more than five stories high. For some people this is the highlight of their visit.

Top of the bill is *Hubble 3-D* narrated by Leonardo di Caprio. Rarely seen NASA footage, computer-generated images, and live-action renditions of the lunar landscape are featured. The other film on offer at the IMAX® Theater is *Space Station 3-D*, which shows astronauts from Europe and America on board a space station. It provides great footage of those views that only astronauts get

to see. The **NASA Art Gallery**, inside the IMAX® Theater, offers more than 200 artworks by some famous artists, including Andy Warhol, Robert Rauschenberg, and Annie Leibovitz.

Kids will probably prefer to see the latest planetary explorer robots, and learn about their interplanetary adventures as revealed in **Robot Scouts**. The popular **Astronaut Encounter** show takes place in the 300-seat Astronaut Encounter Theater at the Visitor Complex. It offers visitors the rare opportunity of meeting a real NASA astronaut. In the daily 30-minute show, an astronaut tells the story of their

particular space mission and takes part in a question and answer session. **Lunch with an Astronaut** sessions offer visitors the opportunity to enjoy a meal and meet a veteran member of NASA's astronaut corps.

In Shuttle Plaza, guests can climb aboard and enjoy a close-up view of **Explorer** – a replica of the space shuttle – while the home of the retired *Atlantis* shuttle is made ready. The **Mission Status Center** alongside offers live briefings throughout the day on the latest mission details. Nearby, a "Space Mirror" reflects sunlight onto the names inscribed on the **Astronaut Memorial**. This honors the 16 astronauts, from the *Apollo 1* to the Space Shuttle *Columbia* missions, who have died in the service of space exploration. The new **Space Shuttle Launch Experience** gives visitors the opportunity to experience the reality of a launch.

The *Explorer*, a life-size replica of the space shuttle

TIMELINE OF SPACE EXPLORATION

1958 First American satellite, the *Explorer 1,* is launched (Jan 31)	**1962** John Glenn orbits the earth in *Mercury* spacecraft	**1968** *Apollo 8* orbits the moon (Dec 24)	**1977** The Space Shuttle *Enterprise* is tested aboard a Boeing 747 (Feb 18)	
		1975 American *Apollo* and Russian *Soyuz* vehicles dock in orbit (Jul 17)	**1981** *Columbia* is the first shuttle in space (Apr 12)	

John Glenn

1960		**1970**		**1980**
1961 On May 5, Alan Shepherd becomes the first American in space. Kennedy commits nation to moon landing	**1966** *Gemini 8* makes first space docking (Mar 16) **1965** Edward White is the first American to walk in space (Jun 3)	**1969** Neil Armstrong and Buzz Aldrin (*Apollo 11*) walk on the moon (Jul 24)		**1983** The first American woman goes into space, aboard Space Shuttle *Challenger* (Jun 18) **1984** First American woman, Kathryn Sullivan, walks in space (Oct 11)

Buzz Aldrin

KSC EXHIBITS & BUS TOURS

The entrance gate, modeled after the International Space Station, welcomes guests to the Visitor Complex. Once inside the complex, there is a fascinating walk-through exhibit, which shows visitors a comprehensive history of the major missions that provided the foundation for the space program. The all-glass rotunda leads to **Early Space Exploration**, which showcases key figures from the early days of rocketry. In the **Mercury Mission Control Room**, visitors view from an observation deck the actual components and consoles from which the first eight manned missions were monitored. Footage and interviews with some of the personnel are highlights of this area. Next to it are displays of some of the authentic *Mercury* and *Gemini* spacecraft, which enable visitors to relive some of the excitement and intensity of early space

The Vehicle Assembly Building, which dominates the flat landscape

Rockets on display at the Cape Canaveral Air Station

exploration. KSC Tour buses leave every few minutes from the Visitor Complex and offer an exceptional tour of the space center's facilities. The tour encompasses two major facilities at the space center: the LC 39 Observation Gantry and the Apollo/Saturn V Center. The tour takes guests into secured areas, where guides explain the inner workings of each of the facilities. Visitors can take as long as they wish to explore each sight.

There are two additional special-interest tours that visitors can take at the center: **Cape Canaveral: Then & Now Tour**, which is a historic tour of the *Mercury*, *Gemini*, and *Apollo* launch pads; and the **Discover KSC** tour, which provides an insider's view of the entire space shuttle program. The NASA Up Close Tour includes within its ambit the International Space Station Center. Here, guests can walk through and peer inside the facility where each shuttle's components are assembled for launch.

SPACE CENTER TOUR

Each self-guided tour can take anything between two and three hours to fully explore the two facilities on the KSCTour. Visitors can get a spectacular bird's-eye view of the gigantic launch pads from the 60-ft (18-m) observation tower at the first stop, the **LC 39 Observation Gantry**. Back on the ground, a film and a range of exhibits tell the story of a NASA space shuttle launch and landing.

A commemoration of the first moon landing of 1969, the spacious **Apollo/Saturn V Center** features a 363-ft (110-m) Saturn V moon rocket. Guests can watch the historic launch of *Apollo 8*, the first manned mission to the moon, in the Firing Room Theater. They can follow this up by viewing a film at the Lunar Theater, which shows footage of the moon landing and the actual *Apollo 14* command module. The only place in the world where you can dine next to a genuine moon rock is also here: the Moon Rock Café.

1988 *Discovery*, the first shuttle since the *Challenger* disaster, is launched (Sep 29)	**2001** Dennis Tito pays US$20 million for one week on the International Space Station	**2003** Space Shuttle *Columbia* explodes on re-entry into Earth's atmosphere (Feb 1)	
1990 Hubble telescope is launched (Apr 24)	**1996** *Mars Pathfinder* gathers data from Mars		*Space Shuttle* Columbia

1990	2000	2010

1986 The *Challenger* explodes, killing all its crew (Jan 28)	Atlantis–Mir insignia (*Jun 1995*)	**2005** *Discovery*, the first mission since the *Columbia* disaster, arrives home safely after dramatic spacewalk repairs
1995 The *Atlantis* docks with Russian *Mir* space station (Jun 29)		**2011** Shuttle program retired, last flights of *Atlantis* and *Endeavor*

The bright lights of Universal CityWalk® at night ▷

TRAVELERS'
NEEDS

WHERE TO STAY

Logo of the Hard Rock Hotel

With a wide range of available accommodations and more than 115,000 hotel rooms in the area, Orlando caters to every budget and taste. A visitor can choose from neighborhood bed-and-breakfasts, off-the-beaten-track motels, resorts with in-room Jacuzzis and championship golf courses, ultra-luxurious penthouse suites, buildings shaped like giant guitars, and even rooms that overlook wandering herds of zebra and wildebeest. Outdoor enthusiasts, looking forward to sleeping under the stars, can access any of the many campgrounds and trailer parks. If you are planning a long trip or are traveling in a big group, there are plenty of condos available for hire. The listings on pages 138–45 recommend a variety of places in Central Florida, all representing the best of their kind and in all the price ranges, from reasonable to extravagant. However, the prices tend to fluctuate depending on the season and the location. The Orlando/Orange County Convention & Visitors Bureau website can provide more detailed information on rooms and availability.

The opulent interior of the renowned Peabody Hotel, International Drive

HOTELS & RESORTS

Most of the larger hotels and resorts in the area are refurbished and modernized regularly. The smaller hotels, on the other hand, tend to be older and are well-established.

Widely prevalent and extremely popular, chain hotels have the advantage of at least being predictable – although prices vary depending on the location. Every chain is represented, from the high-end Radisson and Marriott hotels through the mid-range Holiday Inns to the budget Days Inn chain.

Resorts are large hotel complexes, usually set by the water and surrounded by acres of immaculately kept grounds. Prices are high, but these resorts provide various amenities, from swimming pools and exercise rooms to shops and a wide range of world-class restaurants to choose from. With their well-equipped games rooms and special children's programs, these resorts can be a good option for families. Golf is a major attraction in Central Florida, and many resorts offer championship-level courses and instructors for private lessons. Themed resorts, designed around a particular era or activity such as sports or the films of the 1950s, are very popular.

Also designed to entertain are the traditional hotels, such as the Sheraton Safari with its African motif, the Red Horse Inn, decked out in Southwestern style, and the Doubletree Castle, with its towering spires and the Renaissance era music.

Only lacking the manicured acreage of the resorts, the grand hotels of Orlando are impressive in all other aspects. The Peabody Hotel, for instance, offers a fully-equipped athletic club with an Olympic-sized pool, tennis courts, and two excellent gourmet restaurants.

Disney's Palm Course, golfing paradise for amateurs and pros

THE THEME PARK EXPERIENCE

When the Disney theme parks set up resorts right on their properties, it opened a whole new world of vacation possibilities (see p133 & pp134–5). With several hotels literally within walking distance of a theme park or the Disney shopping area, the goal is to keep the attractions always in sight of the entertainment-hungry

The hotels mentioned here are listed on pp138–45

The brilliant exterior of the Hard Rock Hotel, Universal Studios

A relaxing massage at the Grand Floridian Resort & Spa

visitor. Special package plans often include entry to the parks and transportation. Several shuttles and water-taxies connecting the parks and hotels are exclusively available for hotel guests.

In case parents equate theme parks with kid stuff, Disney property is also home to five 18-hole, PGA championship courses and training camps for the Atlanta Braves, the Orlando Rays, and the Tampa Bay Buccaneers ballteams. Recreational activities – such as surfing at the famous Typhoon Lagoon water park, golf, tennis, swimming, para-sailing, and horseback riding – are all included and within easy reach of the hotels. Universal Orlando is oriented

more toward older children and adults than Disney. This is reflected in the main attractions of the two theme parks, and the "themes" of the three hotels on Universal property (see p133 & p135). The Jurassic Park rides, The Amazing Adventures of Spider-Man®, Back to the Future… The Ride, and Terminator 2®: 3D are not for the Mickey Mouse-aged crowd. The lure of the Hard Rock Hotel, Portofino Bay, and the Loews Royal Pacific Resort is also mainly adult oriented. However, the hotels do offer family-friendly restaurants, kids' programs, games, toys, and kid-themed rooms. Universal CityWalk®, between the two parks, makes for an entertaining and exciting destination.

SPA HOTELS

Disney is the trendsetter of all things spa in Orlando, and hosts three world-class retreats on its property – the Saratoga Springs Resort & Spa, the Grand Floridian Resort & Spa with 900 rooms on an expansive 40-acre (16-ha) spread, and the 9,000-sq-ft (836-sq-m) Buena Vista Palace Resort & Spa (see p139). Although all these are highly expensive stays compared to traditional hotels, the amenities provided here are difficult to find

anywhere else. Grand Floridian, in particular, offers beauty shops, facial, massage and water therapy, and a white-sand beach for relaxing.

The facilities at Westgate Lakes, just outside the Disney main gate on Lake Buena Vista, are typical of what local spas have to offer – personal attendants, facials, massages, steam rooms and saunas, whirlpools, and a full beauty salon. The Relâche Spa at the Gaylord Palms Resort offers guests use of cardiovascular equipment, haircuts, and manicures along with body wraps and saunas. The internationally-renowned Mandara Spa from Indonesia has recently opened a center at Universal's Portofino Bay Hotel (see p141).

The luxurious Grand Floridian Resort & Spa at Walt Disney World® Resort

The Hyatt Regency Hotel, Orlando International Airport *(see p145)*

PLACES TO STAY AWAY FROM THE CROWDS

Hotels in Downtown Orlando and in smaller suburbs can offer high-end accommodations at much lower prices *(see pp141–5)*. Conveniently located inside the Orlando International Airport, Hyatt Regency is a good choice for travel-weary tourists and is only 16 miles (26 km) from Disney. Visitors using the Orlando-Sanford International Airport have a choice of several three- and four-star hotels in Sanford and Lake Mary. You can be far from the crowds at these hotels, and at the same time, within fairly easy reach of the theme parks. The attractive Park Plaza Hotel, in upscale Winter Park, has "garden suites" and bougainvillea-draped balconies. The Art Deco Grand Bohemian Hotel in Downtown Orlando has 247 rooms as well as a AAA Four Diamond Award-winning restaurant. For lower room rates, try La Quinta Inn.

BED-AND-BREAKFASTS

Travel to the north and east of Orlando for cosy and affordable B&Bs. Old-world hospitality and homes with antique furnishings are on offer here. Thurston House in Maitland is a restored Queen Anne Victorian farmhouse with fruit trees, a wraparound porch to unwind on, and lovely flower gardens. The Courtyard at Lake Lucerne is a group of four historic buildings, built between 1883 and 1945; a quiet oasis in the heart of Downtown

Logo of La Quinta Inn *(see p144)*

Orlando. This romantic getaway is popular with honeymooners. The Adora Inn in rustic Mount Dora describes itself as a boutique B&B *(see p145)*. All B&Bs offer short- and long-term stays, and guests often eat together in an informal atmosphere. The ambience and the personal touch of the hosts usually make up for the absence of the amenities offered by a full-service hotel.

CONDO RENTALS

Renting a condominium is a popular alternative to hotels and resorts. This is specially true for long-term stays or large family groups. One and two bedroom apartments tend to be near the theme parks; the larger homes are farther away.

Weekly apartments, townhouses, and full-size home rentals can cost the same as or less than a medium-rate hotel room. However, the in-house kitchens, private pools, and multiple bedrooms are very convenient and are good value for money. Most places require security deposits in advance, and also ask for cleaning fees. There is usually a minimum stay requirement too. If you wish to cancel your reservation, it is a good idea to notify the owners well in advance as the cancelation fees at most condos are fairly high.

A condo rental in Orlando, set amid lush green gardens

The hotels mentioned here are listed on pp141–45

An elegant dining area setting at an Orlando lodging

HOW TO RESERVE

Rooms at the Disney and the Universal resorts can be booked when you buy the theme park tickets. Tickets can be purchased either by phone or online. The closer it is to the busy season, the harder it might be to book a first-choice room, but rarely are resorts or larger hotels sold out. Online brokers such as **Priceline** and **Travelocity** can usually secure rooms, but many hotels hold back rooms for their telephone or website reservations. If a late check-in is expected, notify the hotel in advance. Many multi-day packages are also available from the theme parks as well as through travel agents.

PRICES & SEASONS

Room rates vary greatly, depending on the season and location. The busiest and most expensive periods are the holidays during November–April and summer vacation (June–August). Most hotels, even the high-priced chains, will often negotiate a lower rate if asked, but won't volunteer it. Be sure to ask for any special rates that might be available for senior citizens, students, frequent flyers, or corporate clients. Many resorts and non-park hotels offer packages that include theme park admissions and free shuttle services. Disney hotels will sometimes upgrade a room at no extra charge during "off-season," if asked.

HIDDEN EXTRAS

Room rates are generally quoted exclusive of both sales tax and the so-called resort tax. These add up to 11.5 percent in Orlando and 13 percent in Kissimmee. The cost of making a phone call from a hotel room can be exorbitant. Some hotels offer free local phone calls from rooms, but most will add a surcharge for local calls or when dialing toll-free numbers. Some hotels also charge for Internet connection. Many hotels charge for valet parking too.

TRAVELING WITH CHILDREN

Most hotels provide cribs, fold-away cots, and other facilities for children. The theme park resorts also offer baby-sitting services, child-friendly rooms, family-friendly dining options, and fun-filled activities. Specially designed guided tours for children include the popular Hidden Mickey tours where kids search eagerly for the concealed Disney icon.

DIRECTORY

THEME PARK HOTELS

Walt Disney World® Resorts
http://disneyworld.disney.go.com/wdw/resorts/resortoverview

Downtown Disney Hotels
www.downtowndisneyhotels.com

Universal Orlando® Resorts
www.UniversalOrlando.com

HOTEL RENTALS

Expedia
www.expedia.com

Hotels.com
www.hotels.com

Orlando Hotels
www.orlandohotels.com

Travelocity
www.travelocity.com

Hotwire.com
www.hotwire.com

Priceline
www.priceline.com

BED-AND-BREAKFASTS

AAA Auto Club South
www.aaasouth.com

Florida Bed & Breakfasts Inns
www.florida-inns.com

Bed & Breakfasts Online
www.bbonline.com/fl/orlando.html

CONDO & APARTMENT RENTALS

Villas of the World
www.villasoftheworld.com

Homeaway
www.homeaway.com

Florida Homes & Condos
www.disneycondo.com

A deluxe children's suite; a popular choice at many resort hotels

Staying at the Theme Parks

When Walt Disney started buying untouched Florida wilderness in the late 1960s, he began a multi-billion dollar industry that would change the culture of sleepy citrus town Orlando forever. Currently, the area in and around the theme parks has several thousands of hotel, motel, and resort rooms – and many more are being created – for the never-ending stream of tourists flocking each year to Disney World, Universal Orlando, and SeaWorld. The descriptions on these pages highlight accommodations on theme park property or those located nearby.

Visitor enjoying the slide at Port Orleans Resort *(see p139)*

A giant replica of Woody at All-Star Movies Resort *(see p139)*

WALT DISNEY WORLD® RESORTS

Disney property has the largest collection of resorts in Orlando, with offerings to suit every pocket and taste *(see p133 & pp138–40)*.

The opening of Walt Disney World's Pop Century Resort in 2003 – with 2,880 rooms – was the largest single hotel opening in Disney's history. It joined the ranks of the 23 resort hotels directly owned by the parks. Dedicated to American fashions and fads, Pop Century features icons and relics from the 1950s to the 1990s, such as a larger-than-life Rubik's Cube and Sony Walkman, as well as giant bowling pins and yo-yos. All-Star Resorts, the triple-treat of movie, sports, and music-themed hotels, are the least expensive of all on-site lodgings.

The Animal Kingdom Lodge is advantageously located on the western edge of Disney's Animal Kingdom® theme park. Many of its 1,293 rooms include balconies overlooking three savannas, and provide breath-taking views of more than 200 grazing animals and birds, including giraffes, zebra, ibis, and ostriches. Guest rooms include a Royal Suite, with a domed ceiling, a kitchen and a dining room, and sweeping porches. The resort is also host to several of the best restaurants on Disney property.

The two massive hotels that make up the Swan and Dolphin resorts offer almost 2,270 rooms, including 191 special suites themed to Italian, Egyptian, Japanese, and Southwest decor.

Disney's Port Orleans Resort echoes the majestic mansions and row houses of romantic Louisiana. The Beach Club Resort transports Nantucket Bay to Orlando with access to the 25-acre (10-ha) Crescent Lake facility, where canopy and paddleboats are available, as well as the Stormalong Bay water park for the kids.

HOTELS AT WALT DISNEY WORLD® RESORT

Downtown Disney® hosts excellent hotels on its property *(see pp138–9)*. Those closest to most of the attractions include Best Western Lake Buena Vista, literally a brisk walk from the Downtown Disney® shopping and entertainment area; Hilton, which offers "Extra Magic Hour," which allows guests staying at the hotel to enter the Disney theme parks one hour prior to the general opening; Doubletree Guest

Rooms overlook wild animals grazing at Animal Kingdom Lodge *(see p138)*

The hotels mentioned here are listed on pp138–45

The family-friendly Nickelodeon Family Suites, Lake Buena Vista (see p145)

Suites, with on-site ticket sales and free shuttles to the parks; Holiday Inn, a 323-room hotel featuring a 14-story atrium; Hotel Royal Plaza, with tennis courts and spa; Wyndham Palace, featuring the award-winning Arthur's 27 restaurant and Disney character breakfasts; and last but not the least, Regal Sun Resort, a British-themed complex which offers transport to the parks. The 626-room Regal Sun is heavily steeped in Florida amenities, including Disney character meals for the kids and a huge Aquatic Center with heated swimming pools in lush landscaping, water cannons, a thermal spa, and beach volleyball. Each hotel has at least one full-service restaurant.

UNIVERSAL ORLANDO® RESORTS & HOTELS

Hotels on Universal grounds are located along the perimeter of the two parks – the Islands of Adventure and Universal Studios Florida®. The Loews Royal Pacific takes its cue from a tropical island paradise, offering a lagoon-style swimming pool and sandy beach on which to relax, transportation by water taxi to the parks, and an orchid-draped courtyard. There are also five restaurants, including Emeril's Hawaiian-inspired Tchoup Chop. The Loews Portofino Bay Hotel is a faithful recreation of a traditional seaside resort in Italy, with cobble streets and outdoor cafés, bocce ball courts, and a full spa and fitness center.

The hotel's restaurants offer Italian cuisine, from upscale Bice, which had its beginnings in Milan in 1926 and features Old-World elegance, to Trattoria del Porto, which offers diverse regional cuisine and a poolside pizzeria. For those with rock star dreams, the Hard Rock Hotel features rock memorabilia in every room, an "exclusive" seventh-floor Club level with a lounge and music library, and an under-water audio system in the pool. The hotel's Graceland Suite, a tribute to Elvis, is of gigantic proportions.

All these three hotels are pet-friendly, with special rooms and a room-service menu for four-legged guests.

The Universal Express service, offered by all the hotels, allows guests access to all the park rides without having to wait in long lines.

HOTELS & MOTELS NEAR THE PARKS

Most places to stay form concentric rings around both Disney and Universal, diminishing in price the farther away they get from Main Street. But some of the most affordable hotels are just beyond the front door of the parks. The two Hyatt hotels, with rooms at less than a third of the price at the Hard Rock Hotel, are under a mile (1.6 km) from Universal. The Caribe Royale All-Suites Resort, virtually right outside Disney's doors, and with 1,200 rooms and 120 villas, manages to be less expensive than many of the resorts on Disney property.

Bargains can be found within sight of the parks, many offering amenities such as pools and restaurants. There are thousands of hotels in the area. Sand Lake Road, north of Interstate 4, has several miles of motels and hotels of all ranges, many offering free shuttles to the parks and concierge service for tickets to other attractions. To the south of I-4 is International Drive, a long stretch of commercial properties and outlet malls, with places to stay that range from seedy no-name motels to five-star resorts. To the north and east are the grand hotels of Downtown Orlando and smaller motel chains on Colonial Drive.

Loews Portofino Bay Hotel (see p141), a replica of an Italian seaside resort

Camping & RV Parks

Those with an outdoor spirit and the desire to sleep under the stars can find accommodations in Central Florida that range from a tent in the woods to modern, almost luxurious RV camps, complete with swimming pools and clubhouses. Visitors can choose from a wide range of campsites – on state land and private Kampgrounds of America (KOA) parks, and even right on Disney property. Depending on the season, pitching a tent can be fairly inexpensive or can cost as much as a good hotel. RV parks can help tourists on a tight budget save thousands of dollars. In fact, many regular visitors reserve special spots in these parks for years.

Campers picnicking at Disney's Fort Wilderness Resort & Campground

CAMPING

Offering the finest campsite amenities, Disney World stakes out 700 camping spaces at the **Fort Wilderness Resort & Campground** *(see p73)*, with sites ranging from spartan to luxurious. This pet-friendly resort offers charcoal grills,

Boating in scenic heaven, Wekiwa Springs State Park

electric golf carts, cable TV hook-ups, and campfire singalongs. Prices here range from $40 to $80 per night; cabins start at $265.

Other camping sites also have cabins, priced from $30 to $70 depending on season, which can sleep four to eight people. Many of the Disney-centric campgrounds are located just off US Route 192 in Kissimmee.

Campsites are to be found all across Central Florida. **East Lake Fish Camp** in Kissimmee combines outdoor living with Florida's freshwater bounty, offering some of the best bass fishing in the world.

Of all local campgrounds, **Wekiwa Springs State Park** is the most rustic, and most typical of authentic Florida. Open year-round, it is located on the Wekiva River, with 8,000 acres (3,237 ha) of wild scenery that has remained unchanged for centuries.

RV PARKS

RV camps are very popular with cross-country travelers, especially visitors from the far North. Most camps offer all the amenities of resort living, including pools and fitness centers, clubhouses and movie theaters, laundry facilities, cable television and electrical hook-ups, as well as the splendor of the great Florida outdoors. RV site rates vary and can range from $30 a night to more than $1,000 per month. Permanent spots are available for those who choose to return every year.

Just 5 miles (8 km) from Disney is the largest RV and trailer park in the area, the **Encore RV Resort**. Located in Clermont, it is host to 467 sites with electrical, water, and sewage hook-ups, two heated pools, a fitness center with a Jacuzzi, shuffleboard courts, tennis courts, laundry, cable TV and telephone services, and social activities such as bingo and dances.

KOA Kissimmee/Orlando is Orlando's nearest KOA Campground. It is just 5 miles (8 km) from Disney, 6 miles (9.6 km) from SeaWorld®, and 8 miles (13 km) from Universal. Patio sites with picnic tables are available, as is wireless Internet connection.

The **Tropical Palms Resort** in Kissimmee offers campers access to swimming pools, private cottages with air conditioning and kitchens, watercraft rentals, picnic areas, and nearby restaurants.

Picturesque cabins at Orlando SW/ Fort Summit KOA Campground

DIRECTORY

RV & CAMPING INFORMATION

Florida Association of RV Parks and Campgrounds
1340 Vickers Rd,
Tallahassee.
Tel (850) 562-7151.
www.campflorida.com

Florida Department of Environmental Protection (State Parks)
3900 Commonwealth Blvd, Tallahassee.
Tel (850) 245-2157.
www.dep.state.fl.us/parks

KOA Campgrounds
Tel (800) 562-7791.
www.koa.com

Passport America
Tel (1-800) 681-6810.
www.passportamerica.com

RV on the Go
2650 Holiday Trail,
Kissimmee.
Tel (877) 362-6736.
www.rvonthego.com

CAMPSITES

Canoe Creek Campground
4101 Canoe Creek Rd,
St. Cloud.
Tel (407) 892-7010.

Cypress Cove Nudist Resort & Spa
4425 S Pleasant Hills Rd,
Kissimmee.
Tel (888) 683-3140.
www.cypresscoveresort.com

East Lake Fish Camp
3705 Big Bass Rd,
Kissimmee.
Tel (407) 348-2040.

Elite Resorts Campground
2500 US Hwy 27 S,
Clermont.
Tel (352) 432-5932.

Fort Wilderness Resort & Campground
4510 N Fort Wilderness Trail,
Lake Buena Vista,
Orlando.
Tel (407) 824-2900.

KOA Kissimmee/Orlando Campground
2644 Happy Camper Place,
Kissimmee.
Tel (407) 396-2400.

Orange Blossom RV Resort LLC
3800 W Orange Blossom Trail,
Apopka.
Tel (407) 886-3260.

Orange Grove Campground
2425 Old Vineland Rd,
Kissimmee.
Tel (407) 396-6655.

Orlando Lake Whippoorwill KOA
12345 Narcoossee Rd,
Orlando.
Tel (407) 277-5075.

Orlando SW/Fort Summit KOA
2525 Frontage Rd,
Davenport.
Tel (800) 424-1880.

Orlando Winter Garden Campground
13905 W. Colonial Dr,
Winter Garden.
Tel (407) 656-1415.

Southport Park Campground & Marina
2001 W Southport Rd,
Kissimmee.
Tel (407) 933-5822.

Stage Stop Campground
14400 W Colonial Dr,
Winter Garden.
Tel (407) 656-8000.

Tropical Palms Resort
2650 Holiday Trail,
Kissimmee.
Tel (407) 396-4595.

Twelve Oaks RV Resort
6300 State Route 46,
W Sanford.
Tel (800) 633-9529.

Wekiwa Springs State Park
1800 Wekiwa Circle,
Apopka.
Tel (407) 884-2008.

RV PARKS

Aloha RV Park
4648 S Orange Blossom Trail,
Kissimmee.
Tel (407) 933-5730.

Encore RV Resort
9600 Hwy 192,
West Clermont.
Tel (888) 558-5777.

Fairview Mobile Court
4462 Edgewater Dr,
Orlando.
Tel (407) 293-8581.

Floridian RV Resort
5150 Boggy Creek Rd,
St. Cloud.
Tel (407) 892-5171.

Great Oak RV Resort
4440 Yowell Rd,
Kissimmee.
Tel (407) 396-9092.

Merry D RV Sanctuary
4261 Pleasant Hill Rd,
Kissimmee.
Tel (407) 870-0719.

Orange City RV
2300 E Graves Ave,
Orange City.
Tel (800) 545-7354.

Paradise Island RV Resort
32000 S US Hwy 27,
Haines City.
Tel (863) 439-1350.

Ponderosa RV Park
1983 Boggy Creek Rd,
Kissimmee.
Tel (407) 847-6002.

Sanlan RV Park
3929 US Hwy 98 S,
Lakeland.
Tel (800) 524-5044.

Sherwood Forest RV Park
5300 W Irlo Bronson Hwy,
Kissimmee.
Tel (407) 396-7431.

Southern Palms RV Resort
1 Avocado Lane,
Eustis.
Tel (352) 357-8882.

Sun Resort RV Park
3000 Clarcona Rd #99,
Apopka.
Tel (407) 889-3048.

Choosing a Hotel

The hotels in this guide have been selected across a wide price range for their good value, facilities, and location. These listings highlight some of the factors that may influence your choice. Hotels are listed by area, beginning with the Walt Disney World Resort. All entries are listed alphabetically within each price category.

PRICE CATEGORIES
Price categories for a standard double room per night in high season, including tax and service charges.

- [$] under $100
- [$][$] $100–$150
- [$][$][$] $150–$200
- [$][$][$][$] $200–$250
- [$][$][$][$][$] over $250

WALT DISNEY WORLD® RESORT

ANIMAL KINGDOM® Disney's All-Star Movies Resort [$][$]

1901 W. Buena Vista Dr., 32830 **Tel** *(407) 939-7000* **Fax** *(407) 939-7111* **Rooms** *1,920*

Larger than life characters straight out of Disney's most popular movies tower over guests in every nook and cranny. Among these are favourites from *Toy Story*, *101 Dalmatians*, *The Love Bug*, *Fantasia*, and *The Mighty Ducks*. Rooms are smaller than most but the price is right for those on a budget. **www.disneyworld.com**

ANIMAL KINGDOM® Disney's All-Star Music Resort [$][$]

1801 W. Buena Vista Dr., 32830 **Tel** *(407) 939-6000* **Fax** *(407) 939-7222* **Rooms** *1,604*

The theme is obvious from the walk-through jukebox and the variety of gigantic musical instruments that adorn the resort's many buildings. Calypso, country, and classical music can often be heard in the background. Rooms are small and basic, but the resort offers the benefits of staying at Disney on a budget. **www.disneyworld.com**

ANIMAL KINGDOM® Disney's All-Star Sports Resort [$][$]

1701 W. Buena Vista Dr., 32830 **Tel** *(407) 939-5000* **Fax** *(407) 939-7333* **Rooms** *1,920*

Sports fans will appreciate the oversized sporting equipment both inside and outside the buildings. There are reminders of baseball, basketball, football, tennis, and surfing everywhere. The amenities and rooms are basic, but this is one of only four budget-conscious Disney resorts. **www.disneyworld.com**

ANIMAL KINGDOM® Disney's Pop Century Resort [$][$]

1050 Century Dr., 32830 **Tel** *(407) 938-4000* **Fax** *(407) 938-4040* **Rooms** *2,880*

One of Disney's four "value" resorts, this homage to pop culture is as popular with adults as children. Giant icons represent each of the decades from the 1950s to the 1990s. A giant Walkman, Rubik's cube, flower power daisies, and cell phone are just a sample of what adorns the grounds. **www.disneyworld.com**

ANIMAL KINGDOM® Disney's Coronado Springs Resort [$][$][$]

1000 W. Buena Vista Blvd., 32830 **Tel** *(407) 939-1000* **Fax** *(407) 939-1001* **Rooms** *1,921*

Themes of the American southwest and Mexico are apparent throughout the resort's three distinctive villages of Casitas, Ranchos, and Cabanas. Landscaped plazas and courtyards, an open market-style restaurant, colorful stucco architecture, and a five-story Mayan pyramid further enhance the experience. **www.disneyworld.com**

ANIMAL KINGDOM® Disney's Animal Kingdom Lodge [$][$][$][$]

2901 Osceola Pkwy., 32830 **Tel** *(407) 938-3000* **Fax** *(407) 938-4799* **Rooms** *1,293*

A stay here feels as if you are on a thrilling African game reserve. The impressive glass wall in the lobby overlooks a vast savanna that allows for random sightings of birds, giraffe, and other wildlife. The authentic design, amazingly ornate chandeliers, and high suspension bridge all contribute to the stunning surroundings. **www.disneyworld.com**

DOWNTOWN DISNEY® Best Western Lake Buena Vista [$]

2000 Hotel Plaza Blvd., 32830 **Tel** *(407) 828-2424* **Fax** *(407) 827-6390* **Rooms** *318*

Amidst the collection of "unofficial" Disney resorts along the beautiful tree-lined boulevard is the Best Western. Rooms have private balconies, many offering views of Disney, and there are lushly landscaped grounds. Downtown Disney, with its array of shops, restaurants, and entertainment venues, is close by. **www.orlandofunspots.com**

DOWNTOWN DISNEY® Hilton at the Walt Disney World Resort [$][$]

1751 Hotel Plaza Blvd., 32830 **Tel** *(407) 827-4000* **Fax** *(407) 827-3890* **Rooms** *814*

Popular with both families and business travelers, this resort has a nautical New England theme that is evident in the lobby area with its restaurants, shops, and small market. The decor in the rooms has a modern shaker motif. Two pools, landscaped grounds, and a great location add to the appeal. **www.hilton.com**

DOWNTOWN DISNEY® Hotel Royal Plaza [$][$]

1905 Hotel Plaza Blvd., 32830 **Tel** *(407) 828-2828* **Fax** *(407) 827-3977* **Rooms** *394*

A beautiful interior, spacious well-appointed rooms with French doors separating the living and sleeping areas, and a location close to Disney set this resort apart. One of the oldest resorts around, it offers reasonable rates, exceptional service, and very pleasant decor. **www.royalplaza.com**

Key to Symbols *see back cover flap*

DOWNTOWN DISNEY® Regal Sun Resort $$

1850 Hotel Plaza Blvd., 32830 **Tel** *(407) 828-4444* **Fax** *(407) 828-8192* **Rooms** *626*

An official Walt Disney World® Resort hotel, the Regal Sun provides good value in a great location. The lobby features colonial decor, while outside there are tennis courts. There is a continuous shuttle service to all the Disney theme parks, and guests can have breakfast with Disney characters three days a week. **www.regalsunresort.com**

DOWNTOWN DISNEY® Disney's Port Orleans Resort; French Quarter $$$

2201 Orleans Dr., 32830 **Tel** *(407) 934-5000* **Fax** *(407) 934-5353* **Rooms** *1,008*

A Disney recreation of New Orleans' famous French Quarter, with intricate wrought iron railings, cobblestone walkways, and garden-style courtyards, this resort has a Mardi Gras atmosphere. Children will appreciate the giant sea serpent waterslide, alligator fountains, and extensive recreational activities. **www.disneyworld.com**

DOWNTOWN DISNEY® Disney's Port Orleans Resort; Riverside $$$

1251 Riverside Dr., 32830 **Tel** *(407) 934-6000* **Fax** *(407) 934-5777* **Rooms** *2,048*

This antebellum, Southern-style resort has two distinctive areas alongside a picturesque Mississippi-style waterway. Magnolia Bend features elegant Dixie mansions set among gardens, while Alligator Bayou has Spanish moss draped from gigantic trees, a swimming hole, and rope swings to give rustic appeal. **www.disneyworld.com**

DOWNTOWN DISNEY® Doubletree Guest Suites $$$

2305 Hotel Plaza Blvd., 32830 **Tel** *(407) 934-1000* **Fax** *(407) 934-1015* **Rooms** *229*

This family-friendly resort boasts a pint-sized children's theater, bird aviary, and colorful murals which adorn the lobby. Rooms are large and offer the comforts and conveniences of home. Upon check-in, guests are given a sample of the famous Doubletree chocolate chip cookies. **www.doubletree.com**

DOWNTOWN DISNEY® Buena Vista Palace Resort & Spa $$$$

1900 Buena Vista Dr., 32830 **Tel** *(407) 827-2727* **Fax** *(407) 827-6034* **Rooms** *1,015*

Just a walk across the roadway to Downtown Disney®, this upscale resort provides great views of Disney's evening fireworks from its upper floors and has one of the best restaurants in Orlando. Most of its recreational activities, including the pools, are on a small private inner island. **www.buenavistapalace.com**

DOWNTOWN DISNEY® Disney's Old Key West Resort $$$$$

1510 N. Cove Rd., 32830 **Tel** *(407) 827-7700* **Fax** *(407) 827-7710* **Rooms** *761*

Spread over several acres, this remarkable recreation of Key West is one of Disney's most popular resorts. Palm trees and pastel villas with picket fences are scattered throughout. The recreational facilities, guest services, and amenities are extensive, and the atmosphere is relaxing and welcoming. **www.disneyworld.com**

DOWNTOWN DISNEY® Disney's Saratoga Springs Resort & Spa $$$$$

1960 Broadway, 32830 **Tel** *(407) 827-1100* **Fax** *(407) 827-4444* **Rooms** *840*

This luxurious resort features Victorian cottages in a village setting with sprawling grounds, gardens, hills, and gurgling springs. Relaxation and rejuvenation are the top activities here, with a full-service spa, skin therapy programs, and soothing body treatments on offer. **www.disneyworld.com**

EPCOT® Disney's Caribbean Beach Resort $$$

900 Cayman Way, 32830 **Tel** *(407) 934-3400* **Fax** *(407) 934-3288* **Rooms** *2,112*

Six distinctive "villages", with six different Caribbean islands as their theme, comprise this inviting resort. Playgrounds and a Spanish fortress-themed pool, sandy beaches, a pool in each village, and an abundance of recreational activities will keep everyone busy while allowing for a relaxed atmosphere. **www.disneyworld.com**

EPCOT® Disney's Beach Club Resort $$$$$

1800 Epcot Resorts Blvd., 32830 **Tel** *(407) 934-7000* **Fax** *(407) 934-3450* **Rooms** *583*

Echoing the style of the New England beach cottages of the 1800s, this casually elegant resort features a lengthy list of recreational facilities and restaurants that it shares with its more refined neighbor, the Yacht Club Resort. White wicker furnishings help to create a comfortable yet upscale atmosphere. **www.disneyworld.com**

EPCOT® Disney's Beach Club Villas $$$$$

1800 Epcot Resorts Blvd., 32830 **Tel** *(407) 934-7000* **Fax** *(407) 934-3450* **Rooms** *282*

This resort, whose seaside theme is evident in its brightly painted architecture, shares restaurants and recreational facilities with both the Beach Club and Yacht Club Resorts. Spacious rooms and the convenience of fully equipped kitchens make this the perfect choice for large families or groups. **www.disneyworld.com**

EPCOT® Disney's Yacht Club Resort $$$$$

1700 Epcot Resorts Blvd., 32830 **Tel** *(407) 934-7000* **Fax** *(407) 934-3450* **Rooms** *630*

A short walk from Epcot®, this upscale resort, styled and decorated to resemble a Cape Cod yacht club, shares a wide range of facilities with its more casual neighbor, the Beach Club Resort. An extensive sand-bottom lagoon pool area, sandy beach, shipwreck, and lighthouse complete the picture. **www.disneyworld.com**

EPCOT® Walt Disney World Dolphin $$$$$

1500 Epcot Resorts Blvd., 32830 **Tel** *(407) 934-4000* **Fax** *(407) 934-4884* **Rooms** *1,509*

Home to Tod English's BlueZoo restaurant, a must no matter where you stay, this whimsical resort is best known for the tremendous dolphins that sit atop its exterior. It is only a water taxi ride from Epcot®, which adds to the already lengthy list of dining choices. A full service spa is available. **www.swandolphin.com**

EPCOT® Walt Disney World Swan $$$$$

1200 Epcot Resorts Blvd., 32830 **Tel** *(407) 934-3000* **Fax** *(407) 934-4884* **Rooms** *756*

Like its neighbor, the Dolphin, this resort is whimsical, with giant swans adorning its exterior. A covered walkway connects it to the Dolphin, with which it shares many facilities, including the sandy beach, playgrounds, and pool. The resort caters to business travelers and families alike. **www.swandolphin.com**

MAGIC KINGDOM® Disney's Fort Wilderness Resort & Campground $$

4510 N. Fort Wilderness Tr., 32830 **Tel** *(407) 824-2900* **Fax** *(407) 824-3508* **Rooms** *784 campsites, 408 cabins*

For a more "back to nature" experience, campsites and cabins are scattered throughout a heavily wooded area. The cabins themselves are, however, full of creature comforts. Recreational activities are extensive and often unique to the resort, and also on offer is Disney's best, and most popular, dinner show. **www.disneyworld.com**

MAGIC KINGDOM® Disney's Contemporary Resort $$$$$

4600 N. World Drive, 32830 **Tel** *(407) 824-1000* **Fax** *(407) 824-3539* **Rooms** *1,008*

The monorail passes right through the middle of this concrete resort. The decor is ultra chic and reflects retro-Asian flair. It is moments to the Magic Kingdom® by rail or by foot, and upper-level rooms offer a great view of the park and the evening fireworks. **www.disneyworld.com**

MAGIC KINGDOM® Disney's Grand Floridian Resort & Spa $$$$$

4401 Grand Floridian Way, 32830 **Tel** *(407) 824-3000* **Fax** *(407) 824-3186* **Rooms** *867*

This opulent Victorian-style resort features a magnificent five-story lobby topped by an ornate stained-glass dome. High tea is served daily, and a band often plays 1940s music. The beautifully appointed rooms all offer views of the meticulously maintained grounds. The facilities, services, and amenities are extensive. **www.disneyworld.com**

MAGIC KINGDOM® Disney's Polynesian Resort $$$$$

1600 Seven Seas Dr., 32830 **Tel** *(407) 824-2000* **Fax** *(407) 824-3174* **Rooms** *847*

Lush tropical gardens and waterfalls, a white sand beach, and a lagoon swimming pool with a steaming volcano and torch-lit walkways create the illusion of an island paradise, located on the Magic Kingdom monorail. Furnishings and decor in all the guestrooms are contemporary. **www.disneyworld.com**

MAGIC KINGDOM® Disney's Wilderness Lodge $$$$$

901 W. Timberline Dr., 32830 **Tel** *(407) 824-3200* **Fax** *(407) 823-3232* **Rooms** *765*

The setting resembles that of the great national parks of the Northwest, with towering pines, a spewing geyser, and rough rocky terrain surrounding a spectacular pool. This rustic, though very upscale, lodge features a spectacular stories-high lobby with authentic twin totem poles. Artist Point restaurant is a must. **www.disneyworld.com**

MAGIC KINGDOM® The Villas at Disney's Wilderness Lodge $$$$$

901 W. Timberline Dr., 32830 **Tel** *(407) 824-3200* **Fax** *(407) 823-3232* **Rooms** *181*

Sharing all the facilities of Wilderness Lodge, the villas here are roomy enough for larger groups or families and have either kitchenettes or full kitchens. They also offer forest views and a cabin-style decor. The grand antler chandelier in the lobby is most impressive as are the decor and attention to detail throughout. **www.disneyworld.com**

OTHER THEME PARKS

SEAWORLD® Hilton Garden Inn Orlando SeaWorld $$

6850 Westwood Blvd., 32821 **Tel** *(407) 354-1500* **Fax** *(407) 354-1528* **Rooms** *233*

Large rooms with conveniences such as a fridge and microwave make this a good choice for those seeking comfortable surroundings without too many extras. The pool is small but adequate, and a trolley service transports guests to International Drive's many restaurants and shops. **www.hiltongardeninn.hilton.com**

SEAWORLD® Residence Inn SeaWorld International Center $$

11000 Westwood Blvd., 32821 **Tel** *(407) 313-3600* **Fax** *(407) 313-3611* **Rooms** *350*

Set back from International Drive, yet still close to its many offerings, this casual large-scale resort offers full kitchens in every one-, two-, or three-bedroom suite; free high-speed Internet access; and a complimentary hot breakfast buffet. Palm trees are scattered around the large pool and recreational areas. **www.residenceinnseaworld.com**

SEAWORLD® Renaissance Orlando Hotel at SeaWorld $$$

6677 Sea Harbor Dr., 32821 **Tel** *(407) 351-5555* **Fax** *(407) 351-9991* **Rooms** *778*

An impressive, upscale resort. In the ten-story glass-topped lobby, the ornate aviary and cascading waterfalls ensure that guests take notice of the beautiful surroundings. Rooms are impeccably decorated, combining function and beauty. **www.renaissanceseaworld.com**

UNIVERSAL ORLANDO® Hard Rock Hotel $$$$$

5800 Universal Blvd., 32819 **Tel** *(407) 503-2000* **Fax** *(407) 503-2010* **Rooms** *750*

Mission-style architecture, an impressive collection of musical memorabilia, and an underwater sound system built into the impressive pool make this the hippest of Universal's luxury resorts. The perks of staying on-site if you are heading for the Universal parks are worth investigating, and they have great wedding facilities. **www.hardrockhotelorlando.com**

Key to Price Guide *see p138* **Key to Symbols** *see back cover flap*

UNIVERSAL ORLANDO® Loews Portofino Bay Hotel   🔲 🚻 ♨ 🏃 📺 $$$$$
5601 Universal Blvd., 32819 **Tel** *(888) 430-4999, (407) 503-1000* **Fax** *(407) 503-1,010* **Rooms** *650*

The charm and ambience of the Italian seaside village of Portofino have been meticulously re-created at this lavish resort. Luxurious surroundings await guests both inside and out. There are five restaurants, extensive recreational facilities, a full-service spa, and a water taxi to transport guests to Universal's parks. **www.loewshotels.com**

UNIVERSAL ORLANDO® Loews Royal Pacific Resort at Universal   🔲 🚻 ♨ 🏃 📺 $$$$$
6300 Hollywood Way, 32819 **Tel** *(407) 503-3000* **Fax** *(407) 503-3010* **Rooms** *1,000*

Guests at this resort are stranded on a breathtaking Pacific island paradise, with a lagoon-style pool and play area, Emeril's Tchop Chop restaurant (a must for adults), and superior service. The densely landscaped grounds are worth a tour even if you do not choose to stay here. **www.loewshotels.com**

ORLANDO & CENTRAL FLORIDA

CAPE CANAVERAL Radisson Resort at the Port   🔲 🚻 ♨ 🏃 📺 $$
8701 Astronaut Blvd., 32920 **Tel** *(321) 784-0000* **Fax** *(321) 784-3737* **Rooms** *284*

While not directly on the beach, the resort is not too far away. The suites feature French doors, some have whirlpools, and all have kitchen facilities. Standard rooms are more basic but still pleasant. The tropically landscaped pool area is inviting, and the view of the port and its cruise ships unique. **www.radisson.com/capecanaveralfl**

CAPE CANAVERAL Residence Inn Port Canaveral   🔲 🚻 ♨ 🏃 📺 $$$
8959 Astronaut Blvd., 32920 **Tel** *(321) 323-1100* **Fax** *(321) 323-1029* **Rooms** *150*

This home away from home provides spacious suites with one, two, or three bedrooms and a fully-equipped kitchen; landscaped grounds; and beautiful beachside surroundings. Kennedy Space Center is a short drive away and the best surfing on the east coast is right outside your door. **www.marriott.com**

CAPE CANAVERAL Ron Jon Cape Caribe Resort   🔲 🚻 ♨ 🏃 📺 $$$
1000 Shorewood Dr., 32920 **Tel** *(321) 799-4900* **Fax** *(321) 784-3949* **Rooms** *206*

Even with pristine beaches a short walk away, guests will find the extensive waterpark with pools, river, waterslide, and fountains a fun way to cool off. Mini golf, tennis, basketball, a children's play center, and a movie theater are all available on-site. The comfortable villas can accommodate up to 12. **www.ronjonresort.com**

CELEBRATION Bohemian Hotel Celebration   🔲 🚻 ♨ 📺 $$$
700 Bloom Street, 34747 **Tel** *(407) 566-6000* **Fax** *(407) 566-1844* **Rooms** *115*

In a picture-perfect town, this three-story wooden-framed hotel is straight out of 1920s Florida. The beautiful rooms offer great views of the artificial lake. The atmosphere is romantic, the restaurant elegant, and the entire experience unique. Smart boutiques and restaurants line nearby Market Street. **www.celebrationhotel.com**

COCOA BEACH Comfort Inn & Suites Hotel & Convention Center   🔲 ♨ 🏃 📺 $$
3901 N. Atlantic Ave., 32931 **Tel** *(321) 783-2221* **Fax** *(321) 783-0461* **Rooms** *170*

Close to the beach and a short drive to top attractions such as the Kennedy Space Center, this is a casual and friendly hotel. The large pool area is lined with palm trees and plenty of lounge chairs, perfect for soaking up the Florida sun. Accommodation ranges from standard rooms to multi-room suites. **www.cocoabeachportcanaveralhotel.com**

COCOA BEACH Holiday Inn Express & Suites   🔲 ♨ 🏃 📺 $$
5575 N. Atlantic Ave., 32931 **Tel** *(321) 868-2525* **Fax** *(321) 868-3602* **Rooms** *60*

A wide variety of accommodation, including family suites, kidsuites, and standard rooms, is available here. So, too, is a rather unique pool, which is open to the outdoors yet protected by a roof, making it easy to swim, relax, and enjoy the Florida sunshine without worrying too much about getting sunburnt. **www.hiexpress.com**

COCOA BEACH La Quinta Inn Cocoa Beach   🔲 🚻 ♨ 🏃 📺 $$
1275 N. Atlantic Ave., 32931 **Tel** *(321) 783-2252* **Fax** *(321) 323-5045* **Rooms** *127*

Good-sized rooms provide plenty of space to relax at La Quinta. A mini fridge, free high-speed Internet access, and a 100 per cent satisfaction guarantee are all included in the very reasonable rates. Several restaurants are within walking distance, as are two major surfing retailers for those in need of swim or surf gear. **www.lq.com**

COCOA BEACH International Palms Resort   🚻 ♨ 🏃 📺 $$$
1300 N. Atlantic Ave., 32931 **Tel** *(321) 783-2271* **Fax** *(321) 783-4486* **Rooms** *500*

In this ideal place for families, the accommodation includes kidsuites, villas, and loft rooms sleeping up to six. There is an extensive array of recreational activities scattered throughout the tropically landscaped grounds, as well as direct access to the beach and a pirate-themed pool and play area. **www.internationalpalms.com/cocoabeach**

CYPRESS GARDENS/ WINTER HAVEN Best Western Park View Hotel   🔲 🚻 ♨ 🏃 📺 $$
5665 Cypress Gardens Blvd., 33884 **Tel** *(863) 324-5950* **Fax** *(863) 324-2376* **Rooms** *174*

The attractions of LEGOLAND® are just steps away. The rooms, while not particularly lavish, are comfortable, and there is a mini-golf course, as well as a pool. After eating in one of the two restaurants, guests can dance the night away in the hotel lounge. **www.bestwestern.com**

DAYTONA BEACH Bahama House ⬛🏊🚶🍴 $$$
2001 S. Atlantic Ave., 32118 **Tel** *(386) 248-2001* **Fax** *(386) 248-0991* **Rooms** *95*

Located right on the beach, this friendly Bahamas-themed hotel offers seven large room layouts to choose from. The decor features bleached-wood furnishings, and most rooms have kitchen facilities. Some have Jacuzzis. Planned recreational activities include scavenger hunts, pool games, and movies. **www.daytonabahamahouse.com**

DOWNTOWN ORLANDO The Courtyard at Lake Lucerne $$
211 N. Lucerne Circle East, 32801 **Tel** *(407) 648-5188* **Fax** *(407) 246-1368* **Rooms** *29*

Four historic homes, including the oldest in Orlando, are meticulously maintained. Each is decorated in period with authentic antiques, and both the 19th-century Victorian and 1940s Art Deco styles are represented. Winding walkways and a beautifully landscaped central courtyard add to the ambience. **www.orlandohistoricinn.com**

DOWNTOWN ORLANDO EO Inn & Urban Spa ⬛🍴🍴 $$
227 N. Eola Dr., 32801 **Tel** *(407) 481-8485* **Fax** *(407) 481-8495* **Rooms** *17*

Upscale, chic, and luxurious, the Urban Spa features smart rooms as well as a day spa. The inn also plays host to the trendy Panera Café. Views of Lake Eola are stunning. Downtown Orlando is once again becoming a hot spot for adults seeking to escape the family atmosphere near the theme parks. **www.eoinn.com**

DOWNTOWN ORLANDO The Veranda $$
115 N. Summerlin Ave., 32801 **Tel** *(407) 849-0321* **Fax** *(407) 849-1875* **Rooms** *12*

A complex of historic buildings, this B&B is located in fashionable Thornton Park. Some of Orlando's hottest and hippest restaurants, and the lovely Lake Eola, are all located here as well. The grounds are beautifully landscaped and the attractive central courtyard is the perfect place to sit and relax. **www.theverandabandb.com**

DOWNTOWN ORLANDO The Grand Bohemian ⬛🍴🏊🚶🍴 $$$
325 South Orange Ave., 32801 **Tel** *(407) 313-9000* **Fax** *(407) 313-9001* **Rooms** *250*

In the heart of downtown Orlando, this hotel pays tribute to the arts. Decadently luxurious, it showcases classic and contemporary artwork from local and internationally renowned artists. Catering mainly to business people, the Bohemian also attracts art aficionados who love the museum-like ambience here. **www.grandbohemianhotel.com**

INTERNATIONAL DRIVE Clarion Inn & Suites ⬛🍴🏊🚶🍴 $
9956 Hawaiian Ct., 32819 **Tel** *(407) 351-5100* **Fax** *(407) 352-7188* **Rooms** *223*

Adjacent to the Orlando Orange County Convention Center and a short walk away from numerous restaurants, this casual hotel features standard rooms and one-bedroom suites with kitchen facilities. SeaWorld® is minutes away by trolley, and it is a 10- to 15-minute drive to Disney and Universal. **wwwclarionorlandoidrive.com**

INTERNATIONAL DRIVE Days Inn Convention Center ⬛🍴🏊🚶🍴 $
9990 International Drive, 32819 **Tel** *(407) 352-8700* **Fax** *(407) 363-3965* **Rooms** *220*

Just across the street from the Convention Center and a few blocks from Seaworld®, this functional and comfortable hotel is well situated for transportation, with International Drive trolley stops at the door and free shuttles to the major theme parks. Business facilities are comprehensive, with free Wi-Fi throughout. **www.daysinnorlando.com**

INTERNATIONAL DRIVE Econo Lodge Inn & Suites ⬛🏊🚶🍴 $
8738 International Dr., 32819 **Tel** *(407) 345-8195* **Fax** *(407) 352-8196* **Rooms** *672*

Ideally located on International Drive, with its plethora of restaurants and shops, this is the largest Econo Lodge in the world and is a tempting choice for anyone heading to Orlando. The rooms range from standards to suites, and the list of amenities and guest services is long given the hotel's reasonable rates. **www.econolodge.com**

INTERNATIONAL DRIVE Fairfield Inn & Suites International Cove ⬛🍴🏊🚶🍴 $
7495 Canada Ave., 32819 **Tel** *(407) 351-7000* **Fax** *(407) 351-0052* **Rooms** *200*

Located on a quieter street just off International Drive, the Fairfield Inn & Suites is only steps away from all the action. Featuring large rooms and suites, the inn also offers a daily complimentary breakfast and free high-speed wireless access to the Internet. **www.marriott.com/mcosl**

INTERNATIONAL DRIVE Four Points by Sheraton Orlando Studio City ⬛🍴🏊🚶🍴 $
5905 International Dr., 32819 **Tel** *(407) 351-2100* **Fax** *(407) 345-5249* **Rooms** *302*

This round hotel stands out among the others lining the busy thoroughfare. The Art Deco-style here pays tribute to Hollywood movies, with spotlights reminiscent of a Hollywood movie premiere and glamorous touches throughout. Rates include large rooms and numerous amenities. **www.starwoodhotels.com**

INTERNATIONAL DRIVE Holiday Inn Hotel & Suites at Universal ⬛🍴🏊🚶🍴 $
5905 Kirkman Rd., 32819 **Tel** *(407) 351-3333* **Fax** *(407) 351-6404* **Rooms** *256*

This popular chain offers comfortable rooms and suites, casual on-site dining, and a free shuttle to many nearby attractions. Recreational facilities include an outdoor pool, a toddler pool, and a games room. The atmosphere is friendly and welcoming, and the decor is bright and cheerful. **www.hiuniversal.com**

INTERNATIONAL DRIVE La Quinta Inn ⬛🏊🚶🍴 $
5825 International Dr., 32819 **Tel** *(407) 351-4100* **Fax** *(407) 996-4599* **Rooms** *117*

The interior decor at this western-themed hotel features warm colors, lots of wood, and wrought-iron lanterns. Wet 'n Wild is nearby, or there is the hotel pool for a more relaxing experience. The reasonable rates make it a good choice for those who are budget-conscious. **www.lq.com**

Key to Price Guide *see p138* **Key to Symbols** *see back cover flap*

INTERNATIONAL DRIVE La Quinta Inn & Suites Convention Center

8504 Universal Blvd., 32819 **Tel** *(407) 345-1365* **Fax** *(407) 345-5586* **Rooms** *184*

Located on a quieter street, though only a short walk to the many restaurants and shops of International Drive, this is a reasonably priced hotel with large rooms and suites that include additional conveniences such as a fridge and microwave. The decor is pleasant and the atmosphere friendly. **www.lq.com**

INTERNATIONAL DRIVE Monumental Movieland Hotel

6233 International Dr., 32819 **Tel** *(407) 351-3900* **Fax** *(407) 352-5597* **Rooms** *254*

Within splashing distance of Wet 'n Wild®, minutes from Universal Orlando®, and a walk to many of the area's shops, restaurants, and smaller attractions, this is a friendly hotel that provides comfortable surroundings and over-sized rooms. Services include a free shuttle to Universal and SeaWorld®. **www.monumentalmovielandhotel.com**

INTERNATIONAL DRIVE Quality Suites Universal South

9350 Turkey Lake Rd., 32819 **Tel** *(407) 351-5050* **Fax** *(407) 363-7953* **Rooms** *214*

Just off the beaten track, yet not too far from the area's many attractions, this hotel offers peaceful surroundings and large rooms with a half-wall between the bed and living area. A large tropically landscaped courtyard with palm trees and stone pathways winds around the hotel pool. **www.qualitysuitesuniversalsouth.com**

INTERNATIONAL DRIVE The Enclave Suites

6165 Carrier Dr., 32819 **Tel** *(407) 351-1155* **Fax** *(407) 351-2001* **Rooms** *321*

With a prime location just off International Drive, this hotel provides stunning views from private balconies and terraces. Both the buildings and landscaped grounds, with two outdoor pools, are appealing. The large comfortable rooms and suites, some designed especially for children, have fully equipped kitchens. **www.enclavesuites.com**

INTERNATIONAL DRIVE Wyndham Orlando Resort

8001 International Dr., 32819 **Tel** *(407) 351-2420* **Fax** *(407) 352-8759* **Rooms** *1,059*

Spread out over several blocks along International Drive, this resort has some of the prettiest grounds in the area. The fountains, steps, and statues are reminiscent of a grand Southern plantation. The rooms are large and comfortable, and there is also a handful of child-friendly suites. **www.wyndham.com**

INTERNATIONAL DRIVE Doubletree Hotel Orlando

5780 Major Blvd., 32819 **Tel** *(407) 351-1000* **Fax** *(407) 363-0106* **Rooms** *742*

There is no mistaking this hotel as its two golden buildings shine brightly in the Florida sunlight. The resort offers a free scheduled shuttle to nearby attractions, including Universal, Wet 'n Wild®, and SeaWorld®, each only minutes away. Rooms are spacious and feature a tropical decor. **www.doubletreeorlando.com**

INTERNATIONAL DRIVE Holiday Inn Resort – The Castle

8629 International Dr., 32819 **Tel** *(407) 345-1511* **Fax** *(407) 248-8181* **Rooms** *216*

In the style of a medieval fairytale castle, this popular hotel features fanciful surroundings, gargoyles in the lobby, and a large pool. Suites are standard and fabulous chocolate chip cookies await guests at the check-in desk. Many restaurants and shops are within walking distance or a short trolley ride. **www.thecastleorlando.com**

INTERNATIONAL DRIVE Embassy Suites International Dr. South

8978 International Dr., 32819 **Tel** *(407) 352-1400* **Fax** *(407) 363-1120* **Rooms** *244*

Ornate iron railings adorn the interior balconies, while the inner courtyard is landscaped with lush vegetation. Each room features separate sleeping and living areas and a kitchenette. Free breakfasts and evening receptions are offered too, though several restaurants are nearby. **www.embassysuites.com**

INTERNATIONAL DRIVE JW Marriott Orlando Grande Lakes

4040 Central Florida Pkwy., 32837 **Tel** *(407) 206-2300* **Fax** *(407) 206-2301* **Rooms** *1,000*

Sharing with the Ritz Carlton its spectacular and meticulously kept grounds as well as a long list of amenities, this luxurious property is one of the finest around. A beautifully landscaped river feature, fine dining, spa treatments, and an exclusive golf club with a caddie concierge are all available here. **www.marriott.com**

INTERNATIONAL DRIVE Peabody Orlando

9801 International Dr., 32819 **Tel** *(407) 352-4000* **Fax** *(407) 354-1424* **Rooms** *1,641*

Renowned for its superior service, this luxurious and upscale resort offers fine living and fine dining can be experienced at Napa, one of the few starred restaurants in Orlando. Room decor is subtle and quite tasteful, and the furnishings, in particular the beds, are amazingly comfortable. **www.peabodyorlando.com**

KISSIMMEE Best Western Lakeside

7769 West Irlo Bronson Memorial Hwy., 34747 **Tel** *(407) 396-2222* **Fax** *(407) 396-1399* **Rooms** *651*

Close to Walt Disney World® as well as the many attractions and restaurants that line the busy thoroughfare of US Highway 192, this casual family-friendly resort features a wide variety of amenities and recreational activities. They include a general store, several eateries, a pool, and a mini-golf course. **www.bestwestern-maingate.com**

KISSIMMEE Holiday Inn Express

3484 Polynesian Isle Blvd., 34746 **Tel** *(407) 997-1700* **Fax** *(407) 997-1701* **Rooms** *132*

Often overlooked as it is not on the main thoroughfare, this casual hotel has plenty to offer, including large comfortable rooms, suites for larger families, and a pool. Free high-speed Internet access and a complimentary Continental breakfast are added perks. The Mediterranean-style lobby is inviting. **www.hiexpress.com**

KISSIMMEE Oak Plantation

4090 Enchanted Oaks Cir., 34741 **Tel** *(407) 847-8200* **Fax** *(407) 847-3022* **Rooms** *332*

This park-like gated community provides quiet, peaceful surroundings. There are magnificent oak trees lining the roadways and walkways throughout the grounds. The self-catering apartment-style accommodation has a homely feel and there are abundant recreational facilities. **www.oakplantationresort.com**

KISSIMMEE Radisson Resort Orlando Celebration

2900 Parkway Blvd., 34747 **Tel** *(800) 606-4947* **Fax** *(407) 396-0097* **Rooms** *718*

Beautiful surroundings are the signature of this popular and budget-minded resort. A lavishly landscaped pool features waterfalls, a waterslide, whirlpools, and a children's pool, while the on-site dining options include a casual 1950s-style diner and a full service Mediterranean-style restaurant. **www.radisson.com/orlando-celebration**

KISSIMMEE Ramada Main Gate West

7491 W. Irlo Bronson Memorial Hwy., 32819 **Tel** *(407) 396-6000* **Fax** *(407) 396-7393* **Rooms** *442*

A large indoor pool, casual eateries, and plenty of places to relax can all be found in this resort's large inner courtyard. The rooms are spacious and comfortable. Children will appreciate the activities and in-room video games on offer. Reasonable rates add to the appeal. **www.ramadamaingatewest.com**

KISSIMMEE Seralago Hotel & Suites Main Gate East

5678 W. Irlo Bronson Memorial Hwy., 34746 **Tel** *(407) 396-4488* **Fax** *(407) 396-8915* **Rooms** *614*

Inviting and family-friendly, this hotel has plenty to offer, including kidsuites, a variety of casual restaurants, and a wide array of recreational activities. The atmosphere and service are both upbeat and friendly. Gatorland is a 15-minute drive away, while Disney is just down the road. **www.seralagohotel.com**

KISSIMMEE Summer Bay Resort

25 Town Center Blvd., 34714 **Tel** *(863) 420-8282 (reservations: 1-888-742-1100)* **Fax** *(352) 241-2268* **Rooms** *95*

Given the rather basic accommodation, the bonus of this inn is that it shares facilities with the entire collection of Summer Bay vacation homes and villas. Guest services and amenities are extensive and very family-friendly. There are pools and playgrounds, tennis and basketball courts, scheduled activities, and more. **www.sumerbayresort.com**

KISSIMMEE Comfort Suites Maingate Resort West

7888 W. Irlo Bronson Memorial Hwy., 34746 **Tel** *(407) 390-9888* **Fax** *(407) 390-0981* **Rooms** *150*

Large rooms that can accommodate up to six, a free continental breakfast, and a location that is hard to beat are all on offer here. So, too, is free scheduled transportation to Universal, Wet 'n' Wild®, SeaWorld®, and Disney. The resort has a modern look that is attractive and inviting. **www.comfortsuiteskissimmee.com**

KISSIMMEE Radisson Resort Worldgate

3011 Maingate La., 34747 **Tel** *(407) 396-1400* **Fax** *(407) 396-0660* **Rooms** *566*

As well as beautifully decorated and well-appointed rooms, this reasonably priced resort offers a long list of guest services. Palm trees are scattered throughout the pool area in the central courtyard, giving it a tropical atmosphere. On-site dining is available, but numerous restaurants are only minutes away. **www.worldgateresort.com**

KISSIMMEE Acadia Estates All Star Vacation Homes

7822 West Irlo Bronson Memorial Hwy., 34747 **Tel** *(407) 997-0733* **Fax** *(407) 997-1370* **Rooms** *37 homes*

This quiet, upscale, and gated neighborhood features some very distinctive vacation homes. Each has a secluded patio with a private pool and hot tub, and between four and seven bedrooms. Some include a gameroom, and all are beautifully decorated. Numerous guest services are also available. **www.allstarvacationhomes.com**

LAKE BUENA VISTA Holiday Inn Sunspree Resort

13351 State Rd. 535, 32821 **Tel** *(407) 239-4500* **Fax** *(407) 239-7713* **Rooms** *507*

This family-friendly resort features kidsuites with separate sleeping and play areas, plus kitchenettes. In the play areas children have their own TV, video game system, and pint-sized furnishings. A mini-theater plays child-friendly movies and a supervised activity center provides parents with some time for themselves. **www.hiresortlbv.com**

LAKE BUENA VISTA Quality Suites

8200 Palm Pky., 32836 **Tel** *(407) 465-8200* **Fax** *(407) 465-0200* **Rooms** *123*

Palm Parkway is a quiet tree-lined road filled with newer, somewhat upscale, though casual, hotels. There are many restaurants nearby, as is Downtown Disney®. Spacious suites with kitchens, complimentary breakfast, and evening receptions are standard here. The surroundings are pleasant though not over the top. **www.qualitysuiteslbv.com**

LAKE BUENA VISTA Sheraton Safari Hotel

12205 Apopka-Vineland Rd., 32836 **Tel** *(407) 239-0444* **Fax** *(407) 239-1788* **Rooms** *489*

A wild safari theme ensures that guests' adventures do not end at the theme parks. A giant python resides in the hotel pool, but he is friendly and allows people to slide down him into the pool. Jungle-like landscaping adds to the ambience. The numerous amenities and services ensure guest satisfaction. **www.sheratonsafari.com**

LAKE BUENA VISTA Fairfield Inn & Suites Orlando in the Marriott Village

8615 Vineland Ave., 32821 **Tel** *(407) 938-9001* **Fax** *(407) 938-9002* **Rooms** *388*

Three separate Marriott-brand hotels are situated together in a village-style setting here to offer guests a wide range of room types and services to choose from. A pool is located in the large central courtyard. Also on offer are a free buffet breakfast and wireless high-speed Internet access. **www.marriott.com**

Key to Price Guide *see p138* **Key to Symbols** *see back cover flap*

LAKE BUENA VISTA Springhill Suites Orlando at the Marriott Village $$
8623 Vineland Ave., 32821 **Tel** *(407) 938-9001* **Fax** *(407) 938-9002* **Rooms** *400*

Another of the Marriott Village hotels that has large comfortable rooms with kitchen facilities and other conveniences to ensure a comfortable stay. Also on offer are a shared pool, courtyard, and casual eateries in a village-like setting. Additional restaurants are within walking distance. **www.marriott.com/mcolx**

LAKE BUENA VISTA Staybridge Suites LBV $$
8751 Suiteside Dr., 32836 **Tel** *(407) 238-0777* **Fax** *(407) 238-2640* **Rooms** *150*

Particularly large and uniquely designed rooms, plus a central location and a grocery delivery service, make this the perfect choice for families and groups. The central courtyard is lined with palm trees overlooking the large pool and sundeck. There is a second location on International Drive. **www.sborlando.com**

LAKE BUENA VISTA Gaylord Palms Resort & Convention Center $$$
6000 West Osceola Pkwy., 34746 **Tel** *(407) 586-0000* **Fax** *(407) 586-1999* **Rooms** *1,406*

A recreation of St. Marco, the oldest Spanish castle in America, is among the attractions of this visually stunning upscale resort. Several Florida themes, including St. Augustine and the Everglades, are reflected in the decor of the luxurious bedrooms. Recreational facilities, amenities, and service are top-notch. **www.gaylordhotels.com**

LAKE BUENA VISTA Hyatt Regency Grand Cypress $$$
One Grand Cypress Blvd., 32836 **Tel** *(407) 239-1234* **Fax** *(407) 239-3800* **Rooms** *750*

Waterfalls, caves, grottoes, and rope bridges surround the pool at this upscale resort. There is plenty on offer for guests of every age, including a sandy beach and crystal-blue lake, an equestrian center, golf, tennis, an array of children's activities, and award-winning fine dining at La Coquina. **www.grandcypress.hyatt.com**

LAKE BUENA VISTA Orlando World Center Marriott $$$
8701 World Center Dr., 32821 **Tel** *(407) 239-4200* **Fax** *(407) 238-8777* **Rooms** *2,000*

An array of restaurants, a premier golf club, a spectacularly landscaped pool and play area, and beautifully decorated spacious rooms are all combined with exceptional service. This resort caters to both families and business travelers alike – a combination that is rare and difficult to find. **www.marriottworldcenter.com**

LAKE BUENA VISTA Caribe Royale Orlando $$$$
8101 World Center Dr., 32821 **Tel** *(407) 238-8000* **Fax** *(407) 238-8400* **Rooms** *1,338*

Spread out over 45 acres (18 ha) of beautifully landscaped grounds filled with towering palm trees, this resort features large suites and multi-room villas to accommodate any size of family. The list of guest services, amenities, and recreational activities is extensive, and it is minutes from Disney. **www.thecaribeorlando.com**

LAKE BUENA VISTA Nickelodeon Family Suites by Holiday Inn $$$$
14500 Continental Gateway, 32821 **Tel** *(407) 387-5437* **Fax** *(407) 387-1490* **Rooms** *777*

This child-friendly Nickelodeon-themed resort now sports two waterpark play areas filled with flumes, waterslides, fountains, and more. Entertainment is top priority here. Suites with special separate bedrooms for the children, living areas, and kitchenettes are standard. **www.nickhotel.com**

LAKE BUENA VISTA Waldorf Astoria Orlando $$$$$
14200 Bonnet Creek Resort Lane, 32821 **Tel** *(407) 597-5500* **Fax** *(407) 597-3701* **Rooms** *497*

Set in almost 500 acres (202 ha) of woodlands and waterways, with great access to Orlando's attractions, this luxury hotel is close to all the theme parks. It has two swimming pools, private cabanas, a full-service health spa, and a golf course. **www.waldorfastoriaorlando.com**

MAITLAND Thurston House B&B $$$
851 Lake Ave., 32751 **Tel** *(407) 539-1911* **Fax** *(407) 539-0365* **Rooms** *4*

Built in 1885 and restored in 1991, this period Queen Ann-style Victorian farmhouse sits on a beautiful lakefront. The inn's four rooms are quaint yet elegant and each feature a queen bed; reading area; modern amenities such as a TV, VCR/DVD, and CD player; and complimentary high-speed Internet access. **www.thurstonhouse.com**

MOUNT DORA The Lakeside Inn $$
100 N. Alexander St., 32757 **Tel** *(352) 383-4101* **Fax** *(352) 735-2642* **Rooms** *88*

Built in 1863 and refurbished a century later, this resort is ideal for a period of peaceful solitude. The inn is extremely popular with bird-watchers, anglers, and antique hunters. Children, while welcome, will not find the inn as captivating as adults invariably do. **www.lakeside-inn.com**

MOUNT DORA Adora Inn $$$
610 North Tremain St., 32757 **Tel** *(352) 735-3110* **Rooms** *5*

In the heart of Mount Dora, close to the lake, this beautifully restored Arts & Crafts building dates to 1916, and welcomes guests with a picturesque front porch, pretty gardens, and antique furniture within. Modern touches such as in-room spa treatments, fine dining by arrangement, and Wi-Fi bring it bang up-to-date. **www.adorainn.com**

ORLANDO INTERNATIONAL AIRPORT Hyatt Regency $$$$
9300 Airport Blvd., 32827 **Tel** *(407) 825-1234* **Fax** *(407) 859-9652* **Rooms** *446*

The convenience of not having to leave the airport can save time, money, and stress for many a business traveler. First-rate amenities are at the guests' disposal at this upscale hotel, as are the many shops and restaurants now located at the Orlando International Airport. **www.orlandoairport.hyatt.com**

WHERE TO EAT

A food lover's paradise, the joy of Florida is in the rich and abundant fresh produce it has to offer. From juicy tropical fruits to mouthwatering seafood, every restaurant is overflowing with Florida's natural bounty. Catering to every palate and budget, the region's restaurants range from small cafés

Stone crab claws

to trendy diners to five-star resorts. A vast immigrant population and the constant flow of tourists contributes to a wide variety of ever-changing food choices. See the listings on pages 148–55. Intimate suppers by candlelight, and themed diners ensure that the dining experience is as much about entertainment as sustenance.

Mexican food at its best – Chili's Grill & Bar, I-Drive *(see p153)*

TYPES OF RESTAURANTS

Orlando is a multi-cultural city offering a wide range of cuisines. The large number of Thai and Vietnamese residents guarantees a bounty of high-quality Asian restaurants. Mexican and Cuban eateries are also plentiful and, since this is the South, barbecue is never far away. African, Irish, Lebanese, Pakistani, Polish, and Indian – foods from all over the world are joyfully served to cater to all taste-buds. Almost every regional American cuisine is represented, from Maine to New Orleans, while a breed of innovative chefs has combined Florida's finest local produce with zesty Caribbean flavors to create what is called New Florida or "Floribbean" cuisine. Sushi is available in supermarkets, and every street corner has a pizza joint. "Natural" supermarkets such as Whole Foods and Chamberlain's offer a range of organic meals.

Restaurants of every size and shape serve seafood. In one Florida institution, the "raw bar," you can enjoy deliciously fresh raw oysters or clams and steamed shrimp.

RESERVATIONS

Reservations are usually not required at smaller restaurants. But it would be a good idea to make advance reservations at larger places in upscale areas such as Sand Lake Road, International Drive, and the theme parks, particularly on weekends. Guests staying at the Disney World® and Universal resorts get preferred seating at the attraction-owned restaurants.

DINING ON A BUDGET

There are several ways to reduce your food budget. Most restaurants offer huge and inexpensive breakfasts. Bargain meals are plentiful away from the hotels and

theme parks, particularly at the large number of Indian, Vietnamese, and Thai eateries. Several seafood and Chinese all-you-can-eat buffets can be found along I-Drive. Southern barbecue is also affordable. Check online for discount coupons, which can cut a bill by 25 percent or more.

Some restaurants will cook your own fish for a reduced price. In addition, many state parks have barbecues where you can grill your catch or any other food that you care to bring along. Delis and supermarkets are good for picnic provisions.

EATING OUT LATE

Most restaurants close at 10pm since Floridians prefer to eat early – usually between 7 and 9pm. Some restaurants, however, do stay open until 11pm. The Globe, at 25 Wall Street Plaza in Downtown Orlando, serves food until 2am.

The highly acclaimed Emeril's Restaurant *(see p151)* **at Universal Orlando®**

The Boheme *(see p152)*, Downtown Orlando's luxury hotel and restaurant

Diners on East Colonial Drive such as Denny's (No. 3162), and the 5 & Diner (No. 12286), plus the B-Line at 9801 International Drive, are open 24 hours. Mexican food lovers can drive north on State Road 436 to Beto's at No. 103, near the junction with US 17-92.

CELEBRITY DINING

The new word in Orlando dining is "celebrity." Names that would generally be found attached to big-city restaurants or appearing on the Food Network are popping up all over Central Florida. Emeril Lagasse, who set up Emeril's at Universal and the Tchoup Chop at the Royal Pacific Resort, is now joined by Todd English, who operates Olives in New York and now bluezoo at Disney's Dolphin Hotel *(see p139)*. Norman Van Aken founded Norman's at the Ritz-Carlton (4012 Central Florida Parkway), and innovative chef Melissa Kelly has set up Primo at the JW Marriott. Wolfgang Puck and Roy Yamaguchi own signature restaurants, and a trio of French superstars – Paul Bocuse, Gaston Lenotre, and Roger Verge – run Les Chefs de France at Epcot®.

DINING DISTRICTS

Restaurants emerge in groups in Orlando. The Sand Lake Road "Restaurant Row," near the theme parks, is home to corporate-owned, high-end

eateries such as Seasons 52, Bonefish Grill, Roys, and Timpano Italian Chophouse, as well as stand-alone destinations Essence of India, and Vines. To the west, Bistro 1501 at the Orlando Marriott Hotel offers fine dining in Lake Mary. The ViMi district of Colonial Drive is home to scores of Vietnamese, Thai, and Chinese restaurants. Old favorites such as Little Saigon and Shin Jung sit next to newcomer restaurants. Thornton Park in downtown is host to upscale HUE, City-fish, the Japanese eatery Shari Sushi, and lunchtime favorite Dexters. Nearby College Park draws diners with Jade Bistro, K Restaurant & Wine Bar, Graffiti Junktion, and Juliana's with a taste of the Mediterranean, and the lively Irish-themed pub Scruffy Murphy's.

THEME PARK DINING

Some of the finest dining in Orlando can be found at the parks, including the award-winning Palm at Universal's Hard Rock Hotel. You can be fairly certain that anything consumed, from hot dogs to haute cuisine, at any of the theme parks will be on the expensive side. However, the food is generally worth it.

The parks are full to the brim with themed restaurants. The Coral Reef Restaurant within Futureworld at Epcot® has an 8-ft (2.5-m) high glass wall panorama of the 5.7 million gallon (21.5 million liter) Living Seas aquarium. Epcot®'s World Showcase contains a wealth of dining and snacking options featuring international cuisines, from British fish and chips to a Norwegian buffet spread. Bice Ristorante at Universal's Loews Portofino Bay Hotel transports diners to a full-scale replica of Italy's Portofino harbor, where they dine on Northern Italian cuisine. Also at Universal, CityWalk® treats sports-loving guests to NBA City for basketball-themed goodies, and racing meals at the NASCAR Sports Grille. Disney's Rainforest Café® features hourly thunderstorms amid animatronic gorillas. The parks are also home to the Hard Rock Café®, House of Blues®, and Planet Hollywood®.

The California Grill *(see p150)* at Disney's Contemporary Resort

Choosing a Restaurant

The restaurants in this guide have been selected for their good value, exceptional food, or interesting location. These listings highlight some of the factors that may influence your choice, such as whether you can opt to eat outdoors or if the venue offers live music. Entries are alphabetical within each price category.

PRICE CATEGORIES
Price categories include a three-course meal for one, a glass of house wine, and all unavoidable extra charges including service and tax.
$ under $30
$$ $30–$40
$$$ $40–$50
$$$$ $50–$65
$$$$$ over $65

WALT DISNEY WORLD® RESORT

ANIMAL KINGDOM® Boma – Flavors of Africa $$
Disney's Animal Kingdom Lodge, Bay Lake, 32830 **Tel** *(407) 939-3463*

Tables laden with spicy and unusual African dishes invite exploration at the overwhelming dinner and breakfast buffets at this Disney-themed resort. Dishes are flavored with delicious combinations of tamarind, cumin, coriander, cinnamon, hot chillies, cilantro, papaya, and other uncommon tastes.

ANIMAL KINGDOM® Sanaa $$$$
Disney's Animal Kingdom Lodge, Bay Lake, 32830 **Tel** *(407) 393-3463*

Sanaa serves slow-cooked African cuisine spiced with Indian flavors. The menu is laden with slow-cooked delights, grilled over a wood fire or roasted in a traditional Indian tandoor oven. The food is great, but the best thing is the view. Sitting on a stretch of savanna, Sanaa offers glimpses of passing herds of giraffe, zebra, antelopes, and more.

DISNEY'S HOLLYWOOD STUDIOS® Hollywood Brown Derby $$$
Lake Buena Vista, 32830 **Tel** *(407) 560-4835*

Re-creating the fabled Brown Derby of 1930s Hollywood, the Art Deco interior here echoes the retro menu, which includes a world-famous Cobb salad. Seafood and steaks in fusion style and acclaimed desserts (try the grapefruit cake) round off the offerings. This restaurant is known for serving up the best-mixed drinks in the park.

DISNEY'S HOLLYWOOD STUDIOS® Sci-Fi Dine-In Theater $$$
Lake Buena Vista, 32830 **Tel** *(407) 560-3359*

The theme is drive-in movies and the menu offers appropriate options, with burgers, fries, pasta, ribs, and outrageous milkshakes. The food is expensive for what it is, but the experience of sitting in a replica 1950s car and watching old sci-fi movies is nostalgic for old-timers and provides fun for children too.

DOWNTOWN DISNEY® Olivia's Café $$
Disney Old Key West, 1510 N Cove Road, Lake Buena Vista, 32830 **Tel** *(407) 939-3463*

Diners will think they are in old Key West at this café serving conch-style meals. Check out the Florida paella, conch chowder, and mojo chicken. Floridians feel that Olivia's does Key West pretty good justice with its focus on local flavors. A fun menu and good staff help make it enjoyable for children as well.

DOWNTOWN DISNEY® Wolfgang Puck Café $$
1482 E. Buena Vista Drive, 32830 **Tel** *(407) 938-9653*

Located within Downtown Disney, this is actually several restaurants in one – from a casual, California-influenced express café to fine dining – all powered by the chef's vision and taste. It is an imaginative concept, catering to many different tastes good for the whole family. The fire-roasted pizzas, pastas, and grilled foods are tasty.

DOWNTOWN DISNEY® Bongo's Cuban Café $$$
2426 Viscount Row, 32809 **Tel** *(407) 828-0999*

An unpretentious restaurant – a great Disney antidote – that welcomes families. The food can range dramatically from seafood pltters to shrips sautéed in sauce. Spanish or Neo-Spanish dishes dominate the menu. The bustling, fast-paced energetic environment can detract from conversation at times.

DOWNTOWN DISNEY® Paradiso 37 $$$
1590 E. Buena Vista Drive, 32830 **Tel** *(407) 934-3700*

This high-energy restaurant and bar specializes in street foods of the Americas. Items on the menu represent 37 countries of North, South, and Central America. There's also an interesting wine menu, 37 varieties of tequila, and 10 signature frozen margaritas. Live music adds to the atmosphere at night.

DOWNTOWN DISNEY® Planet Hollywood Orlando $$$
1506 E. Buena Vista Drive, 32830 **Tel** *(407) 827-7827*

Located within a purple neon globe, this institution in Orlando has large video screens and masses of movie memorabilia. The fare is mainstream, with meaty burgers and tasty pizzas. Children will particularly enjoy eating here, but adults may find the dining room too loud for conversation.

Key to Symbols *see back cover flap*

DOWNTOWN DISNEY® Fulton's Crab House 👪 ♿ 🎵 $$$$$

Downtown Disney Market Place ***Tel*** *(407) 939-3463*

Located in a replica of a riverboat dating from the end of the 19th century, this steak and seafood eatery is a treat for adults and children alike. As well as a grand staircase and hand-painted ceiling murals, there are beautiful artifacts reflecting the nautical theme. A children's menu is available.

DOWNTOWN DISNEY® The Outback 👪 ♿ $$$$$

1900 Buena Vista Drive, 32830 ***Tel*** *(407) 827-3430*

An indoor waterfall creates a soothing atmosphere at this Down Under chain bistro. Feast on jumbo stuffed shrimp and steaks. Portions are massive, sides are good, and try to save room for the decadent desserts. This is more of a family or group destination, where the din can get in the way of romance.

EPCOT® Cape May Café 👪 ♿ $$

Disney's Beach Club Resort ***Tel*** *(407) 939-3463*

The buffet breakfast proceedings here are conducted by Admiral Goofy. At dinner, a bell announces the start of the clam bake buffet, where tables are laden with a great array of food from which to choose. Good entertainment is provided for the whole family at every meal every day.

EPCOT® Les Chefs de France 👪 ♿ $$$

Epcot World Showcase, Walt Disney World, 32830 ***Tel*** *(407) 939-3463*

Haute cuisine does not get much higher than that served in a restaurant created by Bocuse, Lenotre, and Verge, three masters of French cooking. From appetizers to classics such as duck *à l'orange*, every dish is a definition of the art. Epcot® admission is necessary for anyone wishing to dine here.

EPCOT® Shula's 👪 ♿ $$$$

Walt Disney World Dolphin Hotel ***Tel*** *(407) 934-1609*

This is one of the resort's finest steakhouses. They also have a fine selection of seafood, and the desserts are spectacular. It is one local eatery where the emphasis is on food and not entertainment, and it shows in each and every dish. Kids are welcome but they will find it tame compared to other resort restaurants.

EPCOT® Todd English's bluezoo ♿ $$$$

Walt Disney World Dolphin Hotel ***Tel*** *(407) 934-1111*

Master restaurateur Todd English celebrates the "bluezoo" of the ocean with innovative seafood creations and stylish decor with an underwater feel. English's hand directs the menu, which has touches of Asian, Tuscan, and American cuisine, and features excellent fish, steak, and free-range chicken dishes. Good wine and cocktails list.

EPCOT Flying Fish Café 👪 ♿ $$$$$

Disney's Boardwalk, Lake Buena Vista, 32830 ***Tel*** *(407) 939-3463*

This restaurant is another good reason to visit the free Disney Boardwalk area, aside from the view of nightly fireworks. The service is superb – the staff seem to anticipate your every need while serving creative American seafood cuisine. The daily specials change according to what is in season.

EPCOT® Yachtsman Steakhouse 👪 ♿ $$$$$

Disney Yacht Club Resort, 32830 ***Tel*** *(407) 939-3463*

This eatery is open all day for hearty favorites, including fish, steak, and pasta, all to be enjoyed in themed nautical surroundings. The scrumptious desserts that are available at the very good dinner buffet are not to be missed. Dining here is likely to be more enjoyable for adults unaccompanied by kids.

FORT WILDERNESS Whispering Canyon Café 👪 ♿ $$

Disney Wilderness Lodge ***Tel*** *(407) 939-3463*

Snap on your six-guns and settle in for an all-you-can-eat campfire buffet in a Wild West setting. The café is also open for frontier-style breakfasts. Families with children will find this particularly appealing. The food is decent and entertainment value quite high. Stop in for a unique local experience.

FORT WILDERNESS Artist Point 👪 ♿ $$$$

Disney's Wilderness Lodge, Lake Buena Vista, 32830 ***Tel*** *(407) 939-3463*

From the size of the plate to the size of the portions, everything here is big. The innovative, Northwestern-themed menu offers exotic items such as sautéed elk sausage, and the service and setting are spectacular. The restaurant has more appeal for adult diners, but children are certainly welcome.

MAGIC KINGDOM® Chef Mickey's 👪 ♿ $$

Disney's Contemporary Resort ***Tel*** *(407) 939-3463*

Very much a family-oriented place, Mickey's offers breakfast and dinner buffets. Diners can enjoy the antics of their favorite Disney characters as they eat dishes from a mixed, unassuming menu that is available throughout the day. The service is quite good and children are especially welcome.

MAGIC KINGDOM® Ohana 👪 ♿ $$

Disney's Polynesian Resort ***Tel*** *(407) 939-3463*

This buzzing, open-plan dining room is the setting for Polynesian-style cuisine. Set-price dinners include meat and shellfish roasted over a fire pit and served on 3-ft (1-m) long skewers. Terrific evening entertainment livens up the dining experience for everyone, whether part of a visiting couple or family

MAGIC KINGDOM® Cinderella's Royal Table
Cinderella's Castle, 32830 **Tel** *(407) 939-3463*

Prime rib and chicken for adults and Disney characters for the kids – this is the traditional Disney breakfast experience taken to the extreme. Little girls love to get a glimpse of Cinderella during their meal. Advance reservations – sometimes as much as three to four months in advance – are mandatory.

MAGIC KINGDOM® California Grill
Disney's Contemporary Resort **Tel** *(407) 939-3463*

This stylish restaurant, with good views and an open-plan kitchen, serves creative West Coast fare such as smoked salmon pizza, and pork and polenta. It is not too trendy for children to find menu items that appeal to them and is a good spot for those who would rather not eat red meat.

MAGIC KINGDOM® Citrico's at the Grand Floridian
Disney's Grand Floridian Resort & Spa, Lake Buena Vista, 32830 **Tel** *(407) 939-3463*

This delightful eatery offers international fare, with a focus on slow-roasted meats. Influenced by French cuisine, everything from breads to desserts is exquisite – even the view of the dramatic action in the open kitchen. Requiring formal attire, it is expensive but worth it. It is closed on Mondays and Tuesdays.

MAGIC KINGDOM® Disney's Spirit of Aloha Dinner Show
Disney's Polynesian Resort, Lake Buena Vista, 32830 **Tel** *(407) 939-3463*

Tropical appetizers and "Island" ribs are the highlights of the menu in this Polynesian-style diner. The food is served to the accompaniment of the traditional music and dances of Tahiti, Samoa, Tonga, New Zealand, and Hawaii. Dining here is enormous fun for both children and adults who like the hula.

MAGIC KINGDOM® Narcoossee's
Disney's Grand Floridian Resort **Tel** *(407) 824-1400*

This restaurant in an octagonal chalet alongside the Seven Seas Lagoon serves delicious meat and fish dishes with fresh local vegetables. The food here is fresh and consistent and the pace not as rushed as elsewhere in the Disney area. Ask about daily specials and for local fish highlights.

MAGIC KINGDOM® Victoria & Albert's
Disney's Grand Floridian Resort **Tel** *(407) 824-1089*

Reservations are a must at this lavish restaurant. The six-course fixed-price menu is superlative, and diners are waited on by a butler and a maid. Ask for the chef's table, the most exclusive one in the house. One of the most delightfully decadent dining experiences in the area, and not one for children.

OTHER THEME PARKS

SEAWORLD® Trade Winds
6677 Sea Harbor Drive, 32821 **Tel** *(407) 351-5555*

Located in the Renaissance Orlando Resort *(see p140)*, across from SeaWorld®, Trade Winds serves upscale American comfort food in a casual environment. Dishes include baby back ribs and fried pork chops, and there is an emphasis on fresh, seasonal ingredients with an organic flair. All dietary needs are catered for.

SEAWORLD® Sharks Underwater Grill
7007 SeaWorld Drive, 32821 **Tel** *(407) 370-1573*

Take the opportunity to enjoy Caribbean and Florida-style seafood inches away from more than 50 sharks at SeaWorld® – a setting that is ideal for children. The menu is upscale and the food is as fresh as getting it directly from the tank – but don't worry, they don't. Admission to SeaWorld® is required.

SEAWORLD® Primo
4040 Central Florida Parkway, 32821 **Tel** *(407) 393-4444*

Organic cuisine is served up at this restaurant located in the enormous JW Marriott Orlando *(see p143)*. From free-range lamb to home-made sausages, care is taken with every ingredient and the result is deliciously successful. Prices are very high, but for anyone looking for a very special meal, Primo is the place to be.

UNIVERSAL ORLANDO® NASCAR Sports Grille
6000 Universal Boulevard, 32819 **Tel** *(407) 224-7223*

Race-car lovers and motorheads will be fascinated by the racing cars and racing memorabilia featured here, as well as the food, which includes steaks, chops, and other barbecued meats. There are also around 40 televisions featuring highlights of great car races. Open until late, this restaurant provides fun for the whole family.

UNIVERSAL ORLANDO® Hard Rock Café Orlando
6050 Universal Boulevard, 32819 **Tel** *(407) 351-7625*

This massive restaurant in CityWalk® overflows with pop memorabilia. The sundaes are great, and the live music in the concert hall (Fridays and Saturdays) makes this an extremely popular hangout. The Hard Rock Café is not an environment for intimate conversation as it has a tendency to be boisterous.

Key to Price Guide *see p148* **Key to Symbols** *see back cover flap*

UNIVERSAL ORLANDO® Jimmy Buffett's Margaritaville
6000 Universal Boulevard, 32819 **Tel** *(407) 224-2155*

Soak up the Key West flavor and Jimmy Buffett tunes at Margaritaville in the very heart of glitzy CityWalk®. There is more appeal in the colorful atmosphere than in the food at this noisy and crowded spot, but the ocean of margarita varieties will easily satisfy your drink-and-be-merry craving.

UNIVERSAL ORLANDO® Latin Quarter
6000 Universal Boulevard, 32819 **Tel** *(407) 224-2800*

Spice up meal times with the culture, cuisine, music, and dance of 21 Latin nations. This popular eatery in upscale CityWalk® serves a huge variety of Latin American dishes, as well as seafood and steaks. It is open for lunch and dinner daily, and usually stays open for late-night revelry until 2am.

UNIVERSAL ORLANDO® Emeril's Restaurant Orlando
6000 Universal Boulevard, 32819 **Tel** *(407) 224-2424*

Savor the casual, contemporary atmosphere, the warm and spicy colors, and first-class service in this CityWalk® restaurant that has become an institution. Highlighting the "Bam!" cuisine of Emeril Lagasse, the menu offers flawlessly prepared items such as the andouille-crusted Texas redfish.

UNIVERSAL ORLANDO® Palm Restaurant
5800 Universal Boulevard, 32819 **Tel** *(407) 503-7256*

The first Palm opened in New York circa 1926, and this Orlando branch within the Hard Rock Hotel *(see p140)* features fine, uncomplicated dishes, including enormous steaks. In contrast to most Universal eateries, free valet parking is provided right at the door.

ORLANDO & CENTRAL FLORIDA

COCOA BEACH The Fat Snook
2464 S. Atlantic Avenue, 32931 **Tel** *321-784-1190*

A culinary oasis, this cosy beachside restaurant uses the freshest ingredients to put together a creative and consistent menu combining Latin flavours with Asian and European highlights and Caribbean flair. You won't find banana polenta or steak glazed with bittersweet chocolate anywhere else in town.

DAYTONA BEACH Aunt Catfish
4009 Halifax Drive, 32127 **Tel** *386-767-4768*

This eatery – popular with travelers and local residents alike – is located on the Intracoastal Waterway. With seafood featuring strongly on the menu, it is especially renowned for its fried catfish and other Southern-style dishes such as crab cakes and clam strips. On Sunday it is open for a popular and varied brunch.

DAYTONA BEACH Down the Hatch
4894 Front Street, Ponce Inlet, 32127 **Tel** *386-761-4831*

Family-oriented and serving fresh fish and a few meat dishes, this restaurant is located on the waterfront, so diners can watch the boats unload their catch at the end of the day. A very casual and friendly environment, with live music from Wednesday through to Sunday, helps to make it popular with local residents.

DOWNTOWN ORLANDO Dragon Court Chinese Buffet
12384 Apoka-Vineland Road, 32834 **Tel** *(407) 238-9996*

For those who love Chinese food head for this no-frills buffet restaurant and its huge selection of dishes, from the traditional favorites you would expect to house specialties – they have a particularly good selection of seafood dishes. Clean and comfortable and very good value.

DOWNTOWN ORLANDO Johnny's Fillin' Station
2631 S. Ferncreek, 32806 **Tel** *(407) 894-6900*

Local critics claim that Johnny's serves the best burgers in Orlando. American food and atmosphere at their purest are on offer at this great family destination that will thrill the kids. The atmosphere is friendly and the staff helpful and upbeat. But there is not much variety on the menu for those who are not particularly meat-inclined.

DOWNTOWN ORLANDO Hawkers
1103 N. Mills Avenue, 32803 **Tel** *(407) 237-0606*

In the heart of the Downtown Vietnamese area, Hawkers specializes in the street food not only of Vietnam but also of mainland China, Hong Kong, and Malaysia. With no dish costing more than $6.50, this is a great place for sharing plates and conversation. There is an extensive wine list, with a good choice served by the glass.

DOWNTOWN ORLANDO Little Saigon
1106 E. Colonial Drive, 32803 **Tel** *(407) 423-8539*

This highly praised restaurant serves the best Vietnamese cuisine in the area. Casual, comfortable, affordable, and authentic are all words used to describe this small, family-friendly place that serves up sizable portions. The staff are happy to describe dishes and guide diners through the menu.

DOWNTOWN ORLANDO Graffiti Junktion American Burger Bar $$
900 E. Washington St., 32801 **Tel** *(407) 426 9502*

This sports bar-style restaurant with graffiti-themed decor serves up great burgers in many flavors, from Tex-Mex to Chicago-style, all served on home-made buns. The menu also includes turkey burgers, fish sandwiches, a vegetarian burger, and freshly cut French fries. The atmosphere is loud and lively, and there's live rock on Sunday afternoons.

DOWNTOWN ORLANDO Il Pescatore $$
651 N. Primrose Drive, 32803 **Tel** *(407) 896-6763*

A simple setting is provided for food that is truly Italian through and through. Traditional house specialties like *trippa del pescatore* (tripe in tomato sauce) make this spot unique in its authenticity. Choosing between the various pasta sauces is pleasingly difficult. This restaurant is closed on Sundays and Mondays.

DOWNTOWN ORLANDO Jade Bistro $$
2425 Edgewater Drive, 32804 **Tel** *(407) 422-7968*

Veteran sushi chefs join seasoned restaurant owners for a truly delightful combination. The pan-Oriental cuisine here is excellent and often exceeds expectations. Although not entirely Japanese, Chinese, or Thai, it still manages to excel in all these areas. Some small children may find the food too adventurous.

DOWNTOWN ORLANDO Napasorn Thai $$
56 E. Pine Street, 32801 **Tel** *(407) 245-8088*

The young yet experienced Napasorn owners wander slightly from traditional Thai food, but serve up well-prepared dishes. The basil duck stands out in particular. The reasonably good sushi bar also helps to make it a most enjoyable destination, though be warned that young children may find the cuisine too experimental.

DOWNTOWN ORLANDO Ceviche Tapas Bar & Restaurant $$$
125 W. Church St., 32801 **Tel** *(407) 281-8140*

The menu here contains 100 different hot and cold tapas, as well as paellas. Ingredients imported from Spain give authenticity to the dishes, and the wine list is exclusively Spanish. Service is good, with knowledgeable waiters who keep the tapas and pitchers of Sangria flowing. Spanish guitarists and dancers provide the entertainment.

DOWNTOWN ORLANDO Le Coq au Vin $$$
4800 S. Orange Avenue, 32806 **Tel** *(407) 851-6980*   **Map** *F2*

Welcoming surroundings and consistently fine rustic French cuisine are the draw to Le Coq au Vin, which is considered to be one of the best French restaurants in the region. The romantic environment is perfect for special occasions. Younger children could, however, become bored with the pace and cuisine.

DOWNTOWN ORLANDO Dexters of Thornton Park $$$
808 E. Washington Street, 32801 **Tel** *(407) 648-2777*

Spacious, light, and airy, with seating at the bar or on barstools at elevated tables. Dexters has a casual ambience and is popular with the urban-professional set. Sandwiches and pastas – small and large portions – are staples, while wines can be ordered both by the bottle and "on tap".

DOWNTOWN ORLANDO Juliana's Restaurant $$$
2306 Edgewater Drive, 32804 **Tel** *(407) 425-1801*

The main street of College Park is the setting for this upscale restaurant where they serve excellent Mediterranean-inspired cuisine, with a particular emphasis on Tuscan fare – their lamb dishes are especially recommended. Juliana's dining rooms are stylish with pleasant artwork, the staff attentive, and there is a decent wine list.

DOWNTOWN ORLANDO The Boheme $$$$
325 S. Orange Avenue, 32801 **Tel** *(407) 581-4700*   **Map** *F2*

One of only two Grand Bosenderfer pianos in the world is the centerpiece this otherwise contemporary setting. Diners can not go wrong with the menu, which features lavishly prepared seafood, game, and pasta. Among the dishes that are highly coveted is the asparagus crusted diver scallops.

DOWNTOWN ORLANDO Fishbones $$$$
6707 Sand Lake Road, 32819 **Tel** *(407) 352-0135*

Fresh selections from the sea are made daily, and diners have the chance to mix various tasty sauces with their selection. Others might opt for the rack of lamb or prime rib at this particularly family-friendly restaurant. It is always worth asking about the catch of the day and local fish and seafood.

DOWNTOWN ORLANDO Gargi's Surfside Restaurant $$$$
1414 N. Orange Avenue, 32801 **Tel** *(407) 894-7907*

A local favorite for more than two decades, the location here on Lake Ivanhoe provides diners with spectacular sunset views of Downtown Orlando. Enjoy a romantic evening with offerings of old-world service and classic traditional Italian food. Take the wine suggestions as gospel.

DOWNTOWN ORLANDO Hue $$$$
629 E. Central Boulevard, 32801 **Tel** *(407) 849-1800*

With decor that has a distinctively big-city look, with large windows and high ceilings, the Hue serves up progressive American cuisine with style. The menu, which changes daily, features dishes such as wood-grilled filet mignon, tamari roasted duck breast, and oven-roasted Chilean sea bass.

Key to Price Guide *see p148* **Key to Symbols** *see back cover flap*

DOWNTOWN ORLANDO K Restaurant & Wine Bar ⚐ $$$$

1710 Edgewater Drive, 32804 **Tel** *(407) 872-2332*

The chef here achieves a grand level of food and service, creating dishes that are both simple and elegantly delicious. From salads to starters to the main course, everything hits the right note, earning the kitchen a sterling reputation. Closed on Sundays.

DOWNTOWN ORLANDO Christini's Ristorante ♪ $$$$$

7600 Dr. Phillips Boulevard, 32819 **Tel** *(407) 345-8770*

This fairly formal restaurant is ideal for a romantic evening. Excellent service, a scenic dining room, and a solid wine list add to the enjoyment of the regional Italian dishes on offer here. The menu varies according to what ingredients are in season, and it is always worth asking about the specials of the day.

DOWNTOWN ORLANDO Hemingway's $$$$$

1 Grand Cypress Boulevard, 32836 **Tel** *(407) 239-1234*

Drawing on the Key West theme intrinsic to the restaurant's name, Hemingway's has a lovely, romantic dining room as well as a deck overlooking a waterfall. Beer-battered coconut shrimp and blackened swordfish with Cajun tartar sauce are among the highlights of the interesting menu.

INTERNATIONAL DRIVE Bahama Breeze ⚐♪ $$

8849 International Drive, 32819 **Tel** *(407) 248-2499*

A menu laden with tastes of the tropics gives diners the chance to indulge their tropical fancy at this eatery. Drinkers might want to sample the delicious *bahamarita*. The light-hearted fun environment helps make it amenable to the whole family, and there are good mingling opportunities for those who are unaccompanied.

INTERNATIONAL DRIVE Chili's Grill & Bar ⚐ $$

7021 International Drive, 32819 **Tel** *(407) 352-7618*

Signature dishes at this casual dining family restaurant include the famous double-basted baby back ribs and enormous burgers. There are also a number of tasty Mexican offerings such as tacos and sizzling fajitas. Outstanding margaritas are available from the full bar.

INTERNATIONAL DRIVE Cedar's Restaurant ⚐♪ $$$

7732 W. Sand Lake Road, 32819 **Tel** *(407) 351-6000*

Cedar's spin on traditional Lebanese food has a lightness of texture and flavor that is both refreshing and inviting. Use the puffy, hot pitas to scoop up *baba ghanoush*, a smooth roasted eggplant and garlic puree with a wonderfully smoky taste. The lunch buffet is a bargain that is well known to locals.

INTERNATIONAL DRIVE Oceanaire Seafood $$$

9101 International Drive, 32819 **Tel** *(407) 363-4801*

Fish is the focus of this upscale national chain that has become a local favorite, often buzzing with the cocktail crowd late at night. The menu changes daily as fresh fish arrives – oysters from Canada and Washington, Scottish salmon, Ecuadorian swordfish, Key West yellowtail, or New England scallops could be among the dishes on offer.

INTERNATIONAL DRIVE Season's 52 ⚐♪ $$$

7700 W. Sand Lake Road, 32819 **Tel** *(407) 354-5212*

The concept here is of fresh seasonal foods. So, be aware that a favorite dish made with pears from Oregon might not be available the next time you go, but you can be sure that something equally impressive will be. The satisfying and occasionally unusual combinations of regional and global ingredients make the food enjoyable.

INTERNATIONAL DRIVE Bonefish Grill ⚐ $$$$

7830 W. Sand Lake Road, 32819 **Tel** *(407) 355-7707*

Moderately priced seafood and a pleasant atmosphere are on offer here. The bar is also popular, and appetizers such as the saucy shrimp and the mussels Josephine are superb, perhaps better than the multiple-choice fish entrées. The seafood offerings change according to what is available on the day.

INTERNATIONAL DRIVE Capital Grille $$$$

9101 International Drive, 32819 **Tel** *(407) 370-4392*

The local chapter in the heart of Convention Center has everything you would expect of this upscale steak-and-seafood chain: dry-aged chops and steaks including a 24-oz porterhouse, oysters from New England, a wood-paneled interior reminiscent of a gentlemen's club, and a staggering choice of 5,000-plus bottles on the wine list.

INTERNATIONAL DRIVE Cuba Libre $$$$

Pointe Orlando, 9101 International Drive, 32819 **Tel** *(407) 226-1600*

Cuba Libre replicates the feel of spicier climes with a two-story Cuban hacienda courtyard, and choreographed floorshows on Saturday nights. Executive chef Guillermo Pernot's award-winning menu features modern contemporary Cuban cuisine. Authentic Cuban rums are used in the delicious cocktails, including the signature mojitos.

INTERNATIONAL DRIVE Everglades ♪ $$$$

9840 International Drive, 32819 **Tel** *(407) 996-9840*

Much better than the average upscale hotel restaurant, Everglades serves creative gourmet dishes inspired by seasonal Florida cuisine. The gator chowder is a colorful touch of Old Florida. Its consistency makes Everglades one of the more popular local restaurants, and there is every chance that kids will enjoy the menu oddities.

INTERNATIONAL DRIVE The Butcher Shop Steakhouse ⬥ $$$$
8445 International Drive, 32819 **Tel** *(407) 363-9727*

Some of the biggest and best steaks along International Drive are on offer here. Diners can even cook their own at the grill for a touch of dinner theater if that is what they fancy doing. The alternative is to sit back and enjoy the good service from staff who deliver cooked-to-order dishes of top quality and consistency.

INTERNATIONAL DRIVE Timpano Italian Chophouse ⬥⬥⬥ $$$$
7488 W. Sand Lake Road, 32819 **Tel** *(407) 248-0429*

The experience of big-city dining with the allure of 1950s New York nightclubs is re-created here. The result is extraordinary quality and impeccable service. The veal *saltimbocca* – thin cutlets served with prosciutto ham and provolone in a subtle garlic and sage sauce – is particularly brilliant.

INTERNATIONAL DRIVE Napa ⬥ $$$$$
9801 International Drive, 32819 **Tel** *(407) 345-4550*

This elegant, formal restaurant in the Peabody Hotel (*see p143*) is named after its southern California-styled cuisine. The menu changes weekly, but is consistently impressive and always includes a vegetarian main course as well as a meat and fish option. This is definitely a destination for special occasions.

INTERNATIONAL DRIVE Roy's Restaurant ⬥⬥ $$$$$
7760 W. Sand Lake Road, 32819 **Tel** *(407) 352-4844*

This upscale restaurant, founded by celebrity chef Roy Yamaguchi, provides a curious fusion of Pacific Rim cuisines, with an emphasis on Hawaiian ingredients. Among typical dishes is the shutome swordfish in a Thai curry sauce. Both the menu and wine list offer a wide variety of selection.

INTERNATIONAL DRIVE Ruth's Chris Steak House ⬥⬥ $$$$$
7501 W. Sand Lake Road, 32819 **Tel** *(407) 226-3900*

Within a gentlemen's club ambience, both the menu and service are delivered with excellence. This New Orleans-based chain serves only aged meats from corn-fed Hereford cows, seared on a 1,800 degree grill – the meat is so tender that a knife is not necessary. This is a restaurant for expense accounts and special occasions.

KISSIMMEE Tropical Breeze ⬥⬥ $
5770 W. Irlo Bronson Memorial Highway, 34746 **Tel** *(407) 397-4004*

Located in Old Town Kissimmee, this good value, casual eating place is well known for its great burgers and good American fare. It is particularly welcoming to children and offers a great selection of dishes and portions with children in mind. There is also outside seating.

KISSIMMEE Black Angus ⬥⬥ $
7516 W. Irlo Bronson Highway, 34747 **Tel** *(407) 390-4548*

This family-friendly restaurant serves flame-broiled steaks, with delicious garlicky mashed potatoes on the side. The New York strip fillet is very popular, and seating is in casual booths and tables. Prices are reasonable, there are nightly steak specials, and kids get a complete dinner at a low cost.

KISSIMMEE Jerusalem Restaurant ⬥⬥ $$
2920 Vineland Road, 34746 **Tel** *(407) 397-2230*

This is a Turkish delight sheltered in a strip mall off the busy US Highway 192. The tabbouli and hummus are made fresh daily, the shish kabob is sizzling hot, and the coffee is bracingly strong. There is authentic couscous for non-meat-eaters, and a great pastry shop next door. Young children may struggle with the menu.

KISSIMMEE Pacino's Italian Ristorante ⬥⬥ $$
5795 W. Highway 192, 34746 **Tel** *(407) 396-8022*

Charbroiled food is the focus of this comfortable and friendly family restaurant, which also provides a free delivery service to nearby hotels. Steaks tend to be the most favored items on the menu, but Pacinos's does a good job of offering a mix of entrées for broad appeal.

MAITLAND Bucca de Beppo ⬥⬥ $
1351 S. Orlando Avenue, 32751 **Tel** *(407) 622-7663*

Think big, big, and bigger at this fun, family-style restaurant with foot-long lasagnes, sandwiches that last a week, and pizzas as big as the table. A good place for those who like to take food home with them; the doggie bags have handles. Reservations for this locals' favorite are highly recommended.

MAITLAND Enzian Theater ⬥⬥ $
1300 S. Orlando Avenue, 32751 **Tel** *(407) 629-1088*

Nachos and hummus with avant-garde films, pasta and salads with thrillers, tiramisu and ice cream with musicals. The premier film and dinner destination all rolled into one, the Enzian shows first-run indie movies with a small but varied menu of dinner and snack items to enjoy while watching the show.

SANFORD Two Blondes & A Shrimp ⬥⬥ $$
112 E. First St., 32771 **Tel** *(407) 688-4745*

This eatery in the heart of Sanford's charmingly restored main street is located in a beautiful renovated building and recreates a Southern seafood-and-steakhouse with an old-fashioned saloon-style bar. It specializes in fresh local seafood – the she crab soup has won awards – and also offers delicious meat dishes and seasonal accompaniments.

Key to Price Guide *see p148* **Key to Symbols** *see back cover flap*

WINTER PARK Brooklyn Pizza
1881 W. Fairbanks Avenue, 32789 **Tel** *(407) 622-7499*

Most in the area – and in the know – consider this to be the best place in town for New York-style pizza. Trading on a family tradition going back over 40 years, Brooklyn Pizza delivers the kind of handmade, authentic pies you had as a child, along with sandwiches, baked dinners, and a few other items.

WINTER PARK Giovanni's
1915 Aloma Avenue, 32792 **Tel** *(407) 673-8800*

This long-time local favorite serves good Italian food, with home-made pizzas and pasta imported from Italy. There is a children's menu, and all dishes are excellent value – meals are reasonably priced and all include bread and salad. Try the chicken marsala or the delicious garlic knots.

WINTER PARK Tijuana Flats
7608 University Boulevard, 32792 **Tel** *(407) 673-2456*

This family-friendly Tex-Mex restaurant has been around since 1995 and features 12 rotating hot sauces, and a variety of Mexican dishes. You stand in line and order your food and they bring it to you. They also have more than 500 hot sauces from around the world on sale. Prices are reasonable.

WINTER PARK Briar Patch
252 N. Park Avenue, 32789 **Tel** *(407) 628-8651*

A perennial favorite on Park Avenue for locals and visitors alike, the front porch coziness and creative menu items keep old fans coming back to the Briar Patch for more. There are long lines at breakfast and weekend lunchtimes – and many who are more then willing to wait. Dining here is fun for the whole family.

WINTER PARK Fiddler's Green
544 W. Fairbanks Avenue, 32789 **Tel** *(407) 645-2050*

One of the largest selections of draft ales, lagers, and stouts in the area is available at this pub, which also serves traditional Irish fare and ambitious offerings such as grilled salmon with champagne sauce. It is all proof that a focus on flavor, presentation, and service can spell "gourmet" for Irish cuisine.

WINTER PARK Miller's Winter Park Ale House
101 University Park Drive, 32789 **Tel** *(407) 671-1011*

Although part of a Florida-based chain they aim to create a neighborhood feel as a local meeting place. The food is excellent value and inlcudes steaks, seafood, and pasta dishes. Children are very welcome and Monday night is free kids night. Fast and friendly service.

WINTER PARK The Boathouse of Winter Park
565 W. Fairbanks Avenue, 32789 **Tel** *(407) 513-4815*

The current occupant of a location that has housed restaurants for decades, the Boathouse serves creative versions of Southern food. High-quality, fresh, and local ingredients turn dishes such as grilled pork chops and fried green tomatoes into something special. Gigantic desserts are made in-house.

WINTER PARK The Cheesecake Factory
520 N. Orlando Avenue, 32789 **Tel** *(407) 644-4220*

Huge, towering interiors, with portions that are almost as large, are typical of this popular chain. More than 30 varieties of mouthwatering cheesecake complement the meal, though you can pick up a piece at the take-out counter for later too. Salads and sandwiches are huge. It is wonderful from beginning to end.

WINTER PARK Café de France
526 Park Avenue S., 32789 **Tel** *(407) 647-1869*

This cozy French bistro serves lighter meals such as crêpes at lunchtime; at dinner, try the rack of lamb or the daily special. A terrific little corner of France in an unlikely location, it can serve as both a great romantic getaway and a special occasion family restaurant. Worth the trip from the central theme park areas.

WINTER PARK Fleming's Steak House
933 N. Orlando Avenue, 32789 **Tel** *(407) 699-9463*

Fleming's is an upscale steakhouse that places great emphasis on the wine. It also offers aged, hand-cut beef in huge, thick-as-a-brick servings and family-style sides, giant seafood entrées, and enormous and highly coveted desserts. Well worth a visit on a special or romantic occasion.

WINTER PARK Luma on Park
290 S. Park Avenue, 32789 **Tel** *(407) 599-4111*

Contemporary American cuisine is served up in cozy surroundings embellished by rich wood and stylish leather trimmings. From the open kitchen appear beautifully presented dishes such as Gulf red snapper, wood-grilled lamb, and Blue Hill Bay mussels with fennel and orange. It is the ideal place for a relaxing meal.

WINTER PARK Park Plaza Gardens
319 Park Avenue S., 32789 **Tel** *(407) 645-2475*

An airy courtyard in a plant-filled atrium provides the setting at this elegant restaurant. The consistently delicious and award-winning American cuisine is served with panache. Good service and a pleasant setting add to the pleasures of the regionally inspired menu. Children may enjoy it, but it is more adult-oriented.

SHOPPING IN CENTRAL FLORIDA

Shopping is one of the major forms of entertainment for visitors to Central Florida. Indoor malls with more than 100,000 sq ft (9,300 sq m) of shopping compete with discount outlet centers, traditional department stores and chain outlets sit side-by-side with unique local shops, and rows of antiques stores are within miles of boutique clothing stores and art galleries. Almost any national retailer can be found on International Drive or in Florida Mall, the state's largest shopping center,

A typical Florida souvenir

while specialty shops sell a wide selection of items, such as antiques, electronics, and sports equipment. Prices range from bargain basement cheap to haute-couture expensive. The theme parks have combined shopping, dining, and entertainment in two massive spending belts running right through their properties, where restaurants and circuses sell souvenirs and souvenir stores offer free magic shows. For listings of malls and factory outlets, see pages 158–9. Shopping districts are described on pages 160–61.

Shops and boutiques along the Park Avenue strip, Winter Park

SALES TAX

Sales tax on clothing is 6.5 percent in Orange County (Orlando) and 7 percent in Osceola County (Kissimmee), where Walt Disney World® is actually situated, so park souvenirs are at the higher rate.

SHOPPING SEASONS

Although actual weather seasons don't vary very much in Central Florida, fashion seasons still turn four times a year. This has led to massive sales in late spring and early fall on clothing and household items.

BOUTIQUE SHOPPING CENTERS

Sitting on the grounds of the first outdoor shopping center in the area, **Winter Park Village** is home to a wide

variety of sleek boutique shops that cater to the latest styles. Fashion can be found at the Ann Taylor Loft store, career-wear at Camille La Vie, and fine men's clothing at Jos. A. Bank. The center offers

The large upscale Mall at Millenia, Orlando

not only clothing, home furnishings, and jewelry stores, but also several fine restaurants, a large Borders bookstore, and, uniquely, condominium lofts above some of the shops.

The Mall at Millenia might also be called a boutique, as it is the only place in Orlando to shop for Jimmy Choo shoes, Max Azria handbags, Betsey Johnson clothing, and Giorgio's of Palm Beach accessories. Shoppers can even find out what they should be buying while watching the latest runway fashions from New York, London, Paris, and Milan on vast screens.

DEPARTMENT STORES

Department stores are still a way of life in Orlando, even with a wealth of smaller specialty shops in malls and neighborhoods. Regional chains such as **Dillard's**, **Bealls**, and **Macy's** dominate the department store scene in Central Florida, offering not only shopping mall outlets but stand-alone stores and discount outlets as well. The Bealls outlets in particular dominate the retail shopping segment, offering discounts on overstock and discontinued goods from the larger stores, and special outlet-only goods and merchandise.

But with the advent of upscale giant malls such as the Mall at Millenia and

An outlet of the exclusive and upscale Saks Fifth Avenue, Orlando

the Florida Mall, national chains are developing a larger presence. Fans of big-city favorites Bloomingdales, Macy's, Nordstrom, Saks Fifth Avenue, and Neiman Marcus can find outlets alongside the more traditional and budget-conscious JC Penney, Sears, and Lord & Taylor in the big malls. For essentials, you need look no further than the no-frills supermarkets such as Target, K-Mart, and Wal-Mart, which can be found anywhere.

Photographic equipment available at a bargain price

SHOPPING FOR BARGAINS

Discount stores and factory outlets carry all kinds of general merchandise, with electronic equipment, household goods and clothing being the biggest draw. Inexpensive designer clothes, sometimes out of season, turn up at local outlets of the TJMaxx, Marshalls, and **Stein Mart** chains at substantial savings over retail. Consignment clothing outlets such as **Deja Vu** and **Orlando Vintage Clothing Co** have deals on pre-owned clothes from modern times back to the 1920s. Shops in the outlet malls have big savings on electronics such as discontinued or factory-second cameras, video equipment, and portable stereos. Then there are the late spring and the fall clearance sales that turn even the high-priced department stores into bargain basements.

One of Florida's many factory outlets, advertising its bargain prices

Shopping Malls

Shopping malls are a quintessential feature of the shopping scene in Florida, where the indoor, air-conditioned mall was invented. They provide all kinds of facilities from movies to restaurants, some even offering personal shoppers and child-minding services. Most malls are conveniently located, often visible from the highway, and in Central Florida range from the Seminole Towne Center on the banks of the St. Johns River to the enormous Florida Mall near the attractions.

Each mall has its own style, some designed as outdoor pavilions, others fully enclosed for all-weather shopping. The discount outlet malls tend to attract large crowds of out-of-town shoppers on the weekends, while the upscale centers fill up during sales. The local Sunday *Orlando Sentinel (see p191)* is a source of sale flyers for the malls. Hotels offer discount cards for most stores, and malls themselves have frequent-shopper programs.

The amazing interior of the Mall at Millenia

The huge food court at the Florida Mall

THE FLORIDA MALL

Sprawling over an area of 200,000 sq ft (18,580 sq m) the Florida Mall is the largest shopping location in Central Florida. It is anchored by the big names of the US shopping industry – Dillard's, JC Penney, Macy's, Saks Fifth Avenue, Sears, and Nordstrom department stores. With more than 250 specialty stores, it's difficult to imagine a category this shopping oasis doesn't cover. Check with guest services for a free discount coupon book.

The Florida Mall is so popular that many local hotels run shuttles to it. It is particularly favored by teens, having an enormous food court and several clothing stores aimed at the younger generation.

For visitors exhausted after hours of shopping, the Florida Mall Hotel has an entrance right on the main Mall concourse. Other hotels in the vicinity include the Howard Johnson, Archway Inn, and the Best Western Florida Mall.

THE MALL AT MILLENIA

Upscale and beyond, the luxury Mall at Millenia offers valet parking, a full service concierge and personal shopper service, and a foreign currency exchange. With its own exit on Interstate 4, the Millenia has Bloomingdales, Macy's, and Neiman Marcus department stores, along with flagship stores from Louis Vuitton, Gucci, Tiffany, Chanel, Apple, IKEA, Tommy Bahama, Burberry, Cartier, St-John, and Cole Haan. Also featured are California Pizza Kitchen, McCormick & Schmick, Brio Tuscan Grille, P.F. Chang's China Bistro, Cheesecake Factory, and Panera Bread.

The atypical food court has more full-service restaurants than many Orlando

The dazzling façade of the Mall at Millenia, one of Orlando's swankiest malls

neighborhoods. Dramatic architectural highlights and dancing fountains add to the glitz of many stores unique to the Orlando area, such as Bang & Olufsen, Japanese Weekend Maternity, Metropolitan Museum of Art Store, and home furnishings specialist Z Gallerie.

DISCOUNT SHOPPING MALLS

One of the most popular malls, the giant **Prime Outlets Orlando** draws as many people as Universal Orlando on a good day. With 170 stores and 700,000 sq ft (6,500 sq m) of outlet shopping, the largest discount center in the country takes up two fully enclosed malls and four strip centers, requiring its own shuttle buses to cover it all. To maximize bargain-hunting time, the mall stays open until 11pm Monday to Saturday, and until 9pm on Sunday.

Factory seconds and overruns cover the spectrum of shopping, from 15 different shoe stores to camera and electronic equipment, from vitamins to bibles, and jewelry to music. Cooks can find discounts on professional knives, while souvenir hunters head for the Universal Studios outlet. Designer labels, such as Geoffrey Beane and Tommy Hilfiger, are all available, along with Mikasa and Pfaltzgraff dishware. Also at Prime Outlets Orlando is the **Off 5th-Saks Fifth Avenue Outlet**, with trendy yet

Orlando Premium Outlets, which stocks designer brands

affordable apparel and sportswear, shoes and accessories, as well as jewelry, luggage, and leather goods.

Orlando Premium Outlets, near SeaWorld, caters to the upscale shopper, offering deep discounts on Burberry, DKNY, Fendi, Nike, Giorgio Armani, and Versace. More than 100 designer brands end up here, from shoes and handbags to apparel and jewelry, as well as a vast selection of housewares and home furnishings.

On the low end of the bargain scale are flea markets, dealing in a mixture of new discount merchandise and recycled bargains. The largest example is **Flea World**, located between Orlando and Sanford. More than 1,700 vendors man booths of antiques, clothing, used books, jewelry, and several more odd assortments of items than can be listed.

DIRECTORY

Flea World

4311 S Orlando Dr,

Sanford, FL 32773.

Tel (407) 321-1792.

www.fleaworld.com

The Florida Mall

8001 S Orange

Blossom Trail,

Orlando, FL 32809.

Tel (407) 851-6255.

www.simon.com

The Mall at Millenia

4200 Conroy Rd,

Orlando, FL32839.

Tel (407) 363-3555.

www.mallatmillenia.com

Off 5th-Saks Fifth Avenue Outlet

5253 International Dr,

Orlando,

FL 32819.

Tel (407) 354-5757.

Orlando Premium Outlets

8200 Vineland Ave,

Orlando, FL 32821.

Tel (407) 238-7787.

www.premiumoutlets.com

Orlando Shopping Mall Information & Maps

www.orlandotourist

informationbureau.

com/shopping/malls.htm

Prime Outlets Orlando

4451 International Dr,

Orlando,

FL 32819.

Tel (407) 352-9611.

www.primeoutlets.com

Seminole Towne Center

220 Towne Center Circle,

Sanford, FL 32771.

Tel (407) 323-2262.

www.simon.com

The Nike Factory Store at Prime Outlets Orlando

Shopping Districts

Retail stores congregate along the high-traffic areas of Orlando, alongside Disney and Universal, and near the large hotels. Aside from the shopping area following the village green of Winter Park, districts tend to be outside of central areas, Downtown Orlando having little shopping of its own. But follow the traffic, and on roads heading southwest to the theme parks and farther west toward the Coast, shopping becomes a journey of discovery. Here, antiques stores and art galleries stand cheek-by-jowl with souvenir stands, and hand-painted furniture is as easily obtainable as a pair of sunglasses.

The Loop shopping center at John Young Parkway, Kissimmee

ORLANDO SHOPPING DISTRICTS

North Orange is a high-traffic strip heading directly out of downtown toward Winter Park. Antiques stores sell tiny knickknacks and several stores cater to home improvement via decorative stone and tile. One of the last great bastions of vinyl and used CDs is **Rock & Roll Heaven**, where you will also find a great selection of posters and vintage magazines for sale. Be sure to check out all the music

memorabilia covering the walls. Comic book fans looking to redecorate can visit **Boom-Art** for furniture and other items decorated in a pop art style by the owners.

A few blocks away from North Orange Street is Mills Avenue, affectionately known as Rainbow Row. This area has more antiques malls, a smattering of art galleries, and several great gay-friendly stores.

The **Orlando International Airport** *(see p192)* has become a major shopping stop, with two Disney Store outlets alongside a Universal Studios store, and two wet-looking shops from SeaWorld in the main concourse. International Drive rewards shoppers by having row upon row of stores catering to every taste. There are brand-name shops

Tile with flamingos

and designer outlet stores, many of which target clothing, shoe, and home decor bargain hunters. Tommy Hilfiger and Armani hold sway at **Pointe Orlando**, an open-air shopping complex replete with palm trees and fountains. The complex also offers several shaded spots where tired shoppers can rest awhile.

Located at the intersection of John Young and Osceola Parkways is **The Loop**, an open-air complex with stores selling electronics, clothing, furniture, and jewelry in a relaxed, fun environment. There is also a diverse range of restaurants to choose from.

WINTER PARK SHOPPING DISTRICTS

Upscale Park Avenue in Winter Park caters to the well-to-do, on a 10-block strip of shops, restaurants, art galleries, and even a museum or two.

Nicole Miller and **Talbots** handle upscale women's clothing, and Banana Republic and The Gap take care of everyone else. Stores such as Williams-Sonoma and Caswell-Massey supply kitchen and makeup items, while **Restoration Hardware** and Pottery Barn fill the home.

Winter Park offers contemporary work from 150 local artists in the Scott Laurent Gallery *(see pp162–3)*, while Timothy's Gallery handles art furniture and home decor. The exemplary gift shop at

A wide variety of shops lined up at Orlando International Airport

Charles Hosmer Morse Museum of American Art gift shop

the **Charles Hosmer Morse Museum of American Art** offers reproductions and apparel based on the museum's collection of Louis Comfort Tiffany artworks. Sample, and get advice about, wines from around the world at **Vino** wine-store.

An expansive outdoor shopping plaza, Winter Park Village *(see pp156–7)* offers an all-round experience, with its many – and varied – clothing shops, home decor and furniture stores, jewelry outlets, a bookstore, fine dining, and a state-of-the-art movie theater.

SHOPPING AT THE THEME PARKS

Souvenirs are not the only expensive things visitors can buy at the theme parks. **Universal CityWalk** *(see pp98–9)* is a center for music and funky dining, but shopping also rules, with a San Francisco-style rambling hill that houses establishments such as the Art Deco jewelry store Silver, and Glow!, which sells only stuff that glows in the dark. The

Souvenirs from Universal Studio

Universal Studios store sells movie memorabilia, while All Star Collectibles offers autographed sports photos and merchandise. After dinner, wander through Cigarz At Citywalk for, yes, cigars, or pick up a realistic – but fake – diamond ring at Elegant Illusions.

Downtown Disney's West Side *(see pp74–5)* is the home of $3,000 sunglasses at Celebrity Eyeworks. At Magnetron, 20,000 magnets come to life every few minutes when the shop's lights are dimmed. The glowing, beeping, ringing magnets come in all shapes and sizes, and there are plenty at reasonable prices. There are also gift shops attached to the House of Blues, Planet Hollywood, and Cirque du Soleil in West Side.

Downtown Disney's Marketplace *(see p75)*, right next door, is home to the LEGO Imagination Center, with a giant Lego dragon towering outside. Disney toys abound in stores at the Marketplace, from the Hasbro Once Upon A Toy store to the World of Disney superstore.

DIRECTORY

ORLANDO

Boom-Art
1821 N Orange Ave,
Orlando, FL 32804.
Tel (407) 281-0246.

The Loop
3208 N John Young
Parkway, Kissimmee,
FL 34744.
Tel (407) 414-3361.
www.attheloop.com

Orlando International Airport
One Airport Blvd,
Orlando, FL 32827.
Tel (407) 825-2001.

Pointe Orlando
9101 International Dr,
Orlando, FL 32819.
Tel (407) 248-2838.
www.pointeorlando.com

Rock & Roll Heaven
1814 N Orange Ave,
Orlando, FL 32804.
Tel (407) 896-1952.

WINTER PARK

Charles Hosmer Morse Museum of American Art
445 Park Ave N,
Winter Park, FL 32789.
Tel (407) 645-5311.
www.morsemuseum.org

Nicole Miller
312 Park Ave S,
Winter Park, FL 32789.
Tel (407) 628-0400.
www.nicolemiller.com

Restoration Hardware
400 Park Ave S,
Winter Park, FL 32789.
Tel (407) 622-1050.
www.restorationhardware.com

Talbots
180 Park Ave N,
Winter Park, FL 32789.
Tel (407) 629-6444.
www.talbots.com

Vino
400 Park Ave S,
Winter Park, FL 32789.
Tel (407) 691-0304.

THEME PARKS

Downtown Disney's Marketplace
10,000 Lake Buena
Vista Blvd,
Lake Buena Vista,
FL 32831.
Tel (407) 824-4321.

Downtown Disney's West Side
Buena Vista Dr,
Lake Buena Vista,
FL 32830.
Tel (407) 828-3058.

Universal CityWalk
1000 Universal Studios
Plaza, Orlando,
FL 33612.
Tel (407) 224-2691.

Specialty Shops

While bargains on clothing is the big retail draw, Central Florida holds its own on more eclectic shopping as well. Indoor and outdoor antiques malls are widespread and popular, cheap electronics hold sway in outlet centers, and Florida's fresh produce can be found in neighborhood farmers' markets almost every day of the week. Work by local artists fills galleries and restaurants alike, and the tourist trade hungers for theme park souvenirs. Orlando's temperate climate means that outdoor sports are a year-round undertaking, which makes sports items a big shopping draw.

Antique Row on Orange Avenue, Orlando

ANTIQUES

The Mecca of antiques in Central Florida is a one-hour drive away from a town called Mount Dora *(see p114)*. The picturesque village on a chain of lakes has the largest collection of antiques dealers and stores in Southern USA. The most dramatic shopping experience is at **Renninger's Antique Center**, with more than 180 shop sites in a 40,000 sq ft (3,716 sq m) air-conditioned building. Open on weekends, the collection of furniture, dolls, silver, and jewelry is difficult to surpass. Dealers here specialize in Art Deco items, World's Fair collectibles, Mission and Arts & Crafts furniture, and art pottery. The area also hosts one of the largest antiques fairs in the US *(see p27)*. This

extravagant event takes place four times a year. There are 20 more antiques shops on the streets of Mount Dora, including **Uncle Al's Time Capsule** for collectible books and souvenirs, and **Fifth Avenue Antique Mall and Emporium**. The North Orange and Mills Avenue areas, in Downtown Orlando, are antiques strips worth exploring. **A & T Antiques** takes on mainly English furniture while **Victoria's Treasure Shop** sells gold and silver jewelry. There are many antique stores in Winter Park, and **American Antiques** is definitely worth a visit.

ART GALLERIES

A growing local arts community means an increasing supply of items for the **Scott Laurent Gallery** in Winter Park, which specializes in local work. **Creative Spirits Art Gallery** displays work from an Orlando artists' guild, while **Millenia Gallery of Fine Art** offers paintings by renowned artists of years past as well as contemporary pieces. **Grand Bohemian Gallery** offers the work of artists from all over the world. Most downtown restaurants have paintings by new artists for sale.

FARMERS' MARKETS

From Friday to Sunday, the **Osceola Flea and Farmers' Market**, starting at 8am, sells locally-grown produce; and every Wednesday at 5:30am there's the **Volusia County Farmers' Market**. At **Top Produce**, which is open every day including Sunday, you can find farm-grown vegetables, herbs, and flowers. Saturday is a fresh treasure-trove for shopping in **Winter Park Farmers' Market**. Sunday means greens from 9am at the **Downtown Orlando Farmers' Market** and the **Celebration Sunday Farmers' Market**.

GIFTS & SOUVENIRS

A popular gift for Florida's visitors are fresh citrus fruits, including the varieties grown in Central Florida such as pink, red, and white grapefruit, Hamlin and Valencia oranges, and tangerines. Not the giant fruit producer it once was, Orlando still has some groves where one can buy fruit or have it shipped directly. Disney and the theme parks have turned merchandising into a fine art, and shopping for souvenirs is a major activity. From concession stands within the parks to shopping arcades, such as Universal's CityWalk® and Disney's West Side, from the authorized **SeaWorld® Stores** at Orlando International Airport to the Universal clearance store at Belz Factory Outlets, it's hard to escape branded gifts. Shops all along International Drive

The bounty at Winter Park Farmers' Market

sell discounted Disney clothing and merchandise. Local museums have stores, such as the **Orlando Science Center Store**, with gifts geared toward current exhibits.

ELECTRONICS OUTLETS

Because of the large influx of foreign tourists, many electronics shops along International Drive and in the outlet malls carry camcorders and video equipment suited for international customers. Sony, Panasonic, Bose, and others have factory outlet shops for bargains on overruns and reconditioned goods. Bang & Olufsen and Sound Advice offer premium equipment not found in the chain outlets.

Ron Jon Surf Shop, one of the best-known sports retailers

SPORTS EQUIPMENT

While an hour from either coast and any ocean, several retailers in Orlando sell scuba equipment and surfboards. The largest of these is **Ron Jon Surf Shop**, a 40-year tradition in Cocoa Beach that opened an outlet in Orlando in 2003 – it features a huge collection of surfboards and swimwear. **Jet Ski Orlando** handles the power water sports toys, while **Play It Again Sports** recycles used golf, tennis, and exercise equipment.

DIRECTORY

ANTIQUES

A & T Antiques
1620 N Orange Ave,
Orlando, FL 32804.
Tel (407) 896-9831.

American Antiques
1500 Formosa Ave,
Winter Park, FL 32789.
Tel (407) 647-2260.
www.webbantiquemalls.
com

**Fifth Avenue
Antique Mall and
Emporium**
130 W 5th Avenue,
Mount Dora, FL 32757.
Tel (352) 735-2394.

**Renninger's
Antique Center**
20651 US Hwy 441,
Mt Dora, FL 32757.
Tel (352) 383-8393.

**Uncle Al's Time
Capsule**
140 E 4th Ave,
Mount Dora, FL 32757.
Tel (352) 383-1958.
www.sign-here.com

**Victoria's Treasure
Shop**
361 E Michigan St,
Orlando, FL 32803.
Tel (407) 849-9719.

ART GALLERIES

**Creative Spirits
Art Gallery**
820 Lake Baldwin Lane,
Orlando, FL 32803.
Tel (407) 898-8343.

**Grand Bohemian
Gallery**
325 S Orange Ave,
Orlando, FL 32801.
Tel (407) 581-4801.

**Millenia Gallery
of Fine Art**
4190 Millenia Blvd,
Orlando, FL 32839.
Tel (407) 226-8701.
www.milleniafineart.com

**Scott Laurent
Gallery**
348 Park Ave N,
Winter Park, FL 32789.
Tel (407) 629-1488.

Timothy's Gallery
236 Park Ave N,
Winter Park, FL 32789.
Tel (407) 629-0707.

FARMERS' MARKETS

**Celebration Sunday
Farmers' Market**
Oct–Jun: 9am–3pm.
Market St, Celebration,
FL 34747. *Tel (407) 892-
1135; (407) 566-1234.*

**Downtown Orlando
Farmers' Market**
9am–2pm Sun.
Central Blvd & Osceola at
Lake Eola Pk, Orlando, FL
32801. *Tel (321) 202-5855.*

**Osceola Flea
and Farmers'
Market**
8am–5pm Fri–Sun.
2801 East Hwy 192,
Kissimmee,
FL 34744.
Tel (407) 846-2811.
www.fleaamerica.com

Top Produce
8am–7pm Mon–Sat,
9am–6pm Sun.
2225 South Goldenrod Rd,
Orlando, FL32822.
Tel (407) 306-8811.

**Volusia County
Farmers' Market**
5:30–11am Wed.
3090 E New York Ave,
Deland, FL 32724.
Tel (386) 734-1614.

**Winter Park
Farmers' Market**
7am–1pm Sat.
New England &
New York Aves.
Winter Park, FL 32789.
Tel (407) 599-3358.

GIFTS & SOUVENIRS

Hollieanna Groves
PO Box 940067, 540 S
Orlando Ave, Maitland, FL
32794. *Tel (407) 644-8803.*
www.hollieanna.com

**Orlando Science
Center Store**
777 E Princeton St,
Orlando, FL 32803.
Tel (407) 514-2245.

SeaWorld Store
Orlando International
Airport, West Hall, One
Airport Blvd, Orlando, FL
32827. *Tel (407) 825-
2642; (407) 825-2632.*

SPORTS EQUIPMENT

Jet Ski Orlando
6801 S Orange Ave,
Orlando, FL 32809.
Tel (407) 859-2005.
www.jetskiorlando.com

Play It Again Sports
2823 S Orange Ave,
Orlando, FL 32806.
Tel (407) 872-3351.

Ron Jon Surf Shop
5160 International Dr,
Orlando, FL 32819.
Tel (407) 481-2555.
www.ronjonsurfshop.com

ENTERTAINMENT IN CENTRAL FLORIDA

Theme parks are just one of the many forms of entertainment available to tourists in Central Florida. This region is home to a wide and varied assortment of theater, dance, and music venues, as well as popular nightspots and bars. The classics are well represented in Orlando by the Philharmonic Orchestra and the several classical music festivals held each year. A thriving Shakespearean company caters to theater patrons, presenting world-class stage productions. The

Advertisement for the Florida Film Festival

annual Florida Film Festival brings independent movie-making closer to home, and offers a launch pad to student filmmakers from local universities who get the opportunity to screen their films alongside professionals. Local theaters such as Enzian showcase an array of art films. Apart from the cultural activities, Orlando also offers nighttime entertainment with nightclubs and dinner shows in Downtown Disney® (see pp74–5), Universal CityWalk® (see pp98–9), and Downtown Orlando.

Scene from a performance in progress, Mad Cow Theatre

SOURCES OF INFORMATION

The two most popular and reliable sources for current and new entertainment listings are the calendar sections of the *Orlando Sentinel*, which is included in Friday's edition of the daily paper, and the free *Orlando Weekly*, which is available on Thursdays. Both can be accessed online as well. You can also check the websites of MSN's City Guide for any additional information.

THEATER

Orlando has a surprisingly rich theater community, and a wide variety of offerings. The not-to-miss event is the **Orlando International Fringe Festival** (*see p25*), which takes place in May each year. The festival brings

more than 60 companies from around the world together for an exciting ten days of almost continuous theatrical activities. A wide range of productions as well as plays of every imaginable kind are showcased here. The **Bob Carr Performing**

Actors dressed in character, Orlando Shakespeare Theater

Arts Center hosts a Broadway series of touring shows with productions such as *The Producers* and *Les Miserables*. With actors constantly drawn to Orlando for work at the theme parks, the local theater has a large pool of talent that organizes both classic and cutting-edge productions at the intimate **Mad Cow Theatre** (*see p109*) and the award-winning **Theatre Downtown**.

The University of Central Florida, Rollins College, and Valencia Community College all have their own individual and unique theater programs. The colleges have full seasons of productions that are open to the public.

At one time only a seasonal theater, the famous Orlando Shakespeare Theater (*see p107*) now mounts high-quality productions of the classics, as well as new plays, throughout the year. The theater has a state-of-the-art center that incorporates four indoor stages.

CLASSICAL MUSIC & DANCE

Orlando's public radio station, WMFE (90.7 FM), broadcasts National Public Radio programs. Broadcasting more than two dozen performances a year on the radio, the highly gifted **Orlando Philharmonic** orchestra also performs more than 100 times each season.

Dancers from the Orlando Ballet performing on stage

They also provide the accompaniment to **Orlando Ballet**, one of the oldest and most renowned professional dance companies in the Southern United States. In addition to its standard productions, the company also presents a Family Season to bring ballet to a younger audience. The Central Florida Ballet is a popular dance company in Orlando. It gives several performances featuring internationally-renowned dancers through the year, as well as other shows that draw on talent within the local community.

Classical music festivals, such as the **Festival of Orchestras** concert series, features five or more internationally acclaimed symphony orchestras each year, including the National Orchestra of France and the New York Philharmonic. The Rollins College **Winter Park Bach Festival** offers perfor-mances from the famous Bach Festival Choir and Orchestra.

DINNER SHOWS

Dinner theater is a popular concept in Central Florida. You can partake of an appetizing dinner while watching an entertaining show. Take a short trip into the Middle Ages as jousting knights fill the arena in front of you at the **Medieval Times Dinner & Tournament** show *(see p170)*. **Pirates Dinner Adventure** is a Broadway-style show alive with swashbuckling stunts and songs. **Arabian Nights Dinner Attraction** is a show that combines magnificent Arabian stallions with gypsy stunt riders and a Wild West show. At **Sleuth Mystery Dinner Shows** one of 13 original comedy mysteries are performed, with improvisation and audience participation. Disney is also home to two dinner

Logo for Auggie's Jammin' Piano Bar

shows with large-scale extravaganzas: Hoop-Dee-Doo Musical Revue at the Fort Wilderness Resort, with a country buffet and Western entertainment, and Disney's Spirit of Aloha *(see p75)*, an evening of hula, fire dancing, and a luau feast at the popular Polynesian Resort.

NIGHTCLUBS & BARS

While clubs and bars are found everywhere, from the theme parks to the coast, the hub of nighttime entertainment is Downtown Orlando. **The Social** is the ideal destination for everything from rock music to the weekly Phat-n-Jazzy show. Most clubs have DJs and places such as **Firestone Live** are perennial hot spots with nights of Latin, hip-hop, and dance music. Giving great views of the Downtown Orlando skyline are the rooftop **Sky 60** and the Amway Center's 67th-floor nightclub **One80 Grey Goose® Lounge**. **Auggie's Jammin' Piano Bar** is a fun nightspot in the Gaylord Hotel featuring dueling pianists. The entertainment starts at 9pm.

The hottest gay club in town is **Parliament House**, which features a restaurant, club, shopping, and guest rooms. Frequent happy hours, free buffets, and headliner acts all contribute to bringing in the crowds.

An exciting chariot race at the central arena, **Arabian Nights Dinner Attraction** show

A karaoke singer at CityWalk®'s RisingStar

LIVE MUSIC AT THE THEME PARKS

Universal's CityWalk® and Disney's BoardWalk are two exciting hot spots for adults. Take center stage at **CityWalk®'s Rising Star** karaoke club. Belt out your favorite songs as the lead singer of a live band.

Nearby, **Bob Marley – A Tribute to Freedom** plays reggae music. Both **Hard Rock Live®** at CityWalk® and **House of Blues®** at Disney's West Side are enormous world-class venues, featuring famous bands from around the globe.

The **Raglan Road® Irish Pub and Restaurant** at Downtown Disney features live music. Disney® also stages the Epcot® Flower & Garden Festival from April to June (see p24), with a Flower Power concert of stars from the 1960s. Universal celebrates Mardi Gras in spring with concerts by stars such as Cyndi Lauper and the Black Eyed Peas.

LIVE MUSIC AWAY FROM THE PARKS

The eclectic nature of Orlando's music scene is reflected at the Orange Avenue strip in Downtown Orlando, which offers hip-hop and avant-garde rock in underground clubs such as Tanqueray's. **The Social** is Orlando's best club for live music. Mid-May brings music lovers to the clubs and open-air stages set up along Orange Avenue for the Florida Music Festival (see p25).

The **Copper Rocket Pub** in Maitland is a local favorite for folk and rock bands. **Backstage at the Rosen Plaza** is a swinging club with live bands in the Rosen Plaza Hotel, while singers at the popular **Red Fox Lounge** croon love songs. **Plaza Live** has become the Florida stopoff for touring big names in jazz, rock, and country, while the high ceilings and dim lighting at **Adobe Gilas** add to the low-key atmosphere of this live-music club. **Will's Pub** on Mills Avenue hosts local bands.

CHILDREN'S ENTERTAINMENT

Apart from Mickey Mouse and the theme parks, there is plenty to entertain kids. The **DisneyQuest®** (see p75) indoor interactive video arcade lets guests design and ride their own thrill ride. Children learn how to draw Disney characters and can record CDs at the Radio Disney Song Maker. The **Orlando Science Center** (see p107) has fun interactive exhibits for kids of all ages and a gigantic CineDome.

The popular Gatorland (see p119), features 110 acres (44 ha) of live alligators, crocodiles, and scenes from Old Florida. A highlight of the park is the Gator Jumparoo where the reptiles leap into the air to be fed by the trainers.

WonderWorks (see p110), set in an "upside-down" building on International Drive, has interactive science exhibits such as virtual roller coasters and a simulated earthquake.

CRUISES & BOAT TRIPS

With thousands of lakes, rivers, springs, and swamps, Florida's waters are a prime source of entertainment. One of the oldest attractions is the Winter Park Scenic Boat Tour (see p113), a one-hour cruise through three lakes interconnected by canals, which takes you past mansions and the sights of natural, unspoiled Florida. Other boat tours in the area navigate Lake Tohopekaliga in Kissimmee, up the north-flowing St. Johns River, or along the vast Intracoastal Waterway that separates Daytona from the Florida mainland. Trips on an authentic Florida airboat guide sightseers along ancient swampland, and dayboats can be hired out for fishing trips.

Live concert performance, Hard Rock Live®, CityWalk®

A family enjoying the day out on a relaxing boating trip

DIRECTORY

THEATER

Annie Russel Theatre
Rollins College, 1000 Holt Ave, Winter Park.
Tel (407) 646-2145.
www.rollins.edu/theatre/annie.html

Bob Carr Performing Arts Center
401 Livingston St, Orlando.
Tel (407) 849-2020.
www.orlandovenues.net

Mad Cow Theatre
54 W Church St, Orlando.
Tel (407) 297-8788.
www.madcowtheatre.com

Orlando International Fringe Festival
398 W Amelia St, Orlando.
Tel (407) 648-0077.
www.orlandofringe.org

Theatre Downtown
2113 N Orange Ave, Orlando.
Tel (407) 841-0083.
www.theatredowntown.net

UCF Conservatory Theatre
4000 Central Florida Blvd, Orlando.
Tel (407) 823-1500.
www.cas.ucf.edu/theatre

CLASSICAL MUSIC & DANCE

Festival of Orchestras
1353 Palmetto Ave, Suite 100, Winter Park.
Tel (407) 539-0245.
www.festivaloforchestras.com

Orlando Ballet
1111 N Orange Ave, Orlando.
Tel (407) 426-1739.
www.orlandoballet.org

Orlando Philharmonic
812 E Rollins St, Suite 300, Orlando.
Tel (407) 896-6700.
www.orlandophil.org

Winter Park Bach Festival
1000 Holt Ave, Winter Park.
Tel (407) 646-2182. www.bachfestivalflorida.org

DINNER SHOWS

Arabian Nights Dinner Attraction
3081 Arabian Nights Blvd, Kissimmee.
Tel (407) 239-9223.
www.arabian-nights.com

Capone's Dinner & Show
4740 W Hwy 192, Kissimmee. *Tel (407) 397-2378.*

Medieval Times Dinner & Tournament
4510 W Irlo Bronson Hwy, Kissimmee.
Tel (407) 396-1518.
www.medievaltimes.com

Pirates Dinner Adventure
6400 Carrier Dr, Orlando.
Tel (407) 248-0590.
www.piratesdinneradventure.com

Sleuth's Mystery Dinner Shows
8267 International Dr, Orlando.
Tel (407) 363-1985.
www.sleuths.com

NIGHTCLUBS & BARS

Auggie's Jammin' Piano Bar
6000 W Osceola Parkway, Kissimmee.
Tel (407) 586-0000.

Firestone Live
578 N Orange Ave, Orlando.
Tel (407) 872-0066.
www.firestonelive.net

One80 Grey Goose® Lounge
400 W Church St, Orlando.
Tel (407) 440-7180.

Parliament House
410 N Orange Blossom Trail, Orlando.
Tel (407) 425-7571.
www.parliamenthouse.com

Sky 60
64 N Orange Ave, Orlando.
Tel (407) 246-1599.

The Social
54 N Orange Ave, Orlando.
Tel (407) 246-1419.
www.thesocial.org

LIVE MUSIC

Adobe Gilas
9101 International Dr, Orlando.
Tel (407) 903-1477.

Backstage at the Rosen Plaza
9700 International Dr, Orlando.
Tel (407) 996-9700.

Bob Marley – A Tribute to Freedom
1000 Universal Studios Plaza, Orlando.
Tel (407) 224-2690.

Copper Rocket Pub
106 Lake Ave, Maitland.
Tel (407) 645-0069.

Hard Rock Live®
6050 Universal Blvd, Orlando.
Tel (407) 351-5483.
www.hardrock.com

House of Blues®
1490 E Buena Vista Dr, Lake Buena Vista, Orlando.
Tel (407) 934-2583.
www.hob.com

Plaza Live
425 N Bumby Ave, Orlando.
Tel (407) 228-1220.
www.plazaliveorlando.com

Raglan Road Irish Pub and Restaurant
3180 Buena Vista Dr, Lake Buena Vista, Orlando.
Tel (407) 938-0300.

Red Fox Lounge
Best Western Mt. Vernon Hotel, 110 S Orlando Ave, Winter Park.
Tel (407) 647-1166.

RisingStar
6000 Universal Blvd, Orlando.
Tel (407) 224-2189.

Will's Pub
1042 N Mills Ave, Orlando.
Tel (407) 898-5070.
www.willspub.org

CHILDREN'S ENTERTAINMENT

Central Florida Zoo and Botanical Gardens
3755 NW Hwy 17-92 Sanford.
Tel (407) 323-4450.
www.centralfloridazoo.org

DisneyQuest®
1486 E Buena Vista Dr, Lake Buena Vista, Orlando.
Tel (407) 828-4600.
www.disneyquest.com

Orlando Science Center
777 E Princeton St, Orlando.
Tel (407) 514-2000.
www.osc.org

CRUISES & BOAT TRIPS

All Orlando Tours
119 N Kirkman Rd, Orlando.
Tel (888) 609-5665.
www.allorlandotours.com

Rivership Romance
433 N Palmetto Ave, Sanford.
Tel (407) 321-5091.
www.rivershipromance.com

WEDDINGS IN CENTRAL FLORIDA

Apart from its fame as an immensely popular vacation spot, Central Florida is now widely recognized as one of the most sought-after wedding and honeymoon destinations. The region's picture-perfect weather is ideal for wedding ceremonies that range from simple, inexpensive backyard affairs to theme park extravaganzas that cost thousands of dollars. Themed weddings are extremely popular and organizers can create anything a couple desires. Private

Bridal bouquet

gardens, cruise ships, Cinderella's Castle, and several attractions from Rivership Romance to SeaWorld® and Walt Disney World® are available as wedding locations to fulfil every fantasy – many a bride with a flowing train has been seen sporting Mickey Mouse ears. Orlando is also famous for its unusual weddings. Couples exchange vows while golfing, fishing, and even in a hot-air balloon. Many local planners offer ceremony and honeymoon packages.

Wedding ceremony in progress at Disney's Wedding Pavilion

INDOOR SPECTACULARS

The Gaylord Palms Resort & Convention Center is a special place to have a wedding. The resort is divided into regions of Florida, so couples can choose whether they would prefer the old-world ambience of St Augustine, the lush mystique of the Everglades, or the festive spirit of Key West. Weddings are conducted under a glass atrium with hundreds of plants and flowers, and there is plenty of banqueting space for large weddings or smaller rooms for more intimate celebrations.

The **Medieval Times Dinner & Tournament** show allows couples to wed against a backdrop of 11th-century

England. Arabian stallions, knights, and fair damsels form a part of the wedding party. The marble halls of Orlando Museum of Art *(see p107)* provide an elegant backdrop for a wedding or a reception. The ceremony is conducted amid a prestigious collection of American artworks.

The Art Deco **Grand Bohemian Hotel** offers a Bohemian-themed wedding with a stay at the upscale hotel. The ceremony is conducted at their rooftop garden. Located at the Universe Shrine Church, the Mary Queen Roman Catholic Chapel can seat a wedding party of up to 2,000 people. The chapel has exquisite stained-glass windows and presents a charming venue for a wedding.

The plush, impressive Grand Ballroom at the **Florida Mall Hotel** holds up to 600 people. It is located within the Florida Mall and gives couples the opportunity to get married at the largest shopping center in Central Florida.

For a more intimate and exclusive gathering, **The Veranda** at Thornton Park is an ideal location. The B&B features a romantic courtyard hidden behind its five historic buildings, and has 10 rooms including a Bridal Suite with a king four-poster bed.

THEME PARKS

Call it romantic, child-like, or corny, a **Walt Disney World® Resort** wedding is always special. With more than 2,000 couples taking the plunge every year, Disney wedding packages start at around $4,500, while the custom wedding arrangements begin at about $10,000. For those not on a budget, a Disney wedding with 100 guests can cost up to $50,000. Weddings at Magic Kingdom® are private and expensive events that are held after the park closes. The bride arrives in Cinderella's glass coach and couples exchange vows in the scenic Rose Garden by Cinderella's Castle. Adding to the revelry are costumed footmen and trumpeters. Animal Kingdom® offers a safari-themed affair, while a bride at the Disney's Hollywood Studios® is driven

A Universal wedding at the Hard Rock Hotel®

around in a limousine and can leave her handprints in front of Mann's Chinese Theater. Celebrants at Epcot can choose the country pavilion they want to get married in. Disney's Wedding Pavilion, a Victorian chapel surrounded by palm trees, can accommodate 300 guests and as many as 12 weddings in a day. Details such as food, flowers, photography, entertainment, and the honeymoon hotel are all taken care of by Disney planners.

Weddings are also held at the Grand Floridian Resort & Spa and Disney's Polynesian Resort *(see p140)*. Weddings can be themed and, of course, Disney characters are very willing to attend. **Universal** *(see p88)* offers weddings in all its hotels,

including the **Hard Rock Hotel®**, where you can celebrate with between 50 and 240 guests in a style fit for rock 'n' roll royalty *(see p140)*.

OUTDOOR EXTRAVAGANZAS

Located near Downtown Orlando, **Harry P. Leu Gardens** *(see p108)* is a lush 50 acres (20 ha) of horticultural splendor. It offers several garden settings for weddings amid rose and camellia collections. The Rose Garden, the Edinburgh Floral Clock, and the Butterfly Garden here are very popular wedding venues. **Kraft Azalea Gardens** is a quiet spot on the banks of Lake Maitland in Winter Park. The garden has flowering trees from January to March and provides a very romantic and beautiful setting for weddings and receptions. The secluded nature of the gardens lends an intimate quality to the event.

Wedding ceremonies at **Albin Polasek Museum & Sculpture Gardens** *(see pp112–3)* in Winter Park are performed on expansive grounds with Polasek's sculptures looking on. Couples can also get married in the garden's romantic chapel.

The **Rivership Romance**, a 100-ft (30-m) steel steamer ship, lives up to its name, creating a magical experience for couples who choose to get married aboard the ship. The natural splendor of Florida's waterways makes a beautiful backdrop for the photographs. A party of up to 200 people can be accommodated on the ship and the package includes a cruise along the St. Johns River and an elaborate dinner, as well as dancing.

Offering 36 holes on two courses, the **Mission Inn Golf & Tennis Resort** combines sport and nuptials. Champagne breakfasts, bridal luncheons, and bachelor party golf outings are all available around the distinctive Spanish architecture. There's a 1930s yacht, *La Reina*, for cruises on Lake Harris. **Historic Bok Sanctuary** *(see p121)* is one of the highest points in Florida and is a National Historic Landmark. Couples can exchange vows here in a romantic setting of palm trees, plants, and a 57-bell carillon.

The English Gardens is a venue offering a secluded tropical setting for ceremonies, receptions, and parties. The gardens are particularly magical at night, when they are lit up. Less than 10 minutes from downtown Orlando, the Gardens can accommodate up to 120 guests, and can help you plan the whole event.

Albin Polasek Museum & Sculpture Gardens

The romantic setting of Disney's Wedding Pavilion, a Victorian chapel surrounded by palm trees and a lake

Orlando Balloon Rides, offering hot-air balloon weddings

THE UNUSUAL

Couples looking for a wedding ceremony that is out of the ordinary have a range of options to choose from. Companies such as **Orlando Balloon Rides** offers delightful hot-air balloon weddings. The package includes transportation to the flight site, a ground-based ceremony followed by a one-hour balloon flight for two, and a champagne toast at touchdown.

Brevard Zoo in Melbourne offers the use of its Serengeti Pavilion, Flamingo Pond, and Australian Aviary for weddings and receptions. As part of the event, zoo staff can conduct train rides through the park, and sometimes guide guests through a Native Florida Wetlands area by kayak. Biker couples get a slice of hog heaven at **Orlando Harley-Davidson®**. The bride and the groom, dressed in biker wedding garb, take a ride on prized Harley bikes, with the processional also following on Harleys. Those in search of even more speed can exchange vows at the **Daytona International Speedway**. The ceremony is performed in the winner's circle and includes a victory lap. At **Fantasy of Flight**, high-flying and airplane-loving couples will find not only a hangar full of vintage aircraft in mint condition and World War II aircraft exhibits, but also facilities to accommodate between 50 and 3,000 guests for a wedding party.

WEDDING PACKAGES

Rather than leave for the honeymoon after the wedding, those getting married in Central Florida can choose from a wide range of wedding and vacation combination packages offered by most of the resorts and hotels.

The Grand Bohemian in Downtown Orlando has three packages – ranging from a simple ceremony with live classical music to a three-course dinner for the couple and ten guests – all including a one-night stay in the Art Deco-inspired hotel. Prices range from $1,600 to more than $3,000.

Disney weddings are highly organized affairs, and offer the celebrating couple many choices. Disney's Escape Weddings offer an elegant, smaller experience and start at about $4,750 plus the required four-day resort accommodations. The package includes an organist and solo violinist, bride's bouquet, wedding cake, a bottle of champagne, limousine, professional Disney photographer, a wedding website, and annual passes for the bride and groom. Locations include Disney's Wedding Pavilion and several resort locations. For a more extravagant affair, the Wishes Wedding can be whatever and wherever you want. Costs start at a minimum of about $15,000.

The Courtyard at Lake Lucerne combines an intimate garden B&B setting, full wedding packages including rehearsal dinners and receptions, and the convenience of a Downtown Orlando setting.

WEDDING DETAILS

There are entire books filled with lists of wedding planners, caterers, tuxedo rentals, coordinators, flower arrangers, and photographers. Invitations can be ordered from local print shops and office supply stores such as Kinkos. There's a wide variety of flower suppliers, from budget dealers such as 1-800-Flowers to boutique florists. Wedding gowns are a hot business, and stand-alone haute couture shops and stores in the high-end shopping malls supply designer dresses. Wedding planners usually take care of all these details.

LEGALITIES

Marriage licenses are available at any court-house in Florida, and some wedding organizers can obtain the license for you by mail. No blood test or waiting period is required for out-of-state residents. Florida residents, however, are required to undergo a three-day waiting period. If previously married, the date of divorce or date of spouse's death must be supplied.

DIRECTORY

FLORIDA COUNTY CLERK'S OFFICES

Clerk of the Court, Orange County
425 N Orange Ave, Suite 355, Orlando.
Tel (407) 836-2067.

Clerk of Circuit Court, Osceola County
2 Courthouse Square, Suite 2000, Kissimmee.
Tel (407) 742-3500.

WEDDING PLANNERS

A Beautiful Wedding
6288 Indian Meadow, Orlando.
Tel (407) 876-6433.
www.orlandowedding locations.com

Just Marry! Just Celebrate!
4785 Blue Major Dr, Windermere.
Tel (407) 839-3244.
www.justmarry.com

Orlando Wedding Group
1225 N Mills Ave, Orlando.
Tel (407) 897-6037.
www.orlandowedding group.com

Weddings Unique
1223-B North Orange Ave, Orlando.
Tel (407) 629-7111.
www.weddingsunique. com

WEDDING SITES

Albin Polasek Museum & Sculpture Gardens
633 Osceola Ave, Winter Park.
Tel (407) 647-6294.
www.polasek.org

Brevard Zoo
8225 N Wickham Rd, Melbourne.
Tel (321) 254-9453.
www.brevardzoo.org

Daytona International Speedway
1801 W International Speedway Blvd, Daytona Beach.
Tel (866) 761-7223.
www.daytonainternation speedway.com

The English Gardens
1871 Minnesota Ave, Winter Park.
Tel (407) 644-3444.
www.englishgarden weddings.com

Fantasy of Flight
1400 Broadway Blvd SE Polk City.
Tel (863) 984-3500.
www.fantasyofflight. com

Florida Mall Hotel
1500 Sand Lake Rd, Orlando.
Tel (407) 859-1500.
www.thefloridamallhotel. com

Gaylord Palms Resort & Convention Center
6000 West Osceola Pkway, Lake Buena Vista.
Tel (407) 586-0000.
www.gaylordhotels.com

Grand Bohemian Hotel
325 S Orange Ave, Orlando.
Tel (407) 313-9000.
www.grandbohemian hotel.com

Harry P. Leu Gardens
1920 N Forest Ave, Orlando.
Tel (407) 246-2620.
www.leugardens.org

Historic Bok Sanctuary
1151 Tower Blvd, Lake Wales.
Tel (863) 676-1408.
www.boksanctuary.org

Hyatt Grand Cypress
1 Grand Cypress Blvd, Orlando.
Tel (407) 239-1234.
www.grandcypresshyatt. com

Kraft Azalea Gardens
Alabama Dr. off Palmer Ave, Winter Park.
Tel (407) 599-3334.
www.cityofwinterpark. org

Medieval Times Dinner & Tournament
4510 W Irlo Bronson Hwy, Kissimmee.
Tel (407) 396-1518.
www.medievaltimes. com

Mission Inn Golf & Tennis Resort
10400 County Rd 48, Howey-In-The-Hills.
Tel (800) 874-9053.
www.missioninnresort. com

Orlando Balloon Rides
Guests meet at Best Western Lakeside, 7769 W Irlo Bronson Hwy, Kissimmee.
Tel (407) 894-5040.
www.orlandoballoonrides. com

Orlando Harley-Davidson®
3770, 37th Street, Orlando.
Tel (877) 740-3770.
www.orlandoharley.com/ wedding

Rivership Romance
433 N Palmetto Ave, Sanford.
Tel (407) 321-5091.
www.rivershipromance. com

The Courtyard at Lake Lucerne
211 Lucerne Circle NE, Orlando.
Tel (407) 648-5188.

The Veranda
115 N Summerlin Ave, Orlando.
Tel (407) 849-0321.

THEME PARK WEDDINGS

Universal Hard Rock Hotel®
Tel (407) 503-2115.
www.loewshotels.com

Walt Disney World® Resort
Tel (321) 939-4610.
www.disneyweddings. com

SPORTS IN CENTRAL FLORIDA

The average temperature of Central Florida is 72°F (22°C). That alone should be enough incentive to think of the Sunshine State as a good sports-oriented vacation destination. The Great Outdoors in Central Florida means fishing, hiking, golf, and more golf. The region's miles of protected land can be explored on foot, bicycle, or boat. Central Florida is the spring training ground for several

Golfers in Orlando

Major League teams and of course, home of Orlando Magic basketball. Then there's car racing, with NASCAR and the Daytona 500 an hour's drive away from Orlando. Indoor sports, water sports, and the odd horse-back ride are available year-round. Disney adds to the mix, not only with their Wide World of Sports athletic complex, but even a sports hotel, the All-Star Sports Resort.

Tiger Woods in action at a tournament at Bay Hill Golf Club

SOURCES OF INFORMATION

Located in Tallahassee, the **Florida Sports Foundation** is the clearing house for state-wide sporting events. The **Department of Environmental Protection** can provide information on outdoor activities. Spectator sports

are listed in the sports section of the *Orlando Sentinel (see p191)*. You can also contact local tourist offices for information about specific areas. Further sources of information are given in individual sections.

GOLF

If golf is your passion, you may already know that Tiger Woods, Arnold Palmer, and 50 or so other PGA Tour players live in the Orlando area. There are over 130 courses within a 45-minute drive of downtown, and Orlando is home to six golf-instruction academies. The tourist comes first, and most of the best courses (several designed by Palmer and Jack Nicklaus) are open to the public.

In Walt Disney World, the **Palm & Magnolia Golf Clubs** challenge even seasoned pros, and host the PGA's Walt Disney World/Children's

Miracle Network Classic. The Arnold Palmer Invitational is held every March at Palmer's **Bay Hill Golf Club & Lodge**, and is considered to be one of the fiercest courses in the country, while Nicklaus chips in with the **Grand Cypress Resort**'s 18-hole New Course, which was inspired by the Old Course at St. Andrews, Scotland. Other top-range courses include **The Oaks, Timacuan, Falcon's Fire Golf Club, Winter Pines Golf Course**, and **Dubsdread Golf Course**, all situated not more than a five-minute drive away from Downtown Orlando.

Combining vacation and golf is easy at resorts such as **Grande Pines Golf Club, Mission Inn Golf & Tennis Resort, Grenelefe Golf & Tennis Resort**, and the **Ventura Country Club. Kissimmee Bay Country Club** was nominated as one of America's best courses by *Golf Digest*.

A game in progress at Falcon's Fire Golf Club in Kissimmee

◁ **A newly wedded couple against the romantic backdrop of Cinderella's Castle**

TENNIS

Orlando serves up more than 800 tennis courts for visitors to raise a racquet everywhere, from public courts and clubs to resorts and apartment complexes. Walt Disney World® has more than 30 of the finest tennis courts in Central Florida, and most of the larger and not-so-large hotels have lit courts.

The city of Orlando runs several public facilities, including the **Orlando Tennis Center** with 16 indoor courts and four outdoor lighted racquetball courts. **Bollettieri Tennis Academy** is the tennis school that produced Andre Agassi and Monica Seles. Situated in West Bradenton, Florida, about a 90-minute drive from Orlando, it is the

Tennis coaching at the Bollettieri Tennis Academy

largest tennis training operation in the world.

Many hotels have courts, and several resorts offer vacation packages that include tennis lessons. Contact the **United States Tennis Association (Florida Section)** at its base in Daytona Beach for information on coaching, clubs, and competitions.

DRIVING SCHOOLS

Central Florida is the home of the Daytona 500 and numerous other NASCAR, Indy, truck, motorcycle, and dirt bike races. The **FinishLine Racing School** offers a three-day program at the New Smyrna Speedway. The program is unique in the racing school industry in that it covers both aspects of race car involvement – stock and NASCAR driving. Drivetech teaches hands-on stock car racing at the USA International Speedway in Lakeland.

Racing fans can enjoy the thrill of the auto-racing experience at two Richard Petty Driving Experience centers *(see p73)* and Test Track *(see p46)* at FutureWorld in Epcot®, offering a 65-mph (104-km/h) simulation on a mile-long electric-car track.

DIRECTORY

SOURCES OF INFORMATION

Department of Environmental Protection
3319 Maguire Blvd,
Orlando, FL 32803.
Tel (407) 894-7555.
www.dep.state.fl.us

Florida Sports Foundation
2930 Kerry Forest Parkway, Tallahassee,
FL 32309.
Tel (850) 488-8347.
www.flasports.com

GOLF

Bay Hill Golf Club & Lodge
9000 Bay Hill Blvd,
Orlando,
FL 32819.
Tel (407) 876-2429.
www.bayhill.com

Disney's Palm & Magnolia Golf Clubs
1950 W Magnolia Palm Dr,
Lake Buena Vista,
FL 32830.
Tel (407) 939-4653.

Dubsdread Golf Course
549 W Par St,
Orlando, FL 32804.
Tel (407) 246-2551.
www.historical
dubsdread.com

Falcon's Fire Golf Club
3200 Seralago Blvd,
Kissimmee, FL 34746.
Tel (407) 397-2777.
www.falconsfire.com

Grand Cypress Resort
1 N Jacaranda,
Orlando, FL 32836.
Tel (407) 239-4700.
www.grandcypress.com

Grande Pines Golf Club
6351 International Golf Club Rd, Orlando,
FL 32821.
Tel (407) 239-6909.
www.marriottgolf.com

Grenelefe Golf & Tennis Resort
3200 State Rd 546,
Haines City,
FL 33844.
Tel (863) 422-7511.
www.thelefe.com

Kissimmee Bay Country Club
2801 Kissimmee Bay Circle,
Kissimmee, FL 34744.
Tel (407) 348-4653.
www.playgolfin
kissimmee.com

Mission Inn Golf & Tennis Resort
10400 County Rd 48,
Howey-in-the-Hills,
FL 34737.
Tel (352) 324-3101.
www.missioninn
resort.com

The Oaks
1500 Oaks Blvd,
Kissimmee,
FL 34746.
Tel (407) 933-4055.
www.kissimmeeoaks
golf.com

Timacuan
550 Timacuan Blvd,
Lake Mary,
FL 32746.
Tel (407) 321-0010.
www.golftimacuan.com

Ventura Country Club
3201 Woodgate Blvd,
Orlando, FL 32822.
Tel (407) 277-2640.
www.venturacountryclub.
org

Winter Pines Golf Course
950 S Ranger Blvd,
Winter Park, FL 32792.
Tel (407) 671-3172.
www.winterpinesgc.com

TENNIS

Bollettieri Tennis Academy
5500 34th St,
W Bradenton, FL 34210.
Tel (800) 872-6425.
www.imgacademies.com

Orlando Tennis Center
649 W Livingston St,
Orlando, FL 32801.
Tel (407) 246-2161.
www.cityoforlando.net/
recreation

United States Tennis Association (Florida Section)
1 Deuce Court, Suite 100,
Daytona Beach, FL 32124.
Tel (386) 671-8949.

DRIVING SCHOOLS

FinishLine Racing School
3113 S Ridgewood Ave,
Edgewater, FL 32141.
Tel (386) 427-8522.
www.finishlineracing.com

Spectator Sports

Those who prefer sports action from the stands can shout out while watching a home game of Orlando Magic basketball at the Amway Center. Also in residence are the Arena Football League Orlando Predators. The University of Central Florida Golden Knights football team plays at the Bright House Networks Stadium. Another sports venue is the Florida Citrus Bowl, where the famed New Year's Day championship is decided, along with the Florida Classic game pitting Bethune-Cookman and Florida A&M.

Unique to Florida is *jai-alai*, a fast-paced game brought to America by Cuban immigrants. Visitors can watch the game at Orlando-Seminole Jai Alai, a place where you can also wager on horseracing.

An Orlando Predators game in progress

A basketball player making a move at a game, Orlando

ESPN WIDE WORLD OF SPORTS®

A jewel in Disney's crown, Wide World of Sports® is a world-class training and exhibition center for sports worldwide. It is the spring training home of the Atlanta Braves and the permanent home of the Amateur Athletic Union. The Wide World of Sports® facilities draw about 250,000 athletes and 1.2 million spectators each year, most of whom come to Central Florida just for the competitions. These cover about 50 sports, including soccer, baseball, slow- and fast-pitch softball, basketball, martial arts, track and field, marathons, cheerleading, and more. There are almost too many pro and amateur events to list: USA Wrestling National Championships, and the USA Judo Championships are but a few. It also hosts the Pop Warner Super Bowl.

The emphasis at EWWS® is on baseball, with football or soccer and other sports events taking place year round.

Visitors can buy tickets to events and to the complex, which boasts four Major League-sized fields, six softball and youth baseball fields, 12 collegiate basketball courts, a 10-court tennis complex, and complete track and field facilities. The 220-acre (89-ha) state-of-the-art complex features the Milk House, a 165,000-sq-ft (15,329-sq-m) field house that seats 5,500 for basketball; the 9,500-seat Champion Stadium ballpark; and the Jostens Center, an 80,000-sq-ft (7,432-sq-m) multi-sport field house. The Hess Sports Fields include four multi-sport fields for soccer, football, lacrosse, and other sports, as well as

four diamonds for baseball and softball. Naturally, there are several sports-related Disney shops. A sports-themed grill rounds out the experience.

BASEBALL

Since World War I, Florida's warm climate has made it a favorite spring training site for Major League baseball teams. Each team returns to the same town every year, pumping millions of dollars into local economy and bringing much prestige. The towns identify strongly with their visitors.

In Central Florida, the training season is from mid-February through March. The Houston Astros spring-train at the **Osceola County Sports Stadium**, which hosts many tournaments and finals.

The gigantic ESPN Wide World of Sports® complex

The Atlanta Braves work out the kinks at the expansive ESPN Wide World of Sports® complex, accommodating as many as 9,500 fans in the only double-decked baseball stadium set up for spring training in Florida; at 100-ft (30.5-m) high, this is also the tallest in the state.

RODEOS

Every February and October since the 1920s, bull riders and cowboys from all over the country have been competing for big purses and top national rankings in Kissimmee's **Silver Spurs Rodeo**, which is billed as the largest in the Eastern United States, that is, east of the Mississippi, and dates back to 1944. Echoing the time when Florida was one of the top cattle producers in the country, the event features competition in bull- and bronco-riding, steer-wrestling, and barrel-racing. The rodeo is held in the state-of-the-art Silver Spurs Arena, which provides climate-controlled comfort for 8,300 people. It is also used for other events, such as concerts and sports.

Bronco-riding at Silver Spurs Rodeo, Kissimmee

Logo of Silver Spurs Rodeo

AUTO RACING

World speed records were made and then broken on the hard, flat sand of Daytona Beach in the 1920s. Since then, Central Florida has been the center of American car racing. **Daytona International Speedway** *(see p118)* is the home of NASCAR, the epitome of speed. In addition to 10 major weekends of racing activity, including the world-famous Daytona 500, the Speedweeks in February, and the motorcycle racing events in March and October, the speedway showcases 190-mph (305-km/h) stock cars, superfast motorcycles, and souped-up, 125-mph (200-km/h) go-karts.

Located just south of Daytona, **New Smyrna Speedway** offers various stock car racing events almost year-round, from the World Series of Asphalt in February to the Florida Governors Cup in November. Stock cars also roar west of Orlando at the USA International Speedway in Lakeland.

Race cars whizzing by at the internationally renowned Daytona 500

The Great Outdoors

Central Florida is a land of thousands of lakes and crystal-clear spring-fed rivers, punctuated by forests, as well as some of the most temperate climate in the country. A pristine beach is never more than a comfortable drive from any spot in the area; it's entirely possible to catch a sunrise surfing in Daytona, canoe down the St. Johns River, ride at a dude ranch, para- or hang-glide, bike a 20-mile (32-km) marathon, and still catch a glorious sunset in Melbourne Beach. With lush state parks and nature sanctuaries dotting the region, Central Florida is also a major ecotourism center, as well as prime hunting and fishing territory. Central Florida, in other words, is just as much fun for an active vacationer as it is for the theme-park lover.

Harry P. Leu Gardens, a lovely, serene park in bustling Orlando

A family enjoying a leisurely cycle ride in an Orlando park

BIKING & BIKE TRAILS

Lake County, the only area that can be said to have hills, is the home of bicycling in Central Florida, with triathlons from May through October, and an annual 100-mile (160-km) Bicycle Festival in October. Clermont is the center of competition biking, including triathlons for kids over 7 and adults over 70.

Central Florida's "rails-to-trails" network affords hikers more than 220 miles (350 km) of reclaimed rail corridors for hiking. The 41-mile (66-km) stretch from Clermont is particularly impressive, running right through the Withlacoochee State Forest and paralleling the river of the same name.

Orange County alone has more than 30 miles (48 km) of trails. The West Orange Trail extends 22 miles (35 km) along the borders of Lake Apopka and connects Oakland, Winter Garden, Ocoee, and Apopka. The trail features running routes, equestrian walkways, and paved paths for cyclists and skaters. The Cross-Florida Trail runs through the Little Big Econlockhatchee Forest, crossing Central Florida from the Gulf of Mexico to the St. Johns River, a 110-mile (177-km) corridor offering off-road biking opportunities as well as paddling along the Ocklawaha and With-lacoochee Rivers. The 12-mile (19-km) Rock Springs Run in the Wekiva River Basin is a designated mountain-biking trail.

PARKS & NATURE WALKS

The city of Orlando alone has 4,000 acres (1,618 ha) of parks, including the **Harry P. Leu Gardens** with the largest camellia collection and formal rose garden in Southern United States (*see p108*). Several nature preserves flourish within the city limits; these include the

A group of youngsters cycling along a scenic country trail near Orlando

Nature viewing the cowboy way in Central Florida

7-acre (3-ha) Delaney Park, near Downtown Orlando, and the beautifully wild Dickson Azalea Park, to the southeast of downtown, surrounded by native ferns, palms, and oaks. Located in Apopka, a short distance from Orlando, **Kelly Park** features Rock Springs, naturally fed and bubbling into a meandering stream. Wekiwa Springs State Park, also in Apopka, is another oasis with beautiful waters and acres of land. **Blue Spring State Park** is a restful spot that wintering manatee call home from December through February *(see p114).*

Fountain in Harry P. Leu Garden

HORSEBACK RIDING

Dozens of riding academies and stables offer trails and lessons to tourists, and two "dude ranches" give a taste of Florida's cowboy past. Located on 750 acres (300 ha) in Kissimmee, **Horse World Riding Stables** offers trail rides for riders of different levels of ability and Western riding lessons. **Florida Eco-Safaris** in St. Cloud offers overnight horseback adventures that reveal the true, old Florida landscape and culture. Journey deep into Forever Florida, a 4,700-acre (1,902-ha) eco-ranch and wildlife conservation area that contains nine distinct Florida ecosystems and an endless array of natural flora and

fauna, including alligators and black bears. Guests can choose their own adventure from a range of fully guided options. There's a two-hour open-air coach safari, which offers an elevated view of the conservation area; the horseback safaris of varying duration cover trails first used by Native Americans; or guests can soar through the treetops 55 ft (17 m) off the ground on the exciting zipline safari.

HANG- & PARA-GLIDING

Several outfitters in Central Florida offer courses in hang- and para-gliding, as well as rides. For hang- and para-gliding lessons, **Quest Air Soaring Center** takes you on flights of up to

60 miles (96 km). Florida's largest glider teaching school, **Seminole-Lake Gliderport** in Clermont, offers introductory sailplane rides for one or two people and sailplane rental.

SURFING & OTHER WATER SPORTS

An hour's drive from Downtown Orlando, the Space Coast offers 72 miles (115 km) of Atlantic shore and white sand beaches. The Easter Surf Festival, sponsored by Ron Jon Surf Shop in Cocoa Beach, is one of the major stops along the professional surfing circuit. Most of the hotels on the beach at Daytona offer wind-surfer rentals, and two large windsurfing schools operate within minutes of Downtown Orlando. To the east, area residents head for New Smyrna Beach, Cocoa Beach, Sebastian Inlet, and the pristine stretches of the Canaveral National Seashore.

Swimming is as natural as breathing to most residents of Florida. Many hotels have pools, but the real joy of Florida is the opportunity to swim in the ocean or in the lakes, springs, and rivers that abound throughout the state. The full range of water sports, from windsurfing to jet skiing, is offered at the region's resorts; waterskiing can also be enjoyed on freshwater lakes and inland waterways.

Jet skiers at a Buena Vista water sports complex

A couple enjoying brisk canoeing on an Orlando waterway

CANOEING

With more than 2,000 lakes and several connected chains, Orlando is prime boating territory. There are 17 miles (27 km) of natural springs leading from the clear, limpid waters of Wekiwa Springs to the St. Johns River, with plenty of camping opportunities for the hardy and riverside restaurants and bars for the casual.

The Harris Chain of Lakes can take you, from the opposite end of the St. Johns, all the way to the Atlantic Ocean. The Econlockhatchee River runs through Orange and Seminole counties, affording ample opportunities to see undisturbed wilderness minutes from developed Florida. Blue Spring State Park's wonderfully clear water is as good for snorkeling and scuba diving as it is for boats. Many inland waterways are suitable for small boats. Houseboats can be rented from several marinas in Sanford on the St. Johns River, for example.

ECOTOURISM

With more species of plants and animals than any other state, Florida is a natural paradise, ranked 11th in the world for ecotourism. Just north of the Kennedy Space Center, the Merritt Island National Wildlife Refuge and the Canaveral National Seashore *(see p123)* is the largest wildlife preserve on the Eastern Seaboard, with more than 310 species of birds, best seen in winter. The Space Coast holds more than 220 sq miles (570 sq km) of protected wildlife refuges and 40 parks. Blue Spring State Park has a 72°F (22°C) spring, and is home to endangered manatees. It features camping, hiking, and canoeing. Speaking of the gentle giants, locally-run "manatee encounters" offer the chance for small groups to actually swim with them in crystal-clear springs.

Florida Eco-Safaris in St. Cloud is an assembly of nature preserves and the Crescent J Cattle ranch, which together makes up 4,700 acres (1,902 ha) of pristine Florida wilderness for trail rides and outdoor camping. The **Enchanted Forest Nature Sanctuary** on the East Coast winds through the ancient Atlantic Coastal Ridge and 393 acres (160 ha) of coastal hardwood forest.

Fun 2 Dive, Scuba & Snorkling Tours in Sanford offers Manatee snorkling trips and scuba diving where no experience is necessary. They also offer other tours, including eco-tours and wildlife photography tours.

FISHING

Florida's many lakes and rivers provide lots of opportunities for freshwater fishing, but it is most famous for its deep-sea sport fishing for species such as the marlin. The Daytona Beach area features some of the best ocean fishing found anywhere. Marlins are found in the Gulf Stream, while grouper and red snapper can be caught from the reefs. Two dozen private charter boats sail daily from the docks at Ponce Inlet. Fishing on Lake Tohopekaliga and

Snowy egrets keeping a lookout for prey in Merritt Island National Wildlife Refuge

A quiet day's fishing in the calm waters of a lake in Kissimmee

the Kissimmee chain of lakes means largemouth bass, and this area produces more bass over 10 lb (4.5 kg) than any other place in the world. Lakes in the Greater Orlando area also offer catfish and bream, and Merritt Island, to the east, is known for sea trout, snook, and tarpon.

HUNTING

About an hour's drive from Orlando, the Ocala National Forest (*see p118*) is the place for hunters, with whitetail deer and wild turkey in season. Seasonal hunting is also permitted in the wildlife management area in Osceola County at the **Triple N Wildlife Ranch**. There's quail, rabbit, raccoon, wild hog and coyote here, as well as large game, including deer.

LICENSING & SEASONS

A separate fishing license is required to fish on Florida lakes and rivers, or in saltwater. Proof of a successfully completed hunter safety course is required before a license to hunt with a firearm or bow is issued. From May to September it is possible to hunt alligators and applicants are selected through a random drawing. December to January is licensed duck season. Antlered deer and wild hog season is November to January, as is wild turkey. The season for quail, turkey, and squirrel is November to March. Saltwater fish season is virtually year-round.

DIRECTORY

BIKING, BIKE TRAILS, NATURE WALKS & PARKS

Blue Spring State Park
2100 W French Ave, Orange City, FL 32763.
Tel (386) 775-3663.
www.floridastateparks.org

City of Orlando Parks Department
www.cityoforlando.net/public_works/parks

Florida Trails
www.floridaconservation.org
www.traillink.com

Florida Triathlon Events Sommer Sports, Inc.
838 W Desoto St, Clermont, FL 34711.
Tel (352) 394-1320.
www.sommersports.com/home

Kelly Park
Kelly Park Dr, Apopka, FL 32712.
Tel (407) 889-4179.

Wekiwa Springs State Park
1800 Wekiva Circle, Apopka, FL 32712.
Tel (407) 884-2008.
www.floridastateparks.org

HORSEBACK RIDING

Florida Eco-Safaris
4755 N Kenansville Rd, St. Cloud, FL 34773.
Tel (407) 957-9794.
www.floridaecosafaris.com

Horse World Riding Stables
3705 Poinciana Blvd, Kissimmee, FL 34758.
Tel (407) 847-4343.
www.horseworldstables.com

HANG- & PARA-GLIDING

Quest Air Soaring Center
6548 Groveland Airport Rd, Groveland, FL 34736.
Tel (352) 429-0213.
www.questair hanggliding.com

Seminole-Lake Gliderport
Clermont, FL 34712.
Tel (352) 394-5450.
www.soarfl.com

ECOTOURISM

Enchanted Forest Nature Sanctuary
444 Columbia Blvd, Titusville, FL 32780.
Tel (321) 264-5185.

Florida Eco-Safaris
4755 N Kenansville Rd, St. Cloud, FL 34773.
Tel (866) 854-3837.
www.floridaeco-safaris.com

Fun 2 Dive, Scuba & Snorkling Tours
503 S French Ave, Sanford, FL 32771.
Tel (407) 322-9696.
www.fun2dive.com

FISHING & HUNTING

Florida Fishing Seasons
Tel (850) 245-2555.
www.fishingfloridakeys.com/fish_seasons.htm

Florida Fish & Wildlife Conservation Commission
620 S Meridian St, Tallahassee, FL 32399.
Tel (850) 488-4676;
1-888-HUNT-FLORIDA (486-8356);
1-888-FISH-FLORIDA (347-4356).
www.myfwc.com

Triple N Wildlife Ranch
5600 Crabgrass Rd, St. Cloud, FL 34773.
Tel (407) 498-0991.

SURVIVAL
GUIDE

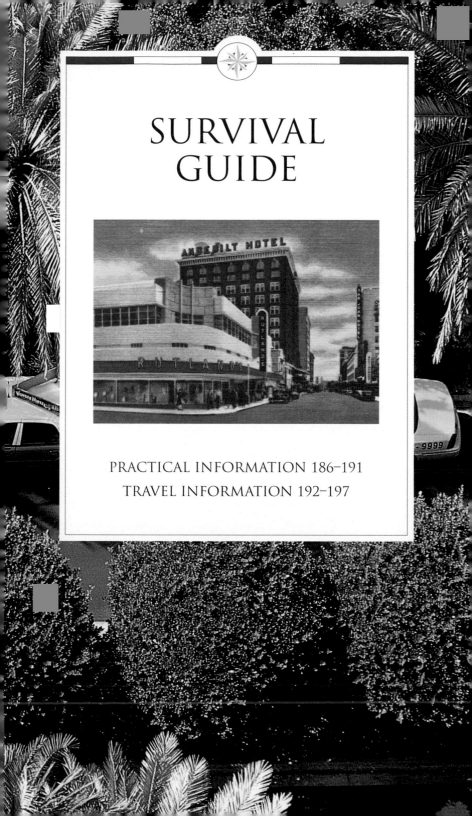

PRACTICAL INFORMATION

Theme parks, perennially gorgeous weather, and a location central to both Florida coasts brings 46 million people to the Orlando area every year, 26 times the number who live there. Not surprisingly, the main industry of Orlando is tourism. With four Disney theme parks, two at Universal, and two marine parks, the emphasis is on entertainment and creating the perfect family vacation. Mickey Mouse and other favorite characters attract children, while world-class museums, cultural events, and theaters appeal to parents. At peak tourist season, during the Thanksgiving, Christmas, and Easter holidays, airfare

The State Seal of Florida

and hotel prices run high, while late winter and early fall bring heavy discounts, shorter lines, and readily available rooms. But there is much more to Orlando than just the theme parks. Central Florida is ranked as one of the best ecotourism destinations in the world, with miles of freshwater lakes, the magnificent St. Johns River, and pristine wildlife sanctuaries spreading to the East Coast. The warm weather also promises a range of sporting activities, such as swimming, horseback riding, para-sailing, waterskiing, and golf. It is impossible to take in everything that Central Florida has to offer in one or even two weeks.

Orlando/Orange County Convention & Visitors Bureau

VISAS

Citizens of Great Britain, New Zealand, Australia, and of many EU countries do not need a visa to enter the US, providing they have a return ticket and their stay does not exceed 90 days. However, they must apply for entry online via the Electronic System for Authorization (ESTA) before travel (https://esta.cbp.dhs.gov). Travelers are advised to register well in advance of their departure date. Canadians need to show a valid passport. Other citizens must apply for a non-immigrant visa from a US consulate.

TOURIST INFORMATION

Some of the information booths at tourist and shopping areas are really time-share dealers offering "half-price tickets" to theme

parks in exchange for several hours of sales pitch. But there are genuinely helpful Orlando Tourist Center booths located downtown, on International Drive, and in larger hotels.

Downtown's **Orlando City Hall** tourist office and the official Information Booth at Orlando International Airport are of particular help for brochures and discount coupons. Both these centers are open daily from 7am to 11pm. Concierge services are available at most hotels, and the customer service centers at the theme parks are an amiable information source. The Official Accommodations Guide to Orlando, including a vacation planning kit, is available from the **Orlando/Orange County Convention**

& Visitors Bureau. Tourists can also call the **Florida State Tourism Board**'s toll-free number to order a visitor's guide to the state. The guest services at both Walt Disney World® and Universal Studios are also extremely helpful. Interested callers can ask for vacation guides, which are mailed to them free of charge.

Both the daily **Orlando Sentinel** and the "alternative" **Orlando Weekly** newspapers publish calendar sections of events in the area, which are duplicated on their websites. The online resource **The Daily City** offers a guide to happenings in town. The monthly **Orlando Magazine** offers advice on restaurants and cultural happenings. Free magazines,

A hotel lobby in Orlando displaying tourist information brochures

◁ **Cabs waiting for passengers on an Orlando street**

A roadside tourist information center, Kissimmee

available at many coffee shops, bars, and restaurants, include *Watermark*, and *Axis*.

ADMISSION CHARGES

Most museums, parks, and other attractions charge an admission fee. This can vary enormously, from $2 at a small museum to over $85 for a day pass at a theme park.

A family outing at a theme park is hence an expensive proposition. The two Universal Orlando® parks are $85 for adults ($79 for kids) per park, while SeaWorld® charges $79.99 for an adult one-day pass and $71.99 for kids aged three to nine. Walt Disney World® tickets for adults are $85 for a single day; kids are $79. Multi-day tickets are available at all parks and offer better value for money. At Disney they're called Park Hopper Tickets, allowing guests unlimited visits to all four Disney parks; the current price is $298 for four days ($279 for kids). Universal Studios offers a "2-Park Flex-Ticket" for unlimited entry at Universal Studios, Islands of Adventure®, and Wet 'n Wild®

for 4 days; the rate is $188.49 per adult and $175.49 for kids. Special rates are offered throughout the year, or through the internet or ticket agencies, but they need to be bought in advance. There are "Florida Resident" rates and passes, in case you know a local.

Many sights of interest offer discounts to children, card-carrying students, and senior cititzens. The Orlando Museum of Art, for instance, charges $8 for adults, $7 for seniors and college students, and $5 for children aged seven to 18; children under six go free.

Reduce the admission price and buy budget meals in local restaurants by using coupons found in brochures available at tourist offices.

OPENING TIMES

Most of the attractions open daily. All the theme parks, for instance, are open 365 days in a year. Most of them open at 9am and close between 7pm and 11pm, depending on the season, with extended opening hours during the high season. State parks are

usually open every day from sunrise to sunset, though the attached visitor centers may close earlier. Some sights close once a week, often on Mondays. Many, including the Orlando Science Center, Orlando Museum of Art, Mennello Museum of American Folk Art, and Morse Museum of American Art *(see p107 & p112)*, have extended hours on Friday and Saturday, and are open only in the afternoon on Sunday. Some sights close on major national holidays: typically New Year, Thanksgiving, and Christmas.

WHEN TO GO

Given its warm climate, Central Florida is a favorite winter destination for most North Americans. Late fall and early winter are very crowded in Orlando, especially at the parks. Book flights and hotels as early as possible. If you're determined to join the crowded tourist season at Disney, planning vacations around the New Year at Magic Kingdom® or the Epcot® International Flower and Garden Festival in April can make the trip more worthwhile.

Plan your family vacation for mid-January–February and September–October to avoid crowds and the summer heat. If you're willing to brave some high temperatures, May is a relatively quiet month at the parks. Theme parks often have off-season multi-day deals, and hotels offer discounted rates.

Visitors strolling along a street near Disney's BoardWalk Resort

Children touching a rock from Mars at the Space Center *(see pp124–7)*

TRAVELING WITH CHILDREN

The reason most children come to Orlando is for the theme parks. However, some rides may be unsuitable for smaller children. Ask the park attendant for a description of the ride. Many so-called "thrill rides" are extremely scary for children, even ones that look safe at first view. New, technologically advanced rides that include 3-D, fog, and motion simulation, such as Men in Black™ – Alien Attack™ *(see p92)* and the Amazing Adventures of Spider-Man® *(see p96)*, can be a little frightening for young kids. Never put a crying child on a ride; every attraction has a rest area off to one side of the doors, and if the child gets too distressed there are medical stations nearby. Also scout out the "lost child" area, and rely on park personnel if your child wanders off.

The glare of Florida's sun can be damaging to young eyes, so remember to take sunglasses as well as sunblock and hats. Small wagons and strollers, even multiple seat strollers, can be rented from Visitor Services just inside the gates at the Disney, Universal, and Sea-World parks. It's worth remembering that Walt Disney World Resort guests are offered an "Extra Magic Hour" entry into the parks, one hour prior to the regularly scheduled park opening

hours on specific dates. This helps families with small children avoid the massive early morning crowds.

Because of Orlando's dependence on tourists, most restaurants and hotels are child-friendly with special seats and menus as well as fun activities. Don't forget what may sound like a joke these days: the "early bird specials." Yes, they do exist. Some family-friendly restaurants in and around Orlando offer the punctual guest heavy discounts for arriving for breakfast before 8am or between 4 and 6pm for dinner.

Theme parks, museums, and other attractions generally have special rates for children between the ages of three and 18, while some allow free admission for

those under three. One of the best child-friendly attractions is Kennedy Space Center *(see pp124–7)*, open every day of the year except December 25.

If you're driving, remember that Florida law requires all occupants of vehicles who are six years of age or older to wear seat belts, and you can receive a ticket for seat belt violations alone. Children up to five years old must be secured in a crash-tested child restraint seat. Car rental agencies will have the right seats available.

SENIOR CITIZENS

Florida has always attracted senior citizens for recreation or permanent settlement. Hotels, car rental agencies, airlines, and many shopping venues offer seniors special discount rates, and it never hurts to ask for a discount anyway. The giant discount malls on International Drive make a point of slashing their already low prices for senior shoppers. Members of the **American Association of Retired Persons (AARP)** are offered many area discounts, including sports and cultural events, and the **National Council of Senior Citizens**, also known as Senior Service America *(see p191)*, can provide hotel and car rental discounts. Amtrak, Greyhound, and the LYNX bus system *(see p196)* have

A senior citizen enjoying a round at Magnolia Golf Club *(see p176)*

Provision for wheelchair users on the Kilimanjaro Safaris® expedition *(see p66)*

special rates for travelers aged 50 and over. The average theme park guest walks between 5 and 7 miles (8–11 km) a day, so it is important to know that standard and motorized wheelchair rentals are available from Visitor Services just inside the gates of all the theme parks.

TRAVELERS WITH DISABILITIES

Always be sure to make hotel management aware of any potentially serious health problems. Walt Disney World® in particular has its own medical staff and facilities to deal with any emergency. Always carry a list of your medications. All of the resorts and the restaurants at the theme parks have rooms that are wheelchair-accessible.

Wheelchair access sign

Concierge services at major hotels can assist in getting handicapped parking placards for cars. At Universal, wheelchairs are available for rental at $12 per day and Electric Convenience Vehicles are available for rental at $45 per day. It is recommended that you call up at least 24 hours in advance to make a reservation. Universal Orlando® has compiled a rider's guide for guests with disabilities, available on its website, that details access for each attraction.

Disney has a limited number of wheelchairs available at the Guest Services Desk, at the entrances to Magic Kingdom®, Epcot®, Animal Kingdom, and Disney-MGM Studios®. Magic Kingdom® and Epcot® also

have motorized wheelchairs. Disney offers a "Guidebook for Guests with Disabilities," and you can get hold of a copy by calling the main information number.

Sign language interpreting services are also available at Universal Studios Florida® and Islands of Adventure®. There is no extra charge for anyone wanting to use this service.

COMMUNICATIONS

Online sources of Orlando information abound, from the websites of the **Orlando Sentinel** and **Orlando Weekly** newspapers, to city guides run by **CitySearch** and **MSN**. These not only give overviews of happenings and restaurants, but also offer bulletin board comments on attractions, restaurants, and other venues from local residents. The major television stations also have Internet calendars. There is a branch of business supply giant, FedEx Office, or one of the major office supply stores – OfficeMax, Office Depot, and Staples – on practically every street corner, making fax and copying services readily available.

Wireless Internet is widely available, with access points in local Starbucks, bookstores and also in public spaces where vistitors can take advantage of free Wi-Fi. Most major hotel chains and many cafés and restaurants, as well as the Orlando International Airport, also offer convenient Internet access.

Newspaper vending machines lined up in a row on a sidewalk in Orlando

Police officers on patrol, Florida-style

PERSONAL SECURITY

Most cities in the region, like elsewhere in the world, have "no-go" areas that should be avoided. The staff at the local tourist office or in your hotel should be able to advise. Note that downtown areas are generally unlike city centers elsewhere; they are first and foremost business districts, which are dead at night and often unsafe.

As beautiful as "The City Beautiful" may look, it also has the potential for less than secure situations. Certain areas of Orlando, such as the Orange Blossom Trail and areas surrounding the downtown main strip of Orange Avenue, should be avoided after dark, and even brightly lit sections of town shouldn't be navigated alone. If in doubt, take a taxi rather than walk. The downtown LYNX bus terminal is not a place to hang around in. Be aware of who is around you in the sprawling parking garages at the theme parks, , and keep an eye on your belongings while enjoying the "party strips" of Downtown Disney as well as Universal CityWalk.

Carry as little money as possible when you go out. If you are attacked, hand your wallet over immediately; do not try to resist.

The major tourist centers of Central Florida are well policed. Given the region's eagerness to both attract and protect tourists, police officers are friendly and helpful to

visitors. Orlando City police are visible in most high-traffic areas; the Mounted Police unit can be seen patroling downtown neighborhoods daily. The theme parks are fanatical about security and visitor service; Disney, for example, has its own fire and police departments and health personnel.

Even if you have only a slim chance of retrieving stolen property, you should report all lost or stolen items to the police. Most credit card companies have toll-free numbers for reporting a loss, as do **Thomas Cook** and **American Express** for lost traveler's checks.

A postcard from the "Sunshine State"

SAFETY FOR DRIVERS

Certain areas of Orlando are better avoided, and keeping alert to highway signs is a must. The well-traveled routes of major highways and main streets are the safest, but even the prominent thoroughfares can suddenly become illogical. The Florida State Police Department has a cellphone emergency 911 service in operation. The Automobile Association of America *(see p197)* places "Good Samaritan" vehicles on the highways to intercept emergencies of various kinds.

Keep some basic rules in mind while driving around

the region. Local drivers change lanes frequently on expressways, so stick to the right and be alert near exits. Speed limits are rigorously enforced, and fines can be as much as $250. Avoid taking short cuts in urban areas. Stick to the main highways if possible. If you need to refer to a map in a city, don't stop until you are in a well-lit or busy area. Avoid sleeping in the car off the highway, although some rest areas on expressways have security patrols. Seat belts are mandatory for all under Florida law. The **Orlando City Hall** website lists road closures.

NATURAL HAZARDS

The major cause of vacation injury in Orlando is the heat. Standing in long lines under the dazzling Florida sun can mean sunburn, rashes, heatstroke, and heat exhaustion. Bring hats, sunglasses, lots of bottled water, and a high SPF waterproof sunscreen – reapply this often, especially at water parks. Plan park visits early in the day or after 5pm.

The natural beauty of Florida can be dangerous. Orlando is riddled with over 1,000 lakes, and chances are the larger ones might contain alligators. There are also several venomous snakes native to Florida. Don't forget to carry insect repellent for mosquitoes and summer gnats.

Florida's beaches are usually well-supervised by lifeguards, but do keep a close eye on young children. Riptides can be dangerous in some places.

A county sheriff, in the regulation dark uniform, and his patrol car

DIRECTORY

TOURIST INFORMATION

Florida State Tourism Board
Tel (866) 972-5280.
www.visitflorida.com

Kissimmee/St. Cloud Convention & Visitors Bureau
Tel (407) 742-8200.
www.visitkissimmee.com

Orlando/Orange County Convention & Visitors Bureau
Tel (407) 363-5872.
www.visitorlando.com

ONLINE INFORMATION

CitySearch
http://orlando.citysearch.com/

MSN City Guide
www.local.msn.com

Orlando City Hall
Tel (407) 246-2121.
www.cityoforlando.net

The Daily City
www.thedailycity.com

MAGAZINES & NEWSPAPERS

El Sentinel (Spanish language edition)
www.orlandosentinel.com/elsentinel

La Prensa
Tel (407) 767-0070.
www.impre.com/laprensafl

Orlando Business Journal
Tel (407) 649-8470.
www.orlando.bizjournals.com

Orlando Leisure Magazine
Tel (407) 647-5557.
www.orlandoleisure.com

Orlando Magazine
Tel (407) 423-0618.
www.orlandomagazine.com

Orlando Sentinel
Tel (407) 420-5000.
www.orlandosentinel.com

Orlando Weekly
Tel (407) 377-0400.
www.orlandoweekly.com

The Wall Street Journal, Orlando office
Tel (407) 857-2600.

WHERE Orlando
www.wheretraveler.com

TV & RADIO

ABC: WFTV-Channel 9
Tel (407) 841-9000.

CBS: WKMG-Channel 6
Tel (407) 521-1323.

Fox: WOFL-Channel 35
Tel (407) 644-3535.

NBC: WESH-Channel 2
Tel (407) 645-2222.

PBS: WMFE-Channel 24
Tel (407) 273-2300.

UPN: WRBW-Channel 65
Tel (407) 644-3535.

WB: WKCF-Channel 18
Tel (407) 645-1818.

WJRR (101.1 FM)
Rock/Alternative
Tel (407) 916-1011.

WLOQ (103.1 FM)
Smooth Jazz
Tel (407) 647-5557.

WMFE (90.7 FM)
Public radio
Tel (407) 273-2300.

WOMX (105.1 FM)
Adult contemporary
Tel (407) 919-1000.

WTKS (104.1 FM)
Talk radio clear channel
Tel (407) 916-7800.

WWKA (92.3 FM)
Country
Tel (407) 298-9292.

OTHER NUMBERS

American Association of Retired Persons
Tel (888) 687-2277.
www.aarp.org

Mobility International
Tel (541) 343-1284.
www.miusa.org

National Council of Senior Citizens; Senior Service America
Tel (301) 578-8900.
www.seniorserviceamerica.org

Seniors First
Tel (407) 292-0177.
www.seniorsfirst.org

EMERGENCY NUMBERS

All Emergencies
Tel 911 for police, fire, or ambulance.

Centra Care
Walk-in medical care.
Tel (407) 200-2273.

Moneygram
Tel (800) 666-3947.

Orlando Police Information Desk
Tel (407) 246-2470.
www.cityoforlando.net

Poison Control
Tel (800) 222-1222.

LOST CREDIT CARDS & TRAVELERS' CHECKS

American Express
Tel (800) 221-7282 (checks).
www.home.americanexpress.com

Diners Club
Tel (800) 234-6377.
www.dinersclub.com

Discover
Tel (800) 347-2683.
www.discovercard.com

MasterCard
Tel (800) 627-8372.
www.mastercard.com

Thomas Cook
Tel (800) 223-7373 (checks).
www.thomascook.com

VISA
Tel (800) 847-2911.
www.visa.com

TRAVEL INFORMATION

More than 51 million visitors flock to the warmth and recreation of Central Florida each year, making it one of the most sought-after tourist destinations in the world. Orlando International is Florida's busiest airport, welcoming millions of visitors every year; and many more arrive by train and bus. The network of interstate highways

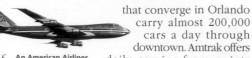
An American Airlines passenger jet

that converge in Orlando carry almost 200,000 cars a day through downtown. Amtrak offers daily service from points North and West, with sleeper cars, and even has room for the family car. Once there, almost all roads lead to the theme parks, with a celebrated public transit system taking some of the burden off the very busy highways.

The brightly illuminated terminal of Orlando International Airport

ARRIVING BY AIR

Orlando's local airports are served by virtually all US domestic carriers and a wide selection of international airlines, including Airtrans, Aerolineas Argentinas, Aer Lingus, Lufthansa, United Airlines and the British favorites Virgin Atlantic and British Airways.

The vast **Orlando International Airport** is the third largest airport in the US and is continuing to expand. The addition of discount carriers such as **Spirit Airlines**, **Sunwing**, and **JetBlue**, is creating a flurry of cheaper flights to this vacation hub.

Orlando-Sanford International Airport has expanded to serve more destinations; carriers include Allegiant Air, Icelandair, Monarch, and Flyglobespan.

Daytona Beach International Airport brings in daily flights from Atlanta on **Delta** and **US Airways**, and flights from the Bahamas on Island Pass Airlines.

AIR FARES

Travel costs to the world's most popular vacation site depend very much on the season. Unfortunately for the vacationer, prime holiday time in Orlando is when fares are at the highest. The difference between late winter (February and March) airfares, when tourist traffic is low, and the height of busy season (November and December) can more than double the price per ticket. The best deals can be found on midweek

flights. Inexpensive fares can usually be found on the online travel websites, but they are geared toward larger carriers and do not include the more popular discount airlines such as JetBlue and **Southwest**. It is better to check online with these airlines directly, as they often have "cyberdeals" only available on the Internet. It can also be an advantage not to plan ahead, with some airlines offering last-minute specials on unsold seats.

AIRPORTS

One of the country's top airports for overall customer convenience, Orlando International Airport boasts state-of-the-art services. Fast intra-airport transportation via monorail and moving walkways leads to shuttle buses, taxis, and public transportation to Downtown Orlando and the parks. Mutilingual tourist information centers by the security checkpoints are open from 7am to 11pm. The airport can also offer an evening's rest, with the Hyatt Regency Hotel and its

A taxi outside the Orlando International Airport

The shopping area at Orlando International Airport

446 rooms right in the main concourse. Banks of rental car agencies are located on the baggage levels in both terminals and taxi and bus-stands are outside Level 1. There are also plenty of shopping and dining opportunities at the airport, with stores from Disney, Universal and SeaWorld®, and the usual selection of airport restaurants right in the terminal. Much quieter than the main Orlando airport, the Orlando-Sanford International is about 30 minutes from Downtown Orlando. It is a major hub for charter flights from Britain and Canada, and is increasingly being used by smaller carriers as a low-pressure alternative.

Daytona Beach International Airport is a small, modern airport located about 4 miles (6 km) out of Daytona. It offers direct flights, mainly with Delta Airlines and US Airways, from

Highway Patrol insignia

various East Coast cities to the world's most famous beach *(see p116)*.

GETTING TO TOWN

The LYNX bus system *(see p196)* runs from Level 1 of the A side of the Main Terminal, departing every 30 minutes from 5:30am to 11:30pm. Travel time to Downtown Orlando is approximately 40 minutes, and to International Drive 60 minutes, at a cost of $2 for either destination. Make sure you have exact fare; the transfers to connecting buses are free. Many hotels have their own courtesy buses, but there are also shuttle buses *(see p196)*: the **Mears Transportation Group** *(see p197)* serves most destinations in the area. Shuttle vans, accommodating up to nine people, have posted rates running at about $17 per person for trips downtown or to Disney. Taxis *(see pp197)* from Orlando International to hotels and theme parks are available at both terminals A and B, just outside baggage claim on Level 1. To avoid costly metered fares, look for a yellow Mears cab for posted flat rate fares to downtown and Walt Disney World®; they accept credit cards. Ground transportation at Orlando-Sanford International is conveniently found right outside the terminal.

The People Mover monorail at Orlando International Airport

Getting Around

Just about a century ago, Central Florida was mostly dirt roads surrounded by orange groves. The present-day convergence of highways, parkways, and six-lane thoroughfares makes Orlando an automotive heaven. Several major roads run through, across, or near downtown, and almost all roads lead to the theme parks. Walt Disney World and Universal Orlando resorts have their own exits on Interstate 4 and the Central Florida Greeneway. Local streets leading to the parks are lined with restaurants and shopping malls.

You can get by without a car in Orlando, but life is much easier with one. If you don't bring your own, car rental rates are among the lowest in the US, and gas is relatively inexpensive. In addition, Floridians are generally courteous and considerate drivers.

Interstate
Highway 4

City parking
restrictions

Speed limit
(in mph)

REST AREA

Rest area,
indicated off an
interstate

Overhead signs at the junction
of two routes

RULES OF THE ROAD

On a two-way street or highway, all drivers moving in either direction must halt for a stopped school bus. At intersections with traffic lights, you may turn right on red if the way is clear and there is no sign prohibiting the turn. Left turns on red from a one-way street into a one-way street are also allowed. Passing is allowed on both sides on any multi-lane road, including interstate highways.

According to Florida law, wearing seat belts while traveling in vehicles is compulsory for all (see p188). Driving under the influence is treated very seriously, so don't drink even one beer. Violators can be fined hundreds of dollars or even be imprisoned for a short period of time.

Most road signs are clear and self-explanatory. If you are caught disregarding instructions, you might be fined. The speed limits in Florida are as follows:
• 55–70 mph (90–105 km/h) on highways.
• 20–30 mph (32–48 km/h) in residential areas.
• 15 mph (24 km/h) near schools.

Speed limits can vary every few miles, so keep a sharp eye out for the signs. On an interstate you can be fined for driving slower than 40 mph (64 km/h). The speed limits are rigorously enforced by the Florida Highway Patrol, whose representatives issue tickets on the spot. A fine can set you back as much as $250.

HIGHWAYS & TOLLS

Metropolitan Orlando is the crossroads of Florida's busy highway system, where the north–south Florida's Turnpike meets east-west Interstate 4. The Beach Line Expressway (State Road 528), which runs east-west, the Central Florida Greeneway (State Road 417) running

An aerial view of Orlando, showing busy, merging highways

south and east into Walt Disney World, and East-West Expressway (State Road 408) connecting Downtown Orlando to I-4, are toll roads. Tolls range between 50 cents and $1.50 per station. Toll roads also operate on an electronic system called SunPass; transmitters can be purchased locally. Florida toll booths do not take bills larger than a $20.

NAVIGATING

The main thoroughfare in Orlando is Interstate 4. Heavily trafficked, it connects all the theme parks and outlet shopping areas in the west with downtown and the bedroom communities to the east. During the morning and the evening rush hours, the highways slow to a virtual standstill, the worst being I-4 through downtown and the area around Walt Disney World, so time your trips accordingly. Be aware that the exit numbers on I-4 were changed in 2003, so older maps and directions will surely be incorrect.

Because of the expense, the toll roads are the least travelled, and while I-4 can sometimes become a parking lot during odd hours, roads such as State Roads 417 and 408 can appear blissfully empty.

Much has been done to improve roads heading west from downtown, and roads such as John Young Parkway can sometimes offer a slower but surer route to the theme parks. The Beach Line is the fastest way from Orlando International Airport to Universal Orlando and

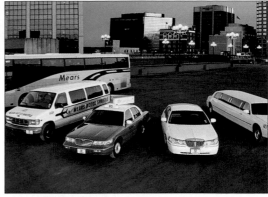

Mears Taxicab dispatch fleet, which includes cars for rent

SeaWorld®, while the Central Florida Greeneway leads directly west to Disney.

Visitors staying at any one of the massive hotels on International Drive will soon discover Sand Lake Road, which leads to the parks as well as to several enormous shopping malls.

CAR RENTAL

To the chagrin of locals, rental car companies offer the best deals to out-of-towners, sometimes as low at $10 a day. Multi-day packages for weekend rentals are usually the best deals, and arranging those deals before you leave home can often mean substantial savings. Check your existing car insurance for rental before you agree to sign the contract. While a Collision Damage Waiver (CDW) is expensive, it sometimes covers damage to the vehicle that insurance will not, even if it was not your fault. Companies differ in their policies concerning gas; some charge for what you use while others will ask that you fill the car before you return it. The major companies *(see p197)* either have rental kiosks right in the airports – Orlando International's are right next to baggage

Logo of the Hertz car rental company

The dreaded rush hour in Orlando

claim; Orlando-Sanford's rentals are right outside the terminal – or a short and free shuttle bus ride away. There are also several agencies in Orlando.

BIKE RENTAL

Orlando is ideal for moving around on a bicycle with its 200 miles (322 km) of bike trails. The Disney resort hotels – Caribbean Beach Resort, Grand Floridian, and others – offer rentals on Disney property, while **David's World Cycle** rents mountain and road bikes.

If you prefer the motorized variety, **American V Twin Motorcycles** rents Harley Davidson motorcycles. **West Orange Trail Bikes & Blades Co.** in Winter Garden offers not only bicycles but also in-line skates. Large groups of 20 or more can schedule guided bicycle tours.

Bike riders on a trail in Walt Disney World® Resort

An Amtrak train moving along a track at the Auto Train yard, Sanford

TRAINS

With a much-discussed light rail system still in the planning stage, rail travel through Central Florida means **Amtrak**. From an Art Deco-inspired station in the heart of the city, Amtrak offers a limited schedule of local travel, including stops in Downtown Orlando, Winter Park, Kissimmee, and points south to Miami. Fares run from $6 for a short hop to Winter Park, to around $30 to Miami, one way. Auto Train is very popular as it provides transport for family and vehicle from Washington, DC to Sanford. But do check for height restrictions on SUVs.

Of course, Amtrak connects across America and into Canada too, with Orlando being one of the more popular destinations. But cross-country rail travel is both time-consuming and expensive when compared to airlines. The 24-hour trip from New York can cost twice the comparable plane flight. A four-day trip from Los Angeles by rail will cost more than $1,100 per person, but that includes the comfort of a bedroom and meals.

LONG-DISTANCE BUSES

Whether you are traveling from other parts of the country or within Florida, Greyhound buses offer the cheapest way to get around. Some services are "express," with few stops en route, while others serve a greater number of destinations. A few routes have "flag stops," where a bus may stop to deposit or collect passengers in places without a bus station. Pay the driver directly, or, if you want to reserve in advance, go to the nearest Greyhound depot. Passes provide unlimited travel for set periods of time – from between four and 60 days – but are useful only if you have a very full itinerary.

PUBLIC TRANSPORT IN CITIES

The award-winning **LYNX** bus system, with more than 60 routes and 4,000 stops through three counties, makes getting around Central Florida inexpensive and easy. The brightly decorated buses fan out from the central station north to Lake Mary, east to Winter Park and Orlando International Airport, and south to Walt Disney World® and Universal Orlando®. The theme park routes in particular are probably the easiest way to the parks if you're staying downtown, with scheduled service from 7am to after 10pm. Look for the signs with pink paw prints denoting LYNX

Orlando's LYNX bus logo

bus stops. A standard, one-way fare throughout the system is only $2, and passes are available for unlimited travel. A Single-Day pass is $4.50, seven days of travel will cost $16, and a month-long pass is $50. Long-term passes can be purchased online at the LYNX website, with Single-Day passes available from the driver when you board any LYNX bus. Downtown visitors have the no-cost advantage of the free LYMMO service, which runs along its own traffic lane every five minutes between 6am and 10pm (midnight on Friday and Saturday). The service connects the Church Street entertainment area to the Amway Center, with stops including the Regional History Center and the Orange County Courthouse.

SHUTTLE BUSES

Most major hotels offer free shuttle buses from the airports to the various resorts. Once you have arrived at your destination, the same hotels

A hotel shuttle bus advertising the Orlando FlexTicket pass

usually have van transportation to Disney, Universal Orlando®, and SeaWorld®. If not, **Mears Transportation** *(see also p193)* offers shuttle vans to various attractions in the area.

The **Daytona-Orlando Transit Service (DOTS)** offers shuttles to and from the airports to the beaches seven days a week. The company also offers single and multiday motor coach tours to various Florida locations, including Key West, Nashville, and Fort Meyers, as well as others that take in the countryside or the fall foliage.

TAXIS

The most readily available taxis are at stands at the Orlando International and Orlando-Sanford airports, taxi-only lanes at most larger hotels, and those circling the theme parks, particularly at the main entrances to the various parks and at Universal CityWalk and Downtown Disney's nightlife entertainment areas. Those operated by **Mears Taxi Dispatch**, with their bright orange paint, and Yellow Cab, are metered and

An I-Ride Trolley for the I Drive area

thought to be the most trustworthy – avoid hiring one of the many "gypsy" cabs, which may end up costing several times what the fare is worth. Reserving a taxi from the airport or by cell phone will give the option of paying by credit card.

Street sign of the I-Ride trolley service

OTHER MODES OF TRANSPORT

One of Orlando's most popular tourist centers,

International Drive provides special transportation for visitors in the form of old-fashioned buses, called the **I-Ride Trolleys**. Trolleys run from the Major Boulevard area and Prime Factory Outlet shops to SeaWorld®, with 83 stops in between; the frequency is 20–30 minutes year-round, seven days a week, from 8am to 10:30pm. Multi-day passes are available. Another old-fashioned way to see the Orlando area is by the **Winter Park Scenic Boat Tour**, on Lake Osceola. Tour boats depart on the hour from 10am to 4pm daily for a 12-mile (19-km) narrated cruise. An even older form of transportation is provided by **Orlando Pedicab** who operates several free human-powered jitneys around downtown. **Discount Mobility USA, Inc.** provides vehicle hire for the disabled.

DIRECTORY

BREAKDOWNS

American Automobile Association (AAA)
Tel (407) 444-7000.
www.aaa.com

AAA General Breakdown Assistance
Tel (800) 222-4357.
NOTE: Rental companies provide 24-hour roadside assistance.

CAR RENTAL

Alamo® Rent a Car
Tel (800) 327-9633.
www.alamo.com

Avis Rent a Car
Tel (800) 831-2847.
www.avis.com

Budget® Rent a Car
Tel (800) 527-0700.
www.budget.com

Dollar® Rent a Car
Tel (800) 423-4704.
www.dollar.com

Enterprise
Tel (800) 736-8222.
www.enterprise.com

Hertz
Tel (800) 654-3131.
www.hertz.com

BIKE RENTAL

American V Twin Motorcycles
Tel (407) 903-0058.
www.amvtwin.com

David's World Cycle
Tel (407) 422-2458.
www.davidsworld.com

West Orange Trail Bikes & Blades Co.
Tel (407) 877-0600.

TRAINS

Amtrak
Tel (800) 525-2550.
www.amtrak.com

BUSES

Daytona-Orlando Transit Service (DOTS)
Tel (800) 231-1965;
(386) 257-5411.
www.dots-daytonabeach.com

LYNX Buses
Tel (407) 841-5969.
www.golynx.com

Mears Transportation Group
Tel (407) 423-5566.

TAXI RENTAL

Mears Taxicab Dispatch
Tel (407) 422-2222.

OTHER MODES OF TRANSPORT

Discount Mobility USA, Inc.
Tel (800) 308-2503, (407) 438-8010.
www.discountmobilityusa.com

I-Ride Trolley
Tel (407) 248-9590.
www.iridetrolley.com

Orlando Pedicab
Tel (321) 217-2233.

Winter Park Scenic Boat Tour
Tel (407) 644-4056.
www.scenicboattours.com

General Index

Acknowledgments

Main Contributor

Phyllis & Arvin Steinberg live in Florida. Phyllis writes about travel for US newspapers, magazines, and websites. She is also a food columnist for 24 newspapers in Florida and cruise editor for a popular travel website. Arvin writes travel articles for US newspapers, magazines, and websites, and is sports editor of a widely read travel website.

Joseph Hayes is a freelance writer for newspapers and magazines around the world, specializing in food, travel, and music. He is also an accomplished playwright, with productions in several countries.

Charles Martin is a Florida-based journalist and radio broadcaster who writes columns and articles on Florida events for numerous local, national, and international lifestyle magazines.

Factchecker

Kia Bocko

Proof Reader

Bhavna Seth Ranjan

Indexer

Shreya Arora

Photography

Dave King, Magnus Rew, Stephen Whitehorn, Linda Whitwam

Illustrations

Arun Pottirayil, Julian Baker

DK London
Publisher

Douglas Amrine

Publishing Managers

Jane Ewart, Fay Franklin

Editorial & Design

Emma Anacootee, Brigitte Arora, Claire Baranowski, Tessa Bindloss, Jane Edmonds, Rhiannon Furbear, Jennifer Greenhill-Taylor, Joseph Hayes, Laura Jones, Juliet Kenny, Esther Labi, Maite Lantaron, Jude Ledger, Carly Madden, Mary Ormandy, Catherine Palmi, Rada Radojicic, Mani Ramaswamy, Susana Smith, Arvin and Phyllis Steinberg, Rachel Symons

Additional Photography

Rough Guides/Demetrio Carrasco

Senior Cartographic Editor

Casper Morris

Senior DTP Designer

Jason Little

DK Picture Library

Hayley Smith, Romaine Werblow, Gemma Woodward

Production Controller

Shane Higgins

Special Assistance

Many thanks for the invaluable help of the following individuals: Kelly Rote, Central Florida Visitors & Convention Bureau; Susan Mclain, Daytona Beach Convention & Visitors Bureau; Georgia Turner, Georgia Turner Group; Dave A. Wegman, Greater Orlando Aviation Authority; Danielle Courtenay, Julie Doyle, Julie A. Fernandez, Orlando/Orange County Convention & Visitors Bureau; Lita O'Neill, Polk County Natural Resources Division; Jacquelyn Wilson, SeaWorld Orlando & Discovery Cove; Susan L. Storey, NBC Universal, Orlando; Jason L. Lasecki, Walt Disney World Resort; Sandra Sciarrino, Wet 'n' Wild; Ian Williams.

Photography Permissions

Dorling Kindersley would like to thank the following for their assistance and kind permission to photograph at their establishments: Albin Polasek Museum & Sculpture Gardens, Audobon National Center for Birds of Prey, Buena Vista Watersports, Falcon's Fire Golf Club, Hard Rock Café Live, Holy Land Experience.

Key: a-above; b-below/bottom; c-centre; f-far; l-left; r-right; t-top.

The publishers would like to thank the following individuals, companies, and picture libraries for their kind permission to reproduce their photographs:

ALAMY: Mark J. Barrett 117cla, Randa Bishop 107bl, Bernie Epstein 8cl; M. Timothy O'Keefe 65br; ANTIQUE & CLASSIC BOAT SOCIETY: 25tl; AQUATICA © SEAWORLD ORLANDO: 86cl.

CENTRAL FLORIDA FAIR: 24 tc; CENTRAL FLORIDA VISITORS & CONVENTION BUREAU: 20tr; THE CHARLES HOSMER MORSE MUSEUM OF AMERICAN ART: 161tl; CORBIS: 21bcr, 129 (inset), 170tc; Archivo Iconografico, S.A 13b; James L. Amos 182b, Tony Arruza 20bl, 103b, 117cra; Yann Arthus-Bertrand 194b; Bettmann 192tc; Gary Braash 21crb; Duomo 116tr; Raymond Gehman 28-29, 102; Martin Harvey 21tr; Lake County Museum 7 (inset), 114tl, 185 (inset), 190c; David Muench 21cla, Marc Muench 117bl; James Randkley 12; Phil Schermeister 17b, 21cr; George Teidmann/ Newsport 27b,179bl; Partrick Ward 24cla; Nick Wheeler 130cl; RAIMUND CRAMM: 123cla.

© DISNEY: 1c, 2–3, 4br; 5tl, 10cl, 15t, 18tr, 18cla, 18clb, 18br, 30, 31b, 32bc, 33tl, "The Twilight Zone™ is a registered trademark of CBS, Inc. and is used pursuant to a license from CBS, Inc." 33cra, La Nouba by Cirque du Soleil ® 33br, 34bl, 36tr, 36br, 37tr, 37br, 38tr, 38bl, 39br, 40tl, 40br, 41tl, 42cla, 43tl, 44b, 46bl, 47tr, 50tl, 50br, 51tl, 52tl, 52b, 53tl, 54bl, 55tl, "The Twilight Zone™ is a registered trademark of CBS, Inc. and is used pursuant to a license from CBS, Inc." 56, 58-59, 60tl, 61b, 62br, 64cl, "It's Tough to be a Bug!" based upon the Disney/Pixar film " A Bug's Life" © Disney/Pixar 64br, 65tl, 66tr, 66b, 67tr, 68-69, 70tr, 70bl, 71tr, 71bl, 72tr, 72cla, 72bl, 73tr, 73cl, 74br, 75tl, *La Nouba* by Cirque du Soleil ® 75c, © LEGO 75br, 130bc, 131tr, 131b, 134tr, "Woody" from the Disney/Pixar film "Toy Story" ©Disney 134cl, 134br, 136cl, 147br, 164-5, 170cl, 171b, 174-75, 178br, 187b, 188br, 189tl, 195br.

ENZIAN THEATER/FLORIDA FILM FESTIVAL: 15c, 24crb, 166tc, 166bc; FALCON'S FIRE GOLF CLUB: 8br; FLORIDA DEPARTMENT OF ENVIRONMENTAL PROTECTION DIVISION OF RECREATION & PARKS: 115b; FLORIDA MALL: 157tl, 158cl; FLORIDA STATE ARCHIVE: 17c; FRANK LANE PICTURE LIBRARY: © David Hosking 180tr.

GAYLORD PALMS RESORT & CONVENTION CENTER: 167c; GENESIS SPACE PHOTO LIBRARY: 20tl, 20c, 20clb, 126bl, 126bc, 126br, 126bc; SEAN GILLIAM: 196t; GREATER ORLANDO AVIATION AUTHORITY: 132tl, 160b, 192cl, 193tl.

HARD ROCK CAFÉ: 130tc, 131tl.

IMG BOLLETTIERI TENNIS ACADEMY IN BRADENTON: 177tl; INDEX STOCK PHOTOGRAPHY. INC., New York: 123cra; INSTITUTE OF SYSTEMIC BOTANY, UNIVERSITY OF SOUTH FLORIDA: Guy Anglin 21clb

KENNEDY SPACE CENTER – VISITORS CENTER, Cape Canaveral: 23c, 124c; 124tr, 125cr, 125ca, 126tr, 188tl; KISSIMMEE ST-CLOUD CONVENTION & VISITORS' BUREAU/Doug Dukane: 180b, 183tl.

LEGOLAND® FLORIDA © MERLIN ENTERTAINMENTS GROUP: Chip Litherland 121tr; THE LOOP, ORLANDO: 160cl; LOEWS HOTELS: 171tl.

MAD COW THEATRE: 109tl; MARINE SCIENCE CENTER, PONCE INLET: 21tl; MARY EVANS PICTURE LIBRARY: 29 (inset); FRED MAWER: 124clb; MEARS TRANSPORTATION GROUP: 195tr.

©NASA: 15br, 22tr, 23tr; NICKOLODEON FAMILY SUITES BY HOLIDAY INN: 135tl.

ORANGE BLOSSOM BALLOONS: 172 tl; ORLANDO HARLEY-DAVIDSON: 74CL; ORLANDO & ORANGE COUNTY CONVENTION & VISITORS BUREAU: 14ca, 27tl, 106br, 108tl, 109br, 112br, 156bc, Walt Disney Company/

Diana Zalucky 26tl; 158tr, 158b, 159tc, 162cl, 162br, 163tr, 166cl, 167tl, 167b, 168br, 176tc, 178tr, 178cl, 179tc, 180tr, 180cl, 181tl, 182tl, 186cl, 197tc; ORLANDO/ORANGE COUNTY COVENTION AND VISITORS BUREAU, INC: 136bl, 195br; ORONOZ, Madrid: 13tc.

PHOTOLIBRARY: Danielle Gali 49-9, Wendell Metzen 110-111; PLANET EARTH PICTURES: 123cra. LA QUINTA: 132cb.

REUTERS: Charles W. Luzier 176cl; RITZ CARLTON ORLANDO GRAND LAKES: 133bl; MARIAN RYAN: 20cl, 20cr.

© SEAWORLD® ORLANDO: 4br, 6-7, 9br, 14bl, 19br, 78, 79b, 80bl, 83cb, 84ca, 84bl, 85tl, 87bl; SILVER SPURS RODEO: 179c; STARWOOD: 133tl; ARVIN STEINBERG: 20cb, 20bcr, 21bcl; PHYLLIS STEINBERG: 116c; SUPERSTOCK: Steve Vidler 3c.

THE MENNELLO MUSEUM OF AMERICAN FOLK ART: *Bird*, Paul Marco 107tr.

© 2008 UNIVERSAL ORLANDO®. ALL RIGHTS RESERVED: 4tr, 9tl, 19tr, 81tr, 88c, 88b, 89cla, 89cb, 89br, 90tl, 90b, 91tl, 91br, 92tl, 92b, 93tr, 94-95, 96tl, 96cl, 96br, 97tl, 97br, 98tl, 98bl, 99br, 135br, 146br, Kevin Kolczynski 168tl.

VILLAS OF GRAND CYPRESS: 16bl.

WET 'N WILD® ORLANDO: 19cr, 25br, 81br, 100tr, 100cla, 100clb, 100bl, 101tl, 101cra, 101crb, 101br, 101bl. ©ZORA NEALE HURSTON NATIONAL MUSEUM OF FINE ARTS: *Festival Girl*, Jane Turner 106cl.

Front endpaper: © DISNEY: cla; SEAWORLD® ORLANDO: tc; CORBIS: Raymond Gehman br.

JACKET
Front: PHOTOLIBRARY: Tim Gartside; Back: ALAMY IMAGES: Greg Balfour Evans tl; DORLING KINDERSLEY: Rough Guides/Dan Bannister cla; DORLING KINDERSLEY: Rough Guides/Demetrio Carrasco clb; DORLING KINDERSLEY: Rough Guides/Dan Bannister bl; Spine: Tim Gartside t.

All other images © Dorling Kindersley. See www.DKimages.com for further information.

Road Map of Greater Orlando

Ocala
APOPKA
441

Lake Apopka
455

FLORIDA'S TURNPIKE (TOLL)

CLARCONA

438

OCEE-APOPKA ROAD
APOPKA-VINELAND ROAD

WINTER GARDEN
OCOEE
PINE HILLS

50
438

← *Gainesville*
27

408 ORLOVISTA
435

545
MARSH ROAD

HARLEM HEIGHTS
TILDEN RD

WINDERMERE ROAD

WINDERMERE

AVALON ROAD

FICQUETTE RD

Lake Butler

CHASE RD

Lake Tibet

Universal Orlando ●

Wet 'n Wild ●

WINTER GARDEN-VINELAND ROAD

REAMS ROAD

Ripley's Believe It or Not ●

i

Magic Kingdom™ ●

Bay Lake

SeaWorld Orlando® ●

WALT DISNEY WORLD® RESORT

LAKE BUENA VISTA

545

Discovery Cove ●

INTERNATIONAL DRIVE

Epcot® ●

Disney's Animal Kingdom® ●

Disney's Hollywood Studios ●

192

417
535
OSCEOLA

Arabian Nights ●

Medieval Times ●

545

CONSERVATION AREA

0 km   5
0 miles   2

Cypress Gardens Adventure Park
Historic Bok Sanctuary ↓

27

4

Fantasy of Flight

17 92

CAMPBELL